D0540582

RAIL CENTRES:
MANCHESTER

Front cover, top: 'Jubilee' class 4-6-0 No 45590 *Travancore* is seen at Exchange station with a service from Scarborough in mid-1963. *Brian Magilton*

Front cover, bottom: No 323 223 departs from Manchester Piccadilly on 14 October 1994 with the 14.40 to Manchester Airport. *Alan Sherratt*

Back cover, top: No 62656 *Sir Clement Royds* on the turntable at Manchester Central, 1952. *Colour Rail*

Back cover, bottom: RES liveried Nos 4630 and 47142 *The Sapper* in Railfreight Grey with Red Stripe, rest between duties at Manchester Victoria on 19 March 1992. *Alan Sherratt*

RAIL CENTRES: MANCHESTER

Stanley Hall MCIT

B L P

Nottingham

Booklaw Publications

First published 1995 by Ian Allan Ltd

© Stanley Hall 1995

All rights reserved. No part of this book may be reproduced or transmitted in any form or by any means, electronic or mechanical, including photocopying, recording or by an information storage and retrieval system, without permission from the Publisher in writing.

This edition published 2008 by Booklaw Publications
382, Carlton Hill, Nottingham NG4 1JA

ISBN 1-901945-29-4

Printed by The Amadeus Press, Cleckheaton, West Yorkshire

Contents

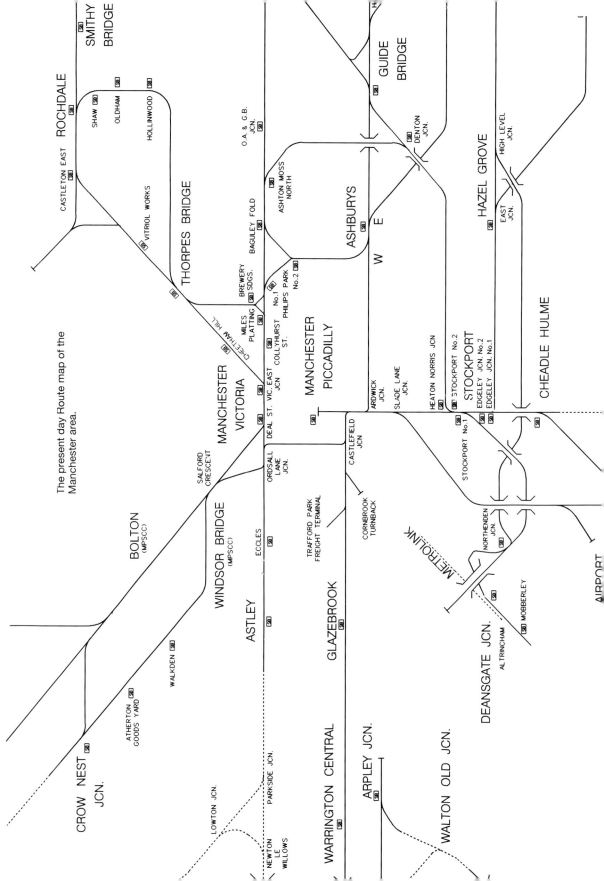

The present day Route map of the Manchester area.

Foreword

To compress the complex and convoluted 170 years' history of Manchester's railways into 50,000/60,000 words is no easy task; there is sufficient material for several volumes, therefore to do justice to the subject, I have confined the geographical area under study to within roughly five miles of Manchester city centre, except where a particular topic deserves a wider canvas.

My association with Manchester started in 1941, when, having travelled from Bradford Exchange on the old 8.15am businessman's train, I stood in my school cap at the end of Platform 11 in Victoria station and marvelled at the hustle and bustle of a seemingly endless stream of passenger trains entering and leaving the station. In the memory they were all headed by Stanier's taper-boilered 2-6-4Ts, but I expect there were a few 'Lanky Tanks' (2-4-2s) amongst them. The Victoria/Exchange complex was a frustrating place for the observer, and necessitated frequent visits to the Exchange end to see what the 'Wessie' was up to. This entailed long walks along that famous No 11 platform.

During a lull in the traffic, the opportunity was taken to walk across to London Road to see what the LNW/GC side had to offer, but it was never as exciting as Victoria. Poor old Manchester had been severely battered by German bombs the previous winter, and the stark ruins of burnt-out buildings and tidied-up bomb sites bore mute testimony to its suffering. However, to a schoolboy everything seemed quite normal; it was just another effect of the war and not unexpected.

My first official visit took place two years later. The LMS was advertising for clerks to replace those who had joined the services and, having applied for such a post, I was summoned to Manchester to sit a written examination in English, geography and arithmetic. This took place in an office on the LNER side of London Road passenger station, long since demolished. A week or so later I was told that I had passed the clerical examination and was informed that I would have to take a medical examination so that I could join the LMS Superannuation Fund. A free ticket was enclosed — to Manchester again, where the medical was held in a specially adapted coach standing against one of the buffer stops at Victoria. I passed, and so my railway career began.

Manchester's railway stations, in fact most railway stations, in those days seemed rather shabby and dingy, the result of many years of relative neglect and being occupied by smoky engines, a world away from today's Piccadilly. Victoria never did improve to any great extent, but ultimately it became a sort of Mecca, the only remaining example of a once-great Victorian railway station. Now, much of Victoria is history, but that wonderful frontage and circulating area are still there.

The story of Manchester's railways is both fascinating and frustrating — the intrigues of the early days; the inter-railway competition to gain a foothold there; the lost opportunities to form a rational network and the lack of municipal interest — culminating despite these drawbacks, in the rich flowering of the railways in the Edwardian era, epitomised for ever by the glorious, solid and proudly prosperous architecture of the Midland Hotel.

Up to World War 1 the railways had prospered and their traffic grew year after year. In the summer of 1914 it must have seemed to railway managers that it would always be so; why should it be otherwise? But the effects of the war that followed led to a great change in the railways' and the country's economic situation. Road transport became a serious competitor; its development accelerated by the war. The grouping of the prewar companies into the Big Four in 1923 was a tremendous distraction, especially to the infant LMS, just at the time when they needed to concentrate on meeting the challenges of the day. Profits slumped and new capital became hard to raise, but the companies managed to achieve a welcome renaissance in the later 30s, helped by government grants and loans. They also recognised the need to diversify, but failed to get to grips with road competition, handicapped as they were by anti-monopoly Victorian legislation.

Once again, war intervened to alter the course of railway history. The railways' 'Square-Deal' campaign to get rid of the incubus of out-dated legislation and improve their competitive position had reached its climax in 1939 and would probably have succeeded had it not been for World War 2. After the war it no longer mattered. A Labour government was returned, committed to the nationalisation of the railways. The railway unions had fondly assumed that nationalisation would ensure that they had job security, improved working conditions and better pay, and perhaps even a say in the running of the railways. They were to be bitterly disappointed. The number of railwaymen employed has dropped by 80% since 1948, and the positive influence of the railway unions on railway policy has been minimal. On the other hand, they have had a very considerable negative influence, born out of frustration, which has ultimately led to the widespread loss of freight traffic and railwaymen's jobs.

After nationalisation in 1948 the railways became the government's millstone, and the last 40 years have seen continual government involvement in railway policy owing to the losses which have occurred. The Treasury has constantly struggled to reduce the drain on public funds used to support the railways, but by far the worst feature has been the lack of any consistent government policy. Secretaries of State seem unable to grasp the fact that railways are a long-term industry, that railway rolling stock has a life of 25/35 years, that signalling installations last for 30 years or more, and that the trackbed and the buildings are there for ever. Perhaps the lack of such appreciation is understandable; Secretaries of State for Transport are rarely with us for more than a year or two and most of them contribute very little. They have a difficult job; they would probably like to do more but the Treasury won't let them. The end result, however, has been a procession of reorganisations, most of them useless in stemming the losses. Whether privatisation will improve matters is now the question; we shall have to wait for the answer.

It is quite probable that Manchester's passengers have noticed little of this, apart from wondering why their train was late, or shabby, or why there wasn't enough room in it. What they have seen since nationalisation is the end of steam, the coming of diesel and electric trains and locomotives of all types, the virtual disappearance of semaphore signalling and its replacement by colour lights, the demise of Central station, and the new Piccadilly. They may also have noticed that the once ubiquitous railway parcels vans and goods delivery lorries that filled Manchester's streets are no longer there.

The recent history of the 'Old Lanky' (as the former Lancashire & Yorkshire Railway is fondly known) is a sad one. No one has seemed to know what to do with it; certainly BR hasn't, so it has been left to wither away gently and become the most neglected area of the whole BR network. The most scandalous omission has been the failure to electrify the Manchester–Bolton–Preston–Blackpool

line. Had that been done it would have reinvigorated the whole corridor. It would have allowed the through running of electric trains from Preston and the north to the Midlands and the south via Manchester. It would have allowed electrically-hauled expresses to serve Blackpool, which now finds itself on a branch line, so far as London is concerned. Yet again the Treasury is cast in the role of villain, but BR has not always given the appearance of being fully committed to the project.

One of the brightest aspects of the postwar railway has been the creation of Passenger Transport Authorities (PTAs), the brainchild of Barbara Castle (a native of Yorkshire, by the way, and educated at Bradford Girls' Grammar School). Without her vision of a properly integrated and efficient system of public passenger transport to meet the needs of conurbations, most suburban and rural train services would simply have ceased to run. It took the Greater Manchester PTA a little time to get its act together; not unexpectedly so, because local authorities had never really bothered their heads about railways, and in any case they too were being reorganised. But now they have grasped the nettle and are enthusiastic supporters of the iron rail. Who would have envisaged, a few years ago, that trains would run through the centre of Manchester, even if they do look like updated trams? And a direct railway to the airport? And ambitious plans for more Metrolink services? The future looks good. Perhaps they should erect a statue to Baroness Castle. And throw brickbats at the Secretaries of State for Transport who deregulated buses and destroyed the concept of integration, and refused to allow PTAs to tender for franchises to operate rail services in their own areas. After all, Manchester used to operate its own buses. What is more natural than that it should be allowed to operate its own trains? Perhaps a future government will allow major cities such as Manchester to decide their own transport policies without interference from central government.

This book does not attempt to give a detailed review of the history of the railways of Manchester. It does not attempt to catalogue every development and list every date. It would be impossible to do so in a single volume, and what is more it would be boring, except as a work of reference. What the book attempts to do is to paint a picture of the development of the railway, set against the region's social, economic and industrial background. It seeks to tell a story and, what is more, to explain why things happened the way they did, or indeed why they didn't happen. It pauses from time to time to look at the contemporary scene through the eyes of the passenger. Whilst the author has structured the book on a chronological basis, he has not stuck rigidly to that format where it has seemed sensible to stray from it to achieve continuity of some aspect of the story.

The author felt that some space should be devoted to the subject of locomotives, whether steam, diesel or electric, in the belief that for many people an important part of the railway scene was, and is, the engine hauling the train. If you are one of those people, I hope you will enjoy reading about your favourite engines. If you are not, please accept my reasons for dealing with the topic, often at some length.

It ought to be mentioned that some of the area covered by this story actually lies within the City of Salford, but I hope its citizens will forgive me for using the term 'Manchester' in a generic sense to avoid confusion.

Manchester was a magnet. It drew the railway companies to it like moths to a candle, and they prospered mightily. The story of Manchester's railways is more complex than that of any other city in Britain, apart from the capital itself. To write about it has been a fascinating exercise and a great pleasure; I hope the reader will gain the same reward.

Finally, a work of this nature could not have been undertaken without a great deal of help from many sources. The National Railway Museum at York once again put its considerable archives at my disposal, and I must also thank the Manchester Central Library. Railway colleagues, both active and retired, willingly assisted. Those still in the railway service have perforce to remain unnamed, but they have my thanks. I might, however, mention John Hammond, a noted railway historian currently with BRT, who has been most helpful. Retired colleagues to whom I am grateful include Ken Appleby (former Area Manager, York); Gerald Aston (former asst. Line Manager, Crewe); George Dodds and Peter Rayner (both former Divisional Operating Superintendents at Manchester) and Charles Armitage, a knowledgeable local railway officer. D. Scott Hellewell, former Chief Planning Officer of SELNEC PTE and its successor the Greater Manchester PTE, and former Operations Director of Metrolink, gave invaluable assistance with the last three chapters. Friends of the National Railway Museum were also of considerable help, especially John Edgington, who performed the very valuable service of checking my photo captions, as well as the text. I would also record with thanks the help willingly given by the *Railway Gazette International* and the Railway Correspondence and Travel Society (publishers of *The Railway Observer*). But, ultimately, the responsibility for what is written in the following pages is mine alone.

Below: Detailed route map of the inner Manchester area, 1920-39

Above: Railway companies often named locomotives after the cities they served, and Manchester's importance was well recognised. The LMS chose No 6246, one of the company's 'Princess Coronation' class 'Pacifics', to carry the proud name *City of Manchester*. The engine was built in 1943 and is seen in wartime black. It was ceremonially named on 3 September 1943 at Manchester Victoria by the Lord Mayor, and driven by Driver W. Wood VC of Newton Heath, whose name was honoured on 'Patriot' class engine No 5536. *National Railway Museum/Crown Copyright Reserved*

Below: Several years elapsed after World War 2 before high-speed running was resumed, and the streamlined casing of the 'Princess Coronations', no longer required for that purpose, was removed to allow easier access for maintenance. *City of Manchester*, now BR No 46246, is seen in this condition as it stands on the turntable at Camden, its home depot, on 8 April 1962. *M. Pope*

Above: The LNER named a number of its 'Sandringham' class 4-6-0s after the more famous football clubs. No 2862, built by Robert Stephenson & Co in January 1937, was chosen to bear the name *Manchester United*. It was renumbered 1662 in 1946, and 61662 by BR. Manchester City football club was not overlooked — its name was borne by engine No 2871 (originally by 2870 before that engine was streamlined in 1937 to work the East Anglian expresses). *National Railway Museum/Crown Copyright Reserved*

Below: The LMS originally chose names carried by previous generations of engines for Nos 6125 to 6149 of its first batch of 50 'Royal Scots', built by the North British Locomotive Co in 1927, but they were later renamed after army regiments. No 6148 was originally named *Velocipede*, but was renamed *The Manchester Regiment* in 1935. The RCTS publication *LMS Locomotive Names* records that the nameplates were presented to the Manchester Regiment at a ceremony at Ashton-under-Lyne on 1 June 1965, upon the withdrawal of the locomotive from service. *National Railway Museum/Crown Copyright Reserved*

1 The Overture
The Development of Manchester

Manchester was not a child of the Railway Age. On the contrary, it was already a major centre with a population approaching 50,000 by 1775, and it was Manchester's astonishingly rapid growth as an Industrial Revolution town in the following half century to 1825 that fathered a demand for a more efficient and cheaper form of transport. That child, the railway, became the key to Manchester's continuing development and expansion right up to the outbreak of World War 1.

Manchester's prosperity and growth were based on the machine manufacture of cotton goods, the raw material being imported, mainly from the southern states of the USA, through the Liverpool docks. Some idea of the growth of that traffic may be gained from the following table giving the average tonnage of vessels handled through the Liverpool docks:

Year	Aggregate Tonnage of Vessels (000s of tons)
1811	611
1831	1592
1851	3737
1871	6131
1889	9291

The importance of cheap and efficient transport between Liverpool and Manchester, not only for the import of raw cotton but also for the export of finished goods, is clearly demonstrated by these figures. These two towns were the biggest in England outside London by the mid-19th century. Between 1760 and 1830 the combined population of Manchester and Salford increased eightfold, and almost doubled again by 1850.

Above left & below left: The last of the 'Princess Coronation' class (often referred to as 'Cities' or 'Duchesses'), No 46257 *City of Salford*, did not enter service until 1948, and was ceremonially named at Manchester Exchange station on 3 June 1948 by the Mayor of Salford, Alderman J. Brenthall. The two photographs show the engine when new, as No M6257, and some years later as BR 46257 leaving Liverpool Lime Street. *National Railway Museum/Crown Copyright Reserved*

It would, however, be misleading to visualise 19th century Manchester as merely a town of cotton mills. Whilst there were some cotton mills in Manchester they increasingly came to be situated in surrounding towns such as Oldham and Ashton, and in the northern river valleys with their plentiful water supply. Manchester itself became the great warehouse and shop window of the cotton trade. This pattern and location of industry created its own demand for efficient transport, not merely for the movement of goods, but also to enable merchants, businessmen, buyers and others engaged in trade, to move around quickly and easily. Hence the rapid development of railways throughout the Lancashire cotton belt, with lines radiating from Manchester like the spokes of a wheel. This unco-ordinated and piecemeal development, whilst adequate at the time, contained the seeds of problems of later years, particularly in the lack of a good north-south route. Manchester became a city (a status granted in 1853) of terminal passenger stations on a scale greater than in any other English city except London.

The half century before the coming of the railways was the great era of canal-building and by 1821 there were three navigable routes between Liverpool and Manchester. The use of canals did not cease immediately upon the opening of the railways, indeed the majority of freight traffic continued to be carried by canal for at least 20 years after the opening of the Liverpool & Manchester Railway. Even after 1850, the canals continued to be used for such bulk commodities as coal and building materials, where speed of delivery was unimportant, but by this time the ownership of canals was passing to the railway companies.

Nor was road transport completely eclipsed. It continued to be used for short distances throughout the canal era and even during the railway era, where the avoidance of double handling at the beginning and end of a transit offered economic or other advantages.

The cotton industry in its turn led to the development of the engineering and chemical industries, which became of major importance in the Manchester area, not only to serve the cotton

industry itself, but in the fields of heavy engineering and the manufacture of machine tools. Manchester — although popularly known as Cottonopolis — became in reality an industrial city and, together with the surrounding district, one of the world's foremost engineering centres, but its fortunes were linked to cotton.

The continuous increase in size and prosperity which characterised the Manchester region for a century after 1775 could not be expected to continue for ever. Manchester may have been the world's first industrial town, but towns in other countries, although starting later, could not be expected to lag behind for ever. It was inevitable that some would challenge Manchester's supremacy, and indeed there were signs of future relative decline even before the end of the 19th century and despite the opening of the Manchester Ship Canal in 1894, which gave Manchester an economic boost up to 1914. 1913 was the record year for the cotton industry. Eighty per cent of the output of cloth was exported, with almost half of it going to India. The immense size and importance of the industry in pre-World War 1 days can be gauged from the fact that two-thirds of the world's cotton cloth was produced on the looms of Lancashire, which made the Lancashire & Yorkshire Railway a very busy and profitable company.

Since then, the story of cotton has been a very sad one. After World War 1, foreign competition and the loss of foreign markets began increasingly to be felt. Exports plummeted and by 1939 they were only a fifth of the 1913 figure. The decline continued after World War 2 until the final virtual

Above: A 'City' of an earlier era, former GC 4-6-0 (LNER Class B2) No 1491 *City of Manchester*, at Immingham in 1947. Before the 1946 renumbering it had been No 5425, and was built at Gorton in 1913. *IAL*

demise of the industry. With a parallel reduction in the engineering industry, the effect on the railways was little short of catastrophic. The loss of their basic traffics of cotton, steel and steel manufactures, and coal, coupled with increasing road competition, crippled their freight traffic to such an extent that the railways of the Manchester area are now little more than passenger carriers. Deserts lie where not long ago there were busy and thriving marshalling yards and goods depots. It is difficult to believe now, that only 30 years ago the railways earned far more revenue from freight than they did from passengers. The railways were built to compete only with each other, on relatively equal terms, and were ill-equipped to deal satisfactorily with road competition, in conditions which were weighted very much in the lorry's favour.

The story of the railways of Manchester is a mirror image of the development and subsequent decline of the area's industrial base, and, in the 20th century, of the growth of road competition, and social change. It is against this background that we shall sketch in the development of the railways, and of changes in the railway scene, starting with the momentous events of 15 September 1830, which ushered in the Railway Era with the opening of the Liverpool & Manchester Railway.

2 The Coming of the Railways
1830 to 1850

Some may argue that the Stockton & Darlington Railway, opened in 1825, was the world's first main-line railway, but it is undeniable that the Liverpool & Manchester Railway was the world's first public railway, operated by steam from the outset over its own tracks. Its success sparked off a wave of investment in schemes for new railways.

The initiative for the building of the railway came chiefly from Liverpool businessmen who saw it as a means of strengthening their hold on the cotton traffic. They held 50% of the shares. By then Liverpool had a considerable overseas trade and its docks were growing rapidly.

Transport facilities between the two towns were quite inadequate to deal with the rapidly increasing goods traffic, and in 1822 the first steps were taken by merchants of both towns. They co-operated in a survey, resulting in a prospectus being issued in 1824. There was intense opposition both from landowners and from the canal companies, who foresaw what a formidable competitor the railway could become. However, the promoters of the bill

for the construction of the line, secured its passage in 1826, after making certain concessions to their opponents. The legal and other charges incurred in securing the passage of a Railway Bill, and in the purchase of the land, were often a substantial proportion of the whole costs of building a railway and were a burden to be borne throughout its life, interest having to be paid on the capital so used.

George Stephenson surveyed the line, although its construction was supervised by his son Robert. It was opened on 15 September 1830, the Manchester terminus being called, appropriately, Liverpool Road. It was an unpretentious terminus, not at all like the imposing structures which were shortly to follow at Birmingham Curzon Street and Euston, and ceased to be used as a passenger station as

Below: A train of the Liverpool & Manchester Railway passes over the Bridgewater Canal at Patricroft in 1830, shortly after the line had been opened. *IAL*

The L&Y route via Littleborough was the easiest of all the trans-Pennine routes, and in great demand in later years for Blackpool excursion trains. Dairycoates Class K3 2-6-0 No 61935 heads an 11-coach Goole to Blackpool Day Excursion past the Dunlop Cotton Mills at Castleton on 11 September 1960. *R. S. Greenwood*

early as 1844. It continued to be used as a goods terminal until 1975, after which it became part of the Manchester Museum of Science and Industry, enabling it to be preserved as the world's oldest passenger station. An interesting feature was the use of Liverpool Road Goods Station by the Great Western Railway, dating from about 1860, using running powers from Walton Junction, Warrington, which might seem to be extending that railway's influence to an excessive degree. Old plans show goods sheds and sidings marked 'Great Western Railway.'

The Liverpool & Manchester Railway was not conceived as anything other than a railway connecting those two major towns, but other schemes were afoot elsewhere which were to have a significant effect upon Manchester's railways. Even whilst the Liverpool & Manchester Railway was being discussed in the 1820s, businessmen in Liverpool & Birmingham were jointly considering a railway line between their two towns, one reason being that the Midlands' industrialists sought an improved transport link for their traffic to Ireland. However, as this scheme developed, the section between Crewe and Liverpool was dropped from the plans in favour of a line from Crewe to Warrington, to join up with an existing line from Warrington to Newton and provide a 'T' junction

with the Liverpool & Manchester Railway. This new line from Birmingham was announced as the Grand Junction Railway and received its Act in 1833. It opened for traffic in 1837, and the following year it enabled through connection to be made between Manchester and London by the use of the London & Birmingham Railway, opened in 1838, whose Birmingham terminus at Curzon Street was adjacent to that of the Grand Junction.

It will have been noted that Liverpool businessmen had been very active in promoting both the Liverpool & Manchester Railway and the Grand Junction; in fact they became known as the 'Liverpool Party', and took a lead in promoting what they regarded as sensible schemes elsewhere. Whether this piqued the citizens of Manchester is not clear but they soon became less than pleased with the prospect of a change of trains and railway companies at Newton, when travelling to Birmingham. They therefore applied to the directors of the Grand Junction Railway for a through route to be provided, avoiding the need to change trains.

The directors of the Grand Junction were not encouraged by this development, as the northern section of their line was still being built and would lose much of its *raison d'être* if they had to construct a new section of line approaching

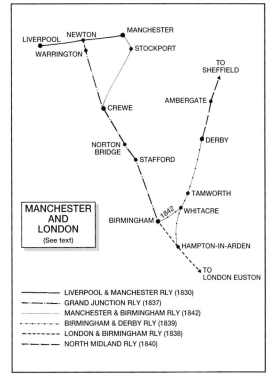

Above left: The original passenger station building at Manchester Liverpool Road, seen in 1965. It was still in use, as the general offices of the goods depot. *John Clarke*

Above: Woodhead station, at the western end of the tunnel, in 1948. *IAL*

Right: Development of the routes from Manchester to London Euston.

Manchester from a more southerly direction. They must also have feared that the Liverpool people would soon make a similar request.

The Manchester people persisted, warning that if the Grand Junction did not provide such a facility, other people would. It was typical of the time that there was no shortage of alternative schemes, including a line from Manchester to Norton Bridge, and one from Manchester to Tamworth, joining there the Birmingham & Derby Junction Railway, which was planning a connection from Whitacre to Hampton-in-Arden, on the line from Birmingham to London. This would have cut out the Grand Junction altogether.

There was yet another scheme, rather grandly titled the Manchester, Buxton, Matlock & Midlands

Junction Railway, which would have provided a different route to London. It was to run from Stockport to a junction with the North Midland Railway at Ambergate, whose line was opened in 1840. It would also have given another route across the Pennines. However, it was a railway whose time had not yet come.

An expensive wrangle developed between the two parties, the legal profession being one of the main beneficiaries, but eventually agreement was reached to form a new railway company, to be known as the Manchester & Birmingham, which would build a line between Manchester and a junction with the Grand Junction line just north of Stafford. The Act was obtained in 1837, but financial and other difficulties ensued, and the plan was amended for a direct line to Crewe, with the Potteries route being abandoned. The portion of line between Manchester and Stockport was opened in 1840, from a temporary terminus at Travis Street, but two years later it was extended to London Road when the line was opened throughout to Crewe.

London Road station was described as a beautiful stone building in the Italianate style, and had a range of buildings 500ft long, with the General Offices of the Manchester & Birmingham Railway being located above the usual station offices. There were initially two platforms, one for arrivals and one for departures.

The Liverpool & Manchester Railway was taken over by the Grand Junction in 1845, but the following year the Grand Junction joined with the Manchester & Birmingham and the London & Birmingham to form the London & North Western Railway, thus effectively ending the squabble between the GJR and the M&BR.

Before leaving the story of London Road station we ought now to look at the fortunes of another railway, which was struggling to reach Manchester from Sheffield. This railway was the Sheffield, Ashton-under-Lyne & Manchester Railway which, for convenience, we shall call the Sheffield & Manchester, although that is not intended to belittle the town of Ashton, which by now was a bustling place with many cotton mills.

At this time, the Pennines formed a formidable barrier to transport between Sheffield and Manchester. There was no canal and only a difficult road. It was thought that a railway would be a profitable project and an Act for the construction of a railway was obtained as early as 1831. The reason for the absence of a canal and a good road soon became clear. The route proposed for the railway entailed so much tunnelling and bridging that it was abandoned as impracticable. A new route was surveyed and another Act was obtained in 1836, but it still required a tunnel at Woodhead, three miles

13yd long, and resulted in some fierce gradients which were to plague the railway operators for well over 100 years.

Construction was slow and the work expensive, and the first section of 8¼ miles between Manchester and Godley was not opened until 1841. Financial problems arose which were to be symptomatic of the fortunes of the line throughout its life, although it would eventually carry a very heavy freight traffic. Not only were construction costs high, so were the operating costs, and they were twin heavy burdens that were bequeathed to the successors of the Sheffield & Manchester Railway (ie the Manchester, Sheffield & Lincolnshire Railway, then the Great Central Railway, and finally the London & North Eastern Railway). The Sheffield & Manchester became part of the Manchester, Sheffield & Lincolnshire Railway in 1849, thus providing a through route between Manchester and Grimsby. The line between Manchester and Sheffield was opened throughout in 1845. At the Manchester end, the Sheffield & Manchester Railway ran into London Road station by virtue of an agreement with the Manchester & Birmingham Railway, dating from the early days in the formation of the two lines, the junction being at Ardwick.

Manchester now had two stations on the south side — Liverpool Road and London Road. The establishment of two terminal stations set the pattern for the development of railways in Manchester. It is not known whether any thought was given to the conversion of Liverpool Road to a through station and starting the Manchester & Birmingham Railway there, but consideration was already being given to the need to connect the two routes. However, it might be more convenient to consider this issue a little further on, after looking at railway development on the north side of Manchester.

The success of the Liverpool & Manchester Railway unleashed a flood of schemes for building railways radiating from Manchester. Only a year after the opening of that railway, proposals were made to convert the Manchester, Bolton & Bury canal into a railway, but it was subsequently decided to retain the canal and build the railway alongside or nearby. The Act was obtained in 1832 and the line was opened in 1838, from a terminus in Salford.

In the 1820s, whilst plans for the Liverpool & Manchester Railway were being developed, thoughts turned to the desirability and the financial attraction of connecting the ports of Liverpool and Hull with a route that went via Leeds. An early scheme for a route following the Leeds & Liverpool canal and running via St Helens and Skipton came to naught. Concurrently, other schemes were being developed for a railway connecting Manchester with Leeds, and in 1835 a proposal was announced for a railway running from Manchester to Normanton, with a junction at the latter place giving access to Leeds by the exercise of running powers over the line of the North Midland Railway.

The term 'Running Powers' appears frequently in the activities of the pre-grouping companies. It indicates that one company had the right to run its own trains with its own engines over the lines of another company. That right could be limited to certain traffics, eg coal and minerals, or it might include all freight traffic but exclude passenger traffic. The company with running powers would normally build its own freight depots, but would use the other company's passenger station. Stops at intermediate stations were often not allowed.

It was frequently in the interests of one company to grant running powers to another company, for it helped to maintain friendly relations with a possible competitor. It was also a valuable bargaining counter, as it provided additional revenue for the granting company (trains using running powers had to pay for the concession), and it avoided the possibility of the construction of a duplicate line which might become a competitor. From the point of view of the company obtaining the running powers, it avoided having to raise additional capital to build that portion of line. The exercise of running powers was paid for out of future revenue.

The Manchester & Leeds Railway received its Act in 1836. Its route across the Pennines, although difficult, was nevertheless one of the easiest in terms of the absence of severe gradients, and it had the advantage of passing through several large towns. Its major work was the Summit Tunnel, one mile 1,125yd in length. The Manchester & Leeds was opened throughout in 1841 from a terminus in Oldham Road, and became incidentally the central part of a through route between Liverpool and Hull; although a change of stations was needed in Manchester, an inconvenience of a type that was to plague Lancashire's railway passengers for a century and a half, and which has only partially been overcome in the present day.

This inconvenience was becoming recognised even before the Manchester & Leeds Railway was opened. Its proposed terminal station at Oldham Road would be one of four in Manchester, if one includes Salford:

Station	Railway Company	Opened
Liverpool Rd	Liverpool & Manchester Rly,	1830
Salford	Manchester, Bolton & Bury Rly	1838
Oldham Rd	Manchester & Leeds Rly	1839
London Rd	Manchester & Birmingham Rly	1842
London Rd	Sheffield & Manchester Rly	1842

The four terminals were completely unconnected and were some considerable distance apart, and the opportunity for one or two grand central stations, on through routes, as were developed in other major cities, eg Newcastle, Leeds, Sheffield, Birmingham and Bristol, was already being lost. Manchester's railways penetrated only a little way into the built-up area, and to have gone further would have incurred enormous cost. Manchester was paying the price of its early development as the world's first industrial city, for it was already established as a major centre by the time of the coming of the railways.

However, consideration was being given to steps that might be taken to improve the situation. A plan was published in 1839 showing connections between (1) Salford and the Manchester & Leeds Railway, (2) Oldham Road and London Road, and (3) both the Liverpool and Bolton lines and London Road. Some of these proposals, which foreshadowed the closure of both Oldham Road and Liverpool Road as passenger stations, did eventually come into being.

These were turbulent times in Manchester so far as railways were concerned, with a seemingly endless list of new schemes being developed and proposed, most of which envisaged no connection with the others. Some proposals failed even before they reached the Bill stage, whilst others failed to obtain their Acts, and whilst Parliament attempted to act as a filter to reject Bills which it thought unsuitable there was little attempt to produce and develop an overall plan. Indeed, to have done so might have blunted the vigour with which new schemes were proposed and developed; and during the period with which we are concerned, the late 1830s/early 1840s, almost all the lines proposed were intended to provide railway communication between major centres where none already existed. The age of competing lines, which gave Britain such a splendid railway system later in the 19th century, albeit at a cost which subsequently proved to be unsustainable, had not yet arrived. The Great Railway Mania of 1844–1846 was still to come. There could have been no concept at the time that formidable competitors for the railways would eventually emerge, in the form of the motor car, the bus and the lorry. Parliament clearly felt, and rightly so, that nothing must be done to stifle or discourage railway development.

In 1839 the Manchester & Leeds promoted a scheme for a through station at Hunts Bank to connect that railway with the Liverpool & Manchester Railway, by means respectively of a line from a junction at Miles Platting and a line from a junction outside the Liverpool Road station. The Liverpool & Manchester was lukewarm at first, but was eventually persuaded to join in, and the

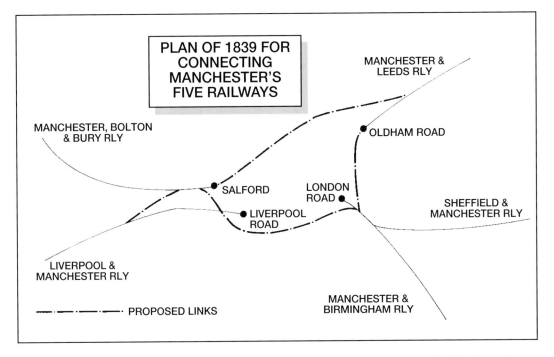

PLAN OF 1839 FOR
CONNECTING
MANCHESTER'S
FIVE RAILWAYS

MANCHESTER &
LEEDS RLY

MANCHESTER, BOLTON
& BURY RLY

OLDHAM ROAD

SALFORD

LONDON
ROAD

SHEFFIELD &
MANCHESTER RLY

LIVERPOOL
ROAD

LIVERPOOL &
MANCHESTER RLY

MANCHESTER &
BIRMINGHAM RLY

— — — — — PROPOSED LINKS

Above: Plan of 1839 for connecting Manchester's five separate railways.

connecting line was built, together with a new through station at Hunts Bank, named Victoria. It had only one platform, but this was long enough for Liverpool trains to be dealt with at one end and Leeds trains at the other. It was opened in 1844, from which date both Oldham Road and Liverpool Road lost their function as passenger stations, although they continued in use as freight depots. The line from Miles Platting was very steeply graded at 1 in 47 and 1 in 60, and for some years a stationary engine was used to haul trains up the bank by means of a wire rope.

The mini-Railway Mania of the mid-1830s was now dying, as shown by the number of Acts passed by Parliament for new railways:

1835	8
1836	29
1837	15
1838	2
1839	1
1840	nil
1841	1

There was a feeling that the railway map of the country was reaching finality, and only 10 Acts for new railways were passed in the first half of the 1840s.

However, before leaving the subject of Victoria station, we ought perhaps to move forward a few years to review the creation of another railway between Manchester and Leeds. The story of

trans-Pennine communication via Standedge started many years earlier, when the Huddersfield Canal across the Pennines (and beneath them through the 3-mile long Standedge Tunnel) was opened in 1811. In 1845 it was proposed to build a railway from Stalybridge to a junction with the Manchester & Leeds Railway at Heaton Lodge, near Mirfield, and to connect with another railway that was being developed from Leeds to Huddersfield via Dewsbury. The newly-formed LNWR took possession of both these new railways (ie the line from Stalybridge and the Leeds to Huddersfield), thus providing more direct access between Manchester and Leeds than was available over the Manchester and Leeds Railway, whose trains ran via Normanton. The latter's direct route to Leeds from Sowerby Bridge was not opened until 1854.

The line from Stalybridge to Huddersfield was opened in 1849, providing the LNWR with a through route between Liverpool and Leeds via Manchester Victoria, with running powers over the Lancashire & Yorkshire's line between Victoria and Stalybridge. Standedge tunnel was bored to take only a single line, but a second single bore was added in 1871. Traffic continued to increase and a third tunnel became necessary. This was built to take two tracks, and was opened in 1894.

This might be a useful point at which to tabulate the dates of formation of the major pre-grouping companies serving Manchester, which were to become household names:

1846 London & North Western Railway, (absorbing the Liverpool & Manchester, the Manchester & Birmingham, and the Huddersfield & Manchester)

1847 Lancashire & Yorkshire Railway, (including the Manchester & Leeds, which had absorbed the Bolton Railway the previous year)

1849 Manchester, Sheffield & Lincolnshire Railway, (including the Sheffield, Ashton-under-Lyne & Manchester Railway)

These new railway companies will henceforth be referred to by their initials — LNWR, L&YR and MS&LR.

It has been mentioned that the LNWR's trains from Liverpool to Leeds ran over L&YR metals between Manchester Victoria and Stalybridge. This short railway received its Act in 1844 and was opened in 1846. The station at Stalybridge was shared with the Sheffield & Manchester Railway's branch from Guide Bridge. Both companies had hopes of extending eastwards, but they were forestalled by the LNWR, which in any event was

much better placed to exploit the route via Standedge as a through trans-Pennine link. A branch was opened by the L&Y from a triangular junction at Philips Park near Miles Platting to a junction with the LNWR Manchester–Crewe line at Ardwick, which allowed the L&Y to operate trains between Victoria and London Road. There was a connection to Beswick Goods depot along the branch.

There is one more railway to consider before we close this chapter. Mention was made earlier of plans to connect the various terminal stations in Manchester, one of which resulted in the creation of Victoria station. Another scheme was developed jointly by the Manchester & Birmingham Railway and the Sheffield & Manchester for a short 1½ mile branch from the joint station at London Road to a junction with the Liverpool & Manchester Railway about ¼ mile outside Liverpool Road station, and a 7½-mile-long railway to Altrincham. Both lines were opened in 1849 and became known as the Manchester, South Junction & Altrincham Railway. This railway, known always as the MSJ&A, although nominally independent, came under the joint control of the LNWR and the MS&L, and ultimately of the LMS and the LNER.

Below: The railway map of Manchester in 1848.

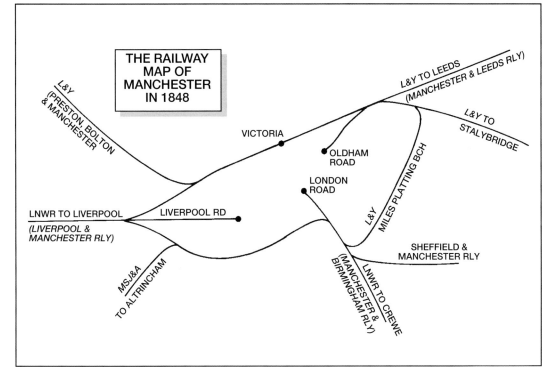

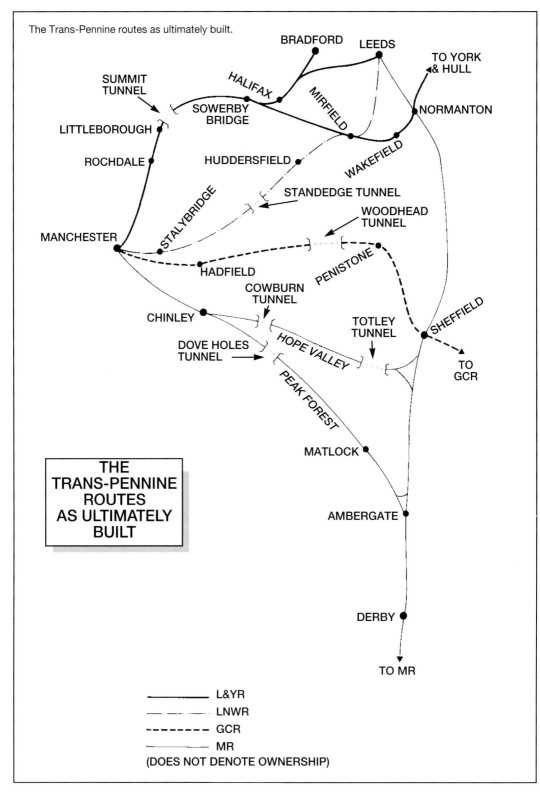

The Trans-Pennine routes as ultimately built.

THE
TRANS-PENNINE
ROUTES
AS ULTIMATELY
BUILT

————————— L&YR

—— · —— · —— LNWR

- - - - - - - GCR

——————— MR

(DOES NOT DENOTE OWNERSHIP)

A casual glance at a railway map might suggest that it would have been more appropriate to have made London Road into a through station and extend the line to Liverpool Road station, but this would have proved very expensive in land acquisition costs. Even the route that was chosen for the MSJ&A required the line to be built at a high level over a maze of streets and canals, on no fewer than 224 arches. A through station at London Road would surely have persuaded the L&YR and the LNWR to build a link from the L&Y's Bolton line to the LNW's Liverpool to Manchester line at Ordsall Lane, thus providing through-train benefits to passengers who were denied them until the Windsor Link was provided about 130 years later.

By the time the Railway Mania got under way the railway map of Manchester had been largely settled until the Midland Railway arrived on the scene, but that is a story for the next chapter. However, the dramatic events of the second half of the 1840s deserve a mention. At the beginning of 1845 there were 2,240 miles of railway open. Five years later this had tripled to 6,621 miles. It is quite astonishing to think of almost 1,000 miles of new railway being opened every year for five years. It would be quite impossible to achieve such a thing today.

During the three years 1844–1846, Parliament sanctioned the building of over 8,000 miles of railway line, which is not far short of the total mileage remaining today. The building programmes involved £180 million of capital. However, some of the authorised mileage was not built, for various reasons — usually financial. Enormous sums were expended in parliamentary and legal costs, not only in meeting the opposition of canal companies and landowners, but also in strife between rival railway companies. The mania subsided almost as quickly as it had risen. Only 16 miles of new line were authorised by Parliament in 1849, and only eight miles in 1850.

It might be useful at this stage to compare the various routes over the Pennines, including those yet to be built, in terms of the general ruling gradient and the length of the main tunnel. *(See table below)*

Except for the Hope Valley route, all these routes carried a very heavy freight traffic in later years. The LNW and L&Y routes had a clear advantage, with heavily laden westbound coal trains on the L&Y route having to face nothing worse than a seven mile climb with a ruling gradient of 1 in 182. However, we are jumping ahead somewhat in our story.

By 1850, LNW and L&Y trains were using Victoria, and LNW and MS&L trains were using London Road. Liverpool Road and Oldham Road stations had become goods depots. The railway map of Manchester had already taken its familiar shape, apart from the major changes caused by the belated arrival of the Midland Railway and the formation of the Cheshire Lines Railway. That story, however, belongs to our next chapter.

	Ruling Gradient		Length of Summit Tunnel
	Eastb'd	Westb'd	
Mid Rly via Peak Forest	90	90	Dove Holes 1m 1100yd
Mid Rly via Hope Valley	90	100	Cowburn 2m 182yd
MS&L via Woodhead	100	120	Woodhead 3m 13yd
LNW via Standedge (from Stalybridge)	125	105	Standedge 3m 60yd
L&Y via Littleborough	152	182	Summit 1m 1,125yd

Apart from the L&Y route, the other routes are very similar in their ruling gradients. However, another factor which has to be taken into account is the length of the sustained climb to the summit:

	Eastbound	Westbound
Mid Rly via Peak Forest	17 miles	15 miles
Mid Rly via Hope Valley	16 miles	2 stretches of 7 miles each from Tapton. 2 stretches of 8 miles & 7 miles from Sheff'ld.
MS&L via Woodhead	17 miles	19 miles
from Barnsley Junc	7 miles	
LNW via Standedge	7 miles	10 miles
L&Y via Summit	7 miles	7 miles

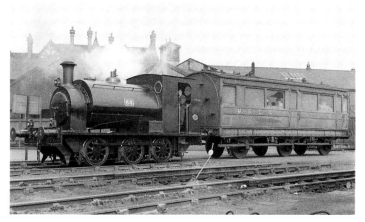

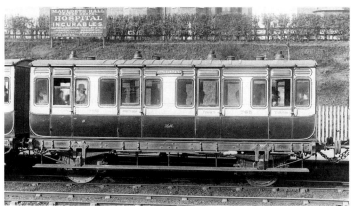

Above: Marple Wharf Junction was situated on the former GC & Mid Joint Line from New Mills to Manchester via Romiley. Ex-LMS Class 5 4-6-0 No 45073 heads the 5.30pm from Sheffield to Manchester Central past the former Midland Railway signalbox on 22 April 1966. The line diverging on the right is the former GC and North Staffs Committee Joint Line to Macclesfield, which now terminates at Rose Hill.
John R. Hillier

Centre left: Manchester Ship Canal 0-6-0ST No 84, with ex-GC six-wheeled saloon brake coach. *IAL*

Below left:
LNW tri-compo coach No 766 at Heaton Chapel. Note the Clarke & Webb chain brake. *IAL*

3 Consolidation and Expansion
1851 to 1880

We have already come across a projected railway with the lengthy title of the Manchester, Buxton, Matlock & Midlands Junction Railway. It issued its prospectus in 1845, at the height of the Railway Mania, to commence its line not in Manchester, but at Cheadle, by a junction with the Manchester & Birmingham Railway (later part of the LNWR). The Act was obtained the following year, with the Manchester & Birmingham (by now the LNWR) being authorised to subscribe over 10% of the capital, and the Midland over 15%. However, the LNW was more concerned with railways in other parts of its system, and the abrupt end of the Railway Mania caused the scheme to be severely reduced in scale. All that was built was the 11½ miles from Ambergate, through Matlock, to Rowsley, opened in 1849 and worked by the Midland. The line was leased jointly to that company and the LNW for 19 years from 1852.

Incidentally, Ambergate was the focal point of another child of the Railway Mania, with an equally grand title — the Ambergate, Nottingham & Boston & Eastern Junction Railway. This line suffered a similar fate, being reduced to a mere 19 miles between Colwick and Grantham (a busy and important line, nonetheless, in later years).

A few years later the LNW was developing a scheme from Stockport to Buxton which interested the Midland, who suggested to the LNW that the Midland could build a line from Rowsley to Buxton and join the LNW's line there, which would provide the Midland with access to Manchester if the LNW would grant running powers. The LNW, however, declined to agree to running powers. It opened its line as far as Whaley Bridge in 1857 but did not arrive in Buxton until 1864.

During this period, railway alliances were both formed and dissolved, accompanied by a certain amount of skullduggery, which convinced the Midland that its only hope of reaching Manchester was over a line of its own, although it has to be said that, set against a background of vigorous railway expansion, and with Manchester such a rich prize, the Midland's attitude had been less than positive.

However, having grasped the nettle, the Midland set about surveying the route. The hand of fate clearly supported the Midland Railway on this occasion, as is evident in the well-known story of

the events of an autumn day in 1861, related by F.S. Williams. The Midland chairman, deputy chairman and general manager were having a reconnaissance of the area, considering all the various options, when they chanced upon a director of the MS&L and two of its officers in a dogcart in a by-lane. Pleasantries were exchanged and the Midland men explained the reason for their presence in the area. The two groups remained together all day, the outcome being that the MS&L people suggested that, rather than the Midland going to the expense of building a new line of its own all the way to Manchester, which would largely run parallel to one of the MS&L's own lines, it might be more advantageous to both sides if the Midland were to use the MS&L line from New Mills to Manchester. In subsequent discussions between the two parties it was agreed that the Midland should run its own trains over the MS&L to or from Manchester, and every other place in Manchester, in Lancashire, or Cheshire, or beyond.

This surprisingly generous agreement was furiously resisted by both the LNW and the Great Northern, a new player in our story, whose presence in Manchester, many miles from its home territory, will be explained later. The Midland had already commenced the construction of its line from Rowsley to Buxton, and it now proposed to build a connecting line to New Mills South Junction, leaving the Rowsley–Buxton line at Miller's Dale. The Act for this work was obtained in 1862.

The line from Rowsley to Buxton was opened throughout in 1863, and from Miller's Dale to New Mills in 1866. From the following year, Midland trains began to run through to London Road station. The line from New Mills to Hyde Junction via Romiley, which had just opened, passed into the joint ownership of the MS&L and the Midland, a very fortuitous partnership. As a postscript, the Ambergate to Rowsley line passed into the sole ownership of the Midland at the expiration of the joint lease with the LNW in 1871.

The Midland, which was one of the big four pre-Grouping companies — LNW, GW, NE and Midland — now had an assured route into Manchester, which was improved in 1875 by the construction of a more direct line from Romiley to Ashburys via Reddish and Belle Vue. However, by this time the

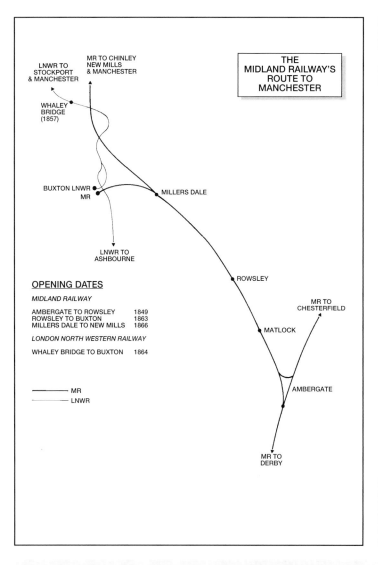

Left: The development of the Midland Railway's route to Manchester.

Right: Map of the Cheshire Lines Railway.

THE MIDLAND RAILWAY'S ROUTE TO MANCHESTER

MR TO CHINLEY NEW MILLS & MANCHESTER

LNWR TO STOCKPORT & MANCHESTER

WHALEY BRIDGE (1857)

BUXTON LNWR MR

MILLERS DALE

LNWR TO ASHBOURNE

ROWSLEY

MR TO CHESTERFIELD

MATLOCK

AMBERGATE

MR TO DERBY

OPENING DATES

MIDLAND RAILWAY

AMBERGATE TO ROWSLEY	1849
ROWSLEY TO BUXTON	1863
MILLERS DALE TO NEW MILLS	1866

LONDON NORTH WESTERN RAILWAY

WHALEY BRIDGE TO BUXTON	1864

———— MR
———— LNWR

Below: Engineer Manchester, a six-foot single, which was formerly LNW No 323 *Greyhound*. It was built in 1853 and transferred to departmental use in 1888, being withdrawn in 1901. *IAL*

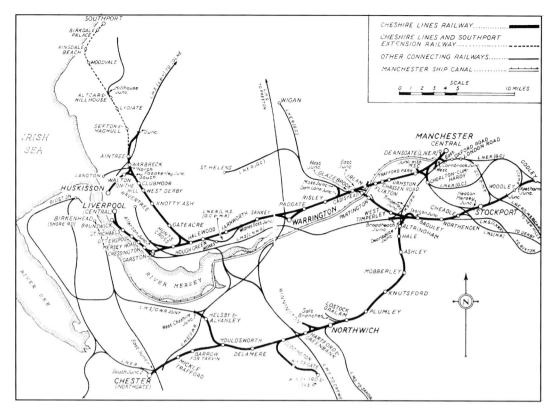

Midland was planning to transfer to a new Manchester terminal to be known as Central, as part of its membership of the Cheshire Lines Committee, to which company we must now turn our attention.

The Cheshire Lines Committee had its origins both in the good working relations which existed between the Great Northern and the MS&L in the 1850s, when they jointly established through working between London King's Cross and Manchester London Road, and in the MS&L's restless ambitions. During the early 1860s a number of small lines were built south of Manchester with MS&L support and encouragement, and aided by the Great Northern, which saw opportunities for expansion. The Midland was later admitted to the MS&L/GN partnership, four local lines being vested jointly by an Act of 1865 in the three parent companies, who then placed the management of these lines in the hands of the Cheshire Lines Committee, the members of that committee being nominated by the three parent companies.

Concurrently, Edward Watkin, the chairman of the MS&L, put forward a scheme for a direct line from Manchester to Garston, connecting there with the Garston & Liverpool Railway — as he wished to be independent of the LNW — whose line was being used at that time by the CLC from Garston to Timperley Junction. He counted upon the support of his two partners in the CLC (the Midland and the Great Northern), who both wished to strengthen their position in the northwest.

Although strongly opposed by the LNW and L&Y, the MS&L was successful in 1865 in obtaining its Act for a direct line, and was authorised to construct a line from a junction with the Manchester, South Junction & Altrincham Railway at Old Trafford to a junction with the Garston & Liverpool Railway near Cressington. The proposed junction at Old Trafford was subsequently amended to a junction at Cornbrook. The new line was opened in 1873, and became part of the CLC, which began to operate trains between Manchester London Road and Liverpool. The Midland very quickly put on a direct service to Liverpool from its own system.

Edward Watkin promoted another ambitious scheme in 1866 to extend the CLC line from Liverpool through the centre of Manchester and join a branch which the Midland intended to build to Ancoats. Through stations were intended to be built at Portland Street and Piccadilly. The Bill passed the Commons but failed in the Lords, Manchester Corporation having withdrawn its support. Such an east-west route would have avoided reversal in London Road, but would have been very expensive both in land acquisition costs and in construction costs. The Midland and the Great Northern may have been able to absorb such costs (the Midland was paying 6%) but the impecunious MS&L was hardly in a position to do so. The scheme was dropped.

Following its entry into Manchester, the Midland began to use the MS&L part of London Road station, but the accommodation there was cramped and it was not long before the MS&L had to tell the Midland to find somewhere else. The CLC line from Garston to Manchester was already being developed as far as Cornbrook, and it was a simple matter, at least in concept (though not in construction) to extend the line to a new terminus, to be called Central.

The three CLC partners all agreed that better station accommodation was required than was currently available at London Road and Oxford Road, but the extra mile or so to the new terminus was bound to be expensive, both in land costs and construction, for the line had to be carried on arches and bridges almost the whole way. This was a problem common to schemes developed in the later part of the 19th century for driving railway lines further in towards city centres. Land prices had risen and compensation costs were higher. It might have been preferable to have improved the MSJ&A route between Cornbrook and London Road, and to have enlarged Oxford Road station, but the LNW, part-owners of the MSJ&A, would not agree to this. They did not trust Edward Watkin.

The extension to Central was finally opened in 1877 to a temporary building on a site which was later used for part of the goods depot. The permanent passenger station was opened on 1 July 1880 and was built with vaults beneath the passenger platforms to provide additional goods warehousing space. This was similar to the arrangement adopted at the Midland's St Pancras station.

The extension to Central immediately gave the CLC a highly competitive route to Liverpool, and an hourly service was introduced at once, the journey taking only 45min. This set a standard for the other companies, the LNW and the L&Y, to aim at. The CLC's route was now only 34 miles, and although it was $2\frac{1}{2}$ miles longer than the LNW route, that company didn't really believe in running trains any faster than it needed to. The L&Y, however, mounted a spirited response over its switchback $39\frac{1}{2}$-mile route, eventually bringing its journey time down to 40min by route improvements and cut-offs which avoided both Bolton and Wigan (see Chapter 4). This is perhaps an illustration of the effects of competition in providing the customer with the best possible service. Today, the trains between Manchester Oxford Road and Liverpool Lime Street are shown in the public timetable to take 49min for

the $34\frac{1}{2}$ miles, with two stops (which might seem excessive by comparison with the timings which were operated a century ago), but the actual running time as shown in the working timetable is only 40min, the remainder being recovery and pathing time.

The Midland obtained its access to the new Central station by a connection just over a mile long, from Romiley, on the New Mills to Manchester London Road line (which it owned jointly with the MS&L), to Bredbury Junction on the CLC east–west route from Godley Junction. It followed the CLC route for about three miles, passing through Stockport Tiviot Dale station, before turning off at Heaton Mersey Junction on to a new line through Didsbury for just over four miles to Chorlton Junction, where it joined the Manchester South District Railway for the final three miles to Central, having joined the line from Liverpool at Throstle Nest East Junction (the section of the Manchester South District Railway between Chorlton Junction and Throstle Nest East Junction was transferred to the CLC in 1886). The Midland endured this somewhat roundabout route until the turn of the century, and its attitude at this time to its Manchester and Liverpool traffic contrasts oddly with its initiative and enterprise in driving a line of its own from Bedford to London St Pancras in the 1860s and from Settle Junction to Carlisle in the 1870s.

The Midland line between Heaton Mersey Junction and Chorlton Junction was not opened until 1880. It had been promoted by an independent company and had been intended to run through Northenden to Alderley, but the Midland, looking for a route to the proposed Central station, purchased it in 1875. It became known as the South District line, and as soon as it was open the Midland diverted most of its services from London Road to Central, several years after the MS&L had given it notice to quit. The MS&L had clearly been very patient.

Before leaving the south side of the city, it might be appropriate to look at the Great Northern's involvement with Manchester. It may have seemed strange to find a GN presence in Manchester, $64\frac{1}{2}$ miles from its own main line from King's Cross to Leeds and the north, at Retford, but the GN was ever an enterprising concern and struck up a friendship with the MS&L as early as 1857, which allowed it to run through trains from King's Cross to Manchester, via Retford and Sheffield, taking only 5hr 20min. This impudent attack upon the LNW's monopoly of Manchester-London traffic stung it into accelerating its best expresses to 4hr 40min. However, the GN trains remained very popular with passengers throughout the remainder of the 19th century, and during the later years its

Above: LNW 'Newton' class 2-4-0 No 1514 *Scott* at Manchester London Road. It was built *c*1866. *IAL*

best expresses took 4½–4¾hr, which matched the Midland and the LNW. There were generally five expresses between King's Cross and Manchester, and there were several express goods trains during the night.

The MSJ&A, which had opened in 1849, had its Manchester terminus at Oxford Road for many years. It seems to have been regarded as mainly a suburban line by its joint owners, the LNW and MS&L, but its traffic developed to the extent that 30 trains a day were being run by 1880. However, no steps were taken to extend the service to London Road, where connections could have been made with the trains of both the owning companies, until 1879 when a few trains were so dealt with. London Road did not become the regular terminus for the Altrincham trains until 1890. The trains were worked by MS&L locomotives, but the MSJ&A had its own carriages.

London Road also saw engines belonging to the North Staffordshire Railway, arising from an agreement with the LNW under which that company worked some of its London trains via Macclesfield and Stoke, using its own engines. Earlier generations of railway enthusiasts, therefore, had a glorious selection of locomotive liveries and owning companies at their disposal. By 1880 these were:

At London Road	LNW, MS&L, NSR
At Central	GN, Midland, MS&L
At Victoria	L&Y, LNW, GW, Midland

Seven companies in all. The Great Western had achieved its access to Manchester as a result,

ultimately, of the misjudged intrigues of the LNW's general manager, Captain Mark Huish, in the development of small railways in the Birkenhead, Chester and Warrington areas. The outcome was that the lines from Chester to both Birkenhead and Warrington became the joint property of both the LNW and the Great Western. Captain Huish eventually resigned and an agreement was reached between the LNW and GW that the latter could have running powers from Warrington to Manchester over the LNW route, using its own engines to work freight trains to Liverpool Road goods depot. It also worked some passenger trains to the LNW platforms at Victoria, being diverted to the LNW's new Exchange station in 1884.

This is the point at which to examine developments on the north side of Manchester, in L&Y territory, where that company eventually had a practical monopoly. By 1850 it had lines to Leeds via Rochdale, and to Bolton, Bury and Stalybridge. There was also a branch to Oldham from the Leeds line at Middleton Junction. A new railway company, known as the Manchester, Bury and Rossendale, received powers in 1844 to join the Manchester to Bolton line at Clifton Junction and exercise running powers to Salford over that route, but it was not long before the Rossendale Railway became part of a newly-formed group — the East Lancashire Railway.

There then ensued a series of disputes between the East Lancs and the L&Y that was typical of the period, with the LNW also causing trouble. Matters reached such a pitch by 1852 that the East Lancs began to consider building its own line from Clifton Junction to Salford. This proposal alarmed the L&Y somewhat and it suggested that the Clifton Junction to Salford line should become the joint property of the two companies, this suggestion being adopted in 1854. They continued to be bad neighbours, but eventually both companies concluded that it would be wiser if they were to work together amicably, and they were amalgamated in 1859.

The L&Y continued to develop its complex of routes. In 1877 it constructed a loop line just over two miles in length from Thorpes Bridge Junction, on the Leeds line, to provide an additional approach to Victoria station via Cheetham Hill; and two years later a new line from Bury to Manchester via Prestwich was opened, joining the loop line at Cheetham Hill Junction. Oldham, a town of considerable industrial importance, had been rather neglected by the L&Y for many years, but an easier and more direct route from Manchester to Oldham was opened from Thorpes Bridge Junction in 1880. Whilst the last half mile into Oldham was up a gradient of 1 in 44, it was somewhat easier than the ¾-mile-long climb at 1 in 27 on the existing line from Middleton Junction.

The story of Victoria would not be complete without a mention of yet another initiative which, although a long time in gestation, finally came to fruition in 1880, four years after the opening of the Midland Railway's Settle Junction to Carlisle line. For many years, there had been plans to connect Blackburn with Clitheroe and thence to a junction with the Skipton to Ingleton line. A railway company called the Blackburn, Clitheroe and North Western Junction had received powers as long ago as 1846 to build such a line, which would have connected with the Skipton to Ingleton line (known as the Little North Western) at Long Preston. A year later the Blackburn company amalgamated with the Blackburn, Darwen & Bolton Railway to form an even longer-titled railway — the Bolton, Blackburn, Clitheroe & West Yorkshire Railway. The Bolton to Blackburn section was opened in 1848.

In the fever of the Railway Mania there had been a number of schemes centred on Clitheroe, and work began on the line to that town from Blackburn. However, enthusiasm for some of the more extravagant schemes soon waned and the line progressed no further towards the Little North Western than Chatburn, which was, and still is, little more than a village. The line was opened in 1850 and, apart from becoming part of the L&Y in 1859, nothing much disturbed its serenity for many years,

until it again assumed potential main line status when the Midland started to build the Settle-Carlisle line. The L&Y thereupon obtained powers to extend the Chatburn line to join the Midland at a new station to be built at Hellifield, rather than at Long Preston, the line being opened on 1 June 1880.

The Hellifield to Blackburn line became an important route for traffic between Lancashire and Scotland, particularly for goods trains, and the Midland also started to run its own Scottish passenger services from both Manchester Victoria and Liverpool. It had now reached those two cities from both the north and the south, despite not owning its own routes through Lancashire. It had made very profitable alliances with both the MS&L and the L&Y, which was a far cheaper option than building its own lines, and benefited all three parties.

The period of railway development between 1850 and 1880 was one of tremendous vitality, fed by the desire of every town of any size to have its own railway facilities, which the competing railway companies were only too happy to provide in areas such as South Lancashire and North Cheshire. It was also a period of intrigue and disputes, with alliances being formed and dissolved, and with friendships between companies waxing and waning. Some of these disputes were settled by amalgamations, or by larger companies absorbing smaller ones. Amalgamations of the bigger companies were often discussed, and the LNW, Midland, L&Y, MS&L and GN were all engaged in such schemes from time to time, but they all came to naught. In later years when some of these companies seriously proposed to amalgamate, as a means of reducing costs and avoiding wasteful competition, Parliament refused to sanction any such move because it feared that an oppressive monopoly might be created.

The turbulent times between 1850 and 1880 led to an unco-ordinated and wasteful development of railway routes, but the competition between rival companies tended to ensure that the customer was the one who benefited, in the provision of quick and efficient services for both passengers and goods. In 1850 there were 6,621 miles of railway open for traffic, and the railways carried 67 million passengers. By 1880, there were almost 18,000 miles of railway in existence, and the railways carried 604 million passengers and 235 million tons of freight. In contrast, in 1993-94 there were 10,275 miles of railway, with BR carrying 713 million passengers but only 103 million tons of freight.

This was a period of tremendous growth and, whilst the rate of building new lines was decreasing by 1880, traffic levels continued to grow substantially year by year right up to the outbreak of World War 1.

4 At The Zenith 1880 –1914
(1) Passenger and General

During this period, Manchester was one of the great trading cities of the world. It had become Cottonopolis, the warehouse and showroom of the cotton industry, surrounded by the manufacturing towns of Lancashire, but it was also an important engineering centre. The population of the Manchester region, which had been one million in 1850, had doubled by the end of the century.

However, by 1900, signs had begun to appear that Manchester's dominance had reached, and even passed, its peak, as foreign rivals who had started later began to catch up and become a serious threat. None the less, trade continued to prosper until 1914, when World War 1 started.

The railways both contributed to, and shared in, this prosperity, and the major railway companies in Manchester were all paying good dividends. In 1889, for example, the LNW was paying an ordinary dividend of 7 ⅜%, whilst the Midland was paying 6%

and the L&Y 4½%. Even the MS&L managed to pay 3%. But there were clouds on the horizon. The Manchester Ship Canal was opened in 1894, which allowed ocean-going ships to sail almost into the heart of Manchester at Trafford Park, robbing the railways of much of their lucrative freight traffic to and from Liverpool. Horse trams were giving way to electric trams, making serious inroads into the railways' short-distance suburban passenger traffic, although whether such railway traffic ever paid its way on some routes, after contributing to terminal costs, is a moot point.

Below: The Midland Hotel in October 1929, showing the covered way from the Central station and a splendid array of vintage taxis. *National Railway Museum/Crown Copyright Reserved*

Above: The various designs of L&YR 2-4-2T were a common feature of the Manchester area for many years. No 301 was built at Norwich in October 1892 and became LMS No 10680 in 1923. It was scrapped in April 1934. *LPC/IAL*

Below: Built for use on the routes from Manchester to Oldham, Rochdale and Bury, the 20 2-6-2Ts designed by H. A. Hoy proved troublesome and were transferred to other duties from 1913. No 744 is pictured at Victoria in 1909. This locomotive was to survive until August 1926. *IAL*

Above: In post-World War 2 days, 'Jubilee' No 45694 *Bellerophon*, bearing a 20A (Holbeck) shedplate, roars past Cheadle Heath North signalbox with an Up express from Manchester Central, and heads towards Disley Tunnel. The line on the left leads to Cheadle Junction signalbox on the Stockport Tiviot Dale–Timperley line. *G. Dawson/John Hammond Collection*

Events across the Channel, in Germany, where Karl Benz produced the world's first petrol-driven motor car in 1885, were destined to have a significant effect upon the railway companies' fortunes. Benz later joined forces with Gottlieb Daimler, another German engineer, to develop his invention, and it is somewhat ironic to learn that Daimler, although born in Württemberg, gained experience at the Whitworth works in Manchester.

However, competition from cars, motorbuses and lorries was not of great significance until after World War 1, and even though the railways' running costs (mainly coal and wages) increased during the period 1900 to 1914, the LNW were still able to pay 8½% on their ordinary shares in 1922.

After 1880 traffic continued to increase year by year, and both passenger and freight traffic levels had almost doubled by 1914. This increase was absorbed by building new lines and cut-offs, by improving facilities, by quadrupling lines, and by running heavier, faster trains.

By the end of the 19th century, express passenger trains on principal routes had become more luxurious, with corridors giving access throughout the train, and with the provision of dining-cars, sleeping-cars and, in some cases, Pullman cars. The railway companies, whose fares had been regulated by Parliament, had to compete with each other on speed, comfort and quality of service. Today's carriage interiors tend to appear spartan and austere to some eyes when pictured beside the comparative luxury on offer in the best pre-World War 1 express trains.

The merchandise business, too, was having to face increased costs. At one time, traders ordered in bulk and kept a reserve stock on their premises, but the high standard of service which inter-railway competition had produced meant that traders could expect, and rely upon, overnight delivery in most cases. They therefore ordered smaller lots, more frequently, rather than have capital tied up in stock. This increased the railways' handling costs, as did the running of reliable and fast overnight merchandise trains between all main centres.

Expansion

In order to be able to deal more satisfactorily with its growing passenger traffic, the L&Y enlarged Victoria station in 1884, and concurrently the LNW opened its own station, which it called Exchange, at the Salford end of Victoria station. The two stations worked as separate entities, and both had through lines and dead-end lines, the L&Y's facing east and the LNW's facing west. The LNW trains to Leeds passed through Victoria on non-platform lines, but the L&Y's westbound services bypassed Exchange. The L&Y had to enlarge Victoria even further to 17 platforms in 1904, when the infrastructure, including the signalling, was largely rebuilt or replaced.

Across at London Road, the LNW's growing suburban traffic was beginning to cause problems of accommodation in the six platforms which were the LNW's share of the station. There was no room available to enable the station to be widened and the LNW built a small suburban terminus a short distance away called, initially, Fairfield Street, and later, Mayfield, which opened in 1910. One of the main reasons for building this station was to accommodate the expected increase in suburban traffic arising from the opening the previous year of the line from Wilmslow via Gatley to Slade Lane Junction, half a mile south of Longsight, which the LNW had built to give themselves a higher-speed route for some of their principal Euston expresses, enabling them to avoid Stockport. In the event, the line became something of a white elephant, as the growing district of Stockport produced a level of patronage which the LNW could not afford to ignore.

The LNW had been prompted to build the Slade Lane line because the Midland had accelerated its best London-Manchester expresses to cover the distance in just over 3½hr, despite the hilly route, and was seriously threatening the LNW's traffic. The Midland had recently opened a new cut-off from New Mills South Junction to Heaton Mersey to speed up its approach to Manchester, and this avoided its expresses having to reduce speed for the various junctions on both sides of Stockport Tiviot Dale station and signal delays in that congested area. The new line, about nine miles long, had little or no intermediate traffic and was expensive to build, requiring a tunnel at Disley two miles 346yd long. It was purely and simply a competitive line to give the Midland the edge over the LNW. The new cut-off was opened in 1902 and it also gave the Midland a much-improved route from the East Midlands to Liverpool via a new curve at Cheadle Heath. It was a product of the intense inter-railway company competition which prevailed in those late-Victorian and Edwardian days. The Midland also built a splendid hotel in Manchester, which was opened on 4 September 1903.

Whether the Midland's shareholders viewed this almost lavish expense with equanimity is not known, but the citizens of Manchester benefited greatly. The Midland's directors, at the turn of the century, could not know the scale and effect of the approaching world war, nor that grouping with the LNW and L&Y would come about in the not-too-distant future. In those optimistic and enterprising days it must have seemed as though railway traffic, and profits, would continue to grow for ever, and that it was essential to stay ahead of the competition by constantly upgrading the product.

The Midland was a railway of tunnels. It was concerned to find a better route between Manchester and Sheffield than the somewhat circuitous one via Ambergate, and it therefore built one, 20 miles long, between Dore, on its St Pancras main line south of Sheffield, and Chinley, on the Derby–Manchester line. Opened in 1893, this was another competitive line, there being little intermediate traffic, and over a quarter of its length was in tunnel, including Totley, at three miles 950yd the longest tunnel in Britain excluding the Severn Tunnel. The new line also passed through Cowburn Tunnel, two miles 182yd long.

One of the main reasons for all this activity was to be found in the realisation of one of Sir Edward Watkin's many ambitions — the opening of the MS&L's London extension to Marylebone in 1899, during the building of which the company renamed itself, appropriately, the Great Central. The newly-named GC promptly instituted a through service of trains between Manchester Central and Marylebone, lightly loaded and fast (at least over the new section of line), but they never became really serious competitors to the well-established and popular trains of the Midland and the LNW for the Manchester–London traffic. The GC trains fared better at intermediate stations, such as Sheffield, Nottingham and Leicester.

The GN's London-Manchester service via Retford — which had been very popular with passengers and had for some years the fastest timings in Britain, on the GN main line south of Grantham — commenced in some cases to run via Grantham, Nottingham and the GC main line to Manchester. Squabbles arose with the GC, and the GN seemed to lose interest in the service. The GN trains were ultimately withdrawn, before grouping made their demise more certain.

However, the GN did not lose interest in Manchester's freight traffic, and it created yet another monument to the great railway age in its Deansgate warehouse, which was opened in 1898. The site alone cost £700,000, and the total cost was in the region of £1 million. Deansgate Goods Depot was reached by a branch just over ¼mile long, carried on bridges and arches from a junction just outside Central station. The GN's King's Cross–Deansgate goods trains used a most interesting route. Deteriorating relations with the GC and an increasing rapport with the Midland

Above: GC Class 11B 4-4-0 (LNER Class D9) No 1024 passing Northwood on a Down express from Marylebone to Manchester in 1904. The engine was built by Sharp, Stewart & Co in 1902. Renumbered 2309 in 1946. *IAL*

Below: L&Y Atlantic No 735, waiting for departure at Platform 12 Manchester Victoria with the 2.45pm to Blackpool on 22 May 1907. The well-polished engine, returning to its home shed, was built in 1899 and was withdrawn in 1927 as LMS 10318. West Junction signalbox can be seen to the right of the engine. *National Railway Museum/Crown Copyright Reserved*

caused the GN to negotiate a route via Grantham, Colwick, the Pinxton branch as far as Brinsley Junction, then across to the parallel Midland Erewash Valley line near Codnor Park. The remainder of the journey then took place over Midland metals, via Ambergate and Miller's Dale.

Finally, in this story of competitive cut-offs and avoiding lines, we must not overlook one of the earlier ones, the L&Y's Wigan avoiding line, three miles long, from a junction near Hindley (at Hindley No 3 signalbox) to Pemberton, shortening the journey by about a mile and avoiding the curvature and junctions through Wigan. It was opened in 1889 and, together with another new line from Windsor Bridge to Hindley, opened a year earlier, shortened the L&Y's Manchester to Liverpool express route by a further three miles. The L&Y was now in a position to compete for the lucrative passenger traffic between the two cities, and it ran its expresses in 40min, a feat which now seems almost incredible over such a hilly route, full of freight trains, signals and junctions. Yet again, the competitive urge, indeed the competitive necessity, had provided the citizens of Manchester with an almost profligate supply of trains and routes to Liverpool. In strict economic terms it might nowadays be regarded as wasteful over-provision, and the railways later found themselves saddled with capital costs which became increasingly difficult to service.

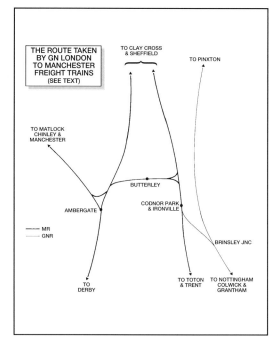

Above: Route of GN London to Manchester freight trains through the Midlands.

Below: The Lancashire and Yorkshire Railway's competitive cut-off and Wigan avoiding line on its route from Manchester to Liverpool.

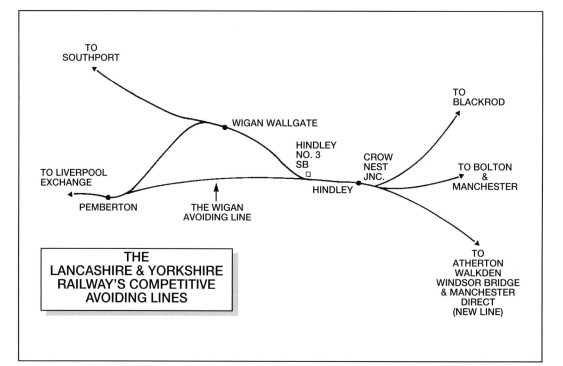

Competition —
The Electric Tram

The horse trams common in the 1880s and 1890s provided little competition for the railways, but when the tramway systems were taken over by the municipalities and were electrified, they started to pose a serious threat to short-distance suburban railway traffic. Manchester Corporation started to operate its own electric trams in 1901 and the network was quickly expanded. Neighbouring towns were similarly engaged, and it was soon possible to travel from one town to another by tram. By 1902 trams were running between Manchester and Stockport and in 1907 services started to run to Oldham and Ashton. By then, Manchester Corporation owned more than 500 trams and operated over 80 miles of track. It was possible, ultimately, to travel by tram all the way from Liverpool to Littleborough. Fares were lower than by rail and the railway companies' chickens were coming home to roost. The high capital costs of land and construction which the railways had had to bear meant that they could not match tramcar competition on price. The trams, with relatively low capital costs, and with municipal support, were in a strong position. There was no question of integrating the tram services with railway stations. Municipal authorities would have scorned to do so, and such integration had to wait another 60 years for the passage of the Transport Act 1968, which specifically provided for it in major conurbations such as Greater Manchester.

Suburban Railway Electrification

The main-line railways had become interested in the possibility of electrifying their suburban routes to combat tramcar competition and to develop new traffic, but they were surprisingly slow to develop the idea. The L&Y electrified its Liverpool–Southport service in 1904, and the success of that operation might have persuaded it to undertake more conversions, but nothing else was done for several years, although in 1913 the Holcombe Brook branch from Bury was electrified as a trial site by the firm of Dick, Kerr & Co at its own expense, in connection with a possible export order to Brazil. The experimental coaches were stored until 1928, when they were converted to an unsuccessful four-car diesel-electric unit for use on the Fylde coast.

The Midland undertook a small scheme from Lancaster to Morecambe and Heysham, which perhaps indicated that they wanted it to be as far

Below: A brand new five-coach electric set built for the Bury service, photographed in 1915. *National Railway Museum/Crown Copyright Reserved*

away from Derby as possible, and the other companies did nothing. A golden opportunity for competing with the trams, for developing new suburban traffic and for reducing the costs of running trains, was lost. Perhaps this was an indication that the enterprising zeal and entrepreneurial skills which had given the country 20,000 miles of railway, and a train service which was generally excellent, were beginning, as the apt metaphor has it, to run out of steam.

However, the L&Y, which was an enterprising railway, and a provincial one at that with no grand expresses to worry about, had its eyes on the growing suburban traffic to the residential areas north of the city. With the experience of the Liverpool–Southport electric service in mind, which demonstrated that electrified suburban services generated traffic and at the same time reduced the running costs, the L&Y decided to electrify the line from Victoria to Bury (Bolton Street) via Prestwich, at 1,200V dc, with the current being collected from a side-contact third rail. A fourth, return-current rail, was also provided but was removed later.

The new service came into operation on 17 April 1916 with a frequency of three trains per hour, and with reduced journey times, although some steam trains ran for another four months as there was a shortage of electric stock, Horwich Works being engaged on war production. The trains used

Platforms 1, 2 & 3 at Victoria, then ran parallel to the Miles Platting line before turning left to pass under that line in Collyhurst tunnel. A little further along, the line divided at Irk Valley Junction, the Bury line diverging left and a spur to Smedley Viaduct Junction on the Rochdale line diverging to the right. At Queens Road Junction a spur trailed in on the left from Cheetham Hill Junction, also on the Rochdale line.

The five-car sets provided for the new service had a distinctly American look about them, but in fact they were built in the L&Y's carriage works at Newton Heath. They were of all-metal construction, with steel frames and aluminium sides, roof and interior fittings. Electric lighting and heating were provided and the seating was arranged in open saloons. The trains were gangwayed throughout, and were a big improvement on anything the Bury line passengers had previously experienced.

Signalling

Modern technology was also beginning to appear in the signalling system. The forward-looking L&Y

Below: Layout of Exchange and Victoria passenger stations post-World War 1.

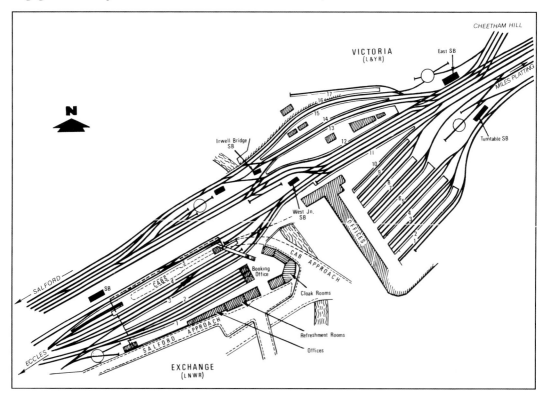

were involved in one of the first power-signalling installations, at Bolton West Junction in 1903, introduced as part of the new Trinity Street station which was opened in 1904. The new signalbox incorporated electro-pneumatic operation of points and signals, controlled by miniature levers arranged in an interlocking frame. The levers themselves had a check-lock feature to ensure that the points had moved to their desired position before the controlling lever could be moved fully home to free the appropriate interlocking. This installation continued in use until as recently as 1992.

The GC employed a low-pressure system to operate its signalling equipment on the main line between London Road and Newton, over a distance of approximately seven miles, using air pressure from a main pipe to operate signals and points by means of an air relay valve.

Below: The suburban concourse at Manchester Victoria, seen in January 1913. Much of this scene has now disappeared, but the buildings have been preserved. The 'ghosting' of the figures was caused by the long time-exposure needed in the poor lighting conditions. *National Railway Museum/Crown Copyright Reserved*

The LNW installed its 'Crewe' all-electric system at Crewe, Euston No 4, Camden and Manchester London Road (the latter in 1909), whilst the Midland tried the Siemens all-electric system, but only at Way & Works, Derby. The setback caused by World War 1, the subsequent government control, and the Grouping of 1923 were to ensure that further schemes were considerably delayed.

Passenger Stations and Train Services 1900–1914

a) The Lancashire & Yorkshire Railway

The L&Y's main station in Manchester was Victoria. It had been enlarged from time to time throughout the 19th century and finally reached the form which was to become so familiar for over half a century following its enlargement in the first decade of the 20th century. It then had 10 dead-end platforms, Nos 1 to 10, which faced east and were used for the heavy suburban traffic, and six through platforms, Nos 11 to 16, for its through expresses and its westbound starting trains, many of which were expresses to such towns as Blackpool, Liverpool and Southport. There was also a dead-end Platform 17, but it was used mainly for parcels traffic. Salford

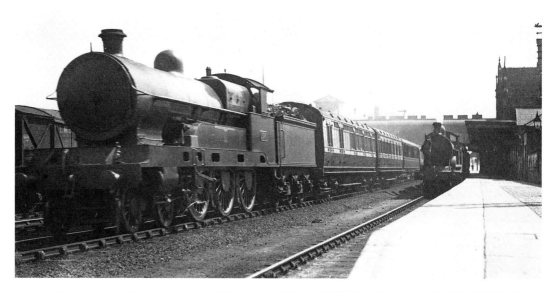

station, less than a mile to the west of Victoria, served to relieve some of the pressure on Victoria, as several suburban trains heading towards Bolton and the East Lancashire Section started their journeys there.

There were through running lines between Platforms 11 and 12, and these were used by freight trains and the LNW expresses from Liverpool and Manchester Exchange to Huddersfield, Leeds and Newcastle. The latter would stride through Victoria in the grand manner as if to demonstrate that they represented the premier line, and were not to be confused with the provincial businessmen's and tradesmen's railway which surrounded them. And always at the east end of a line next but one to Platform 12 would stand two or three engines, usually 0-6-0s, quietly simmering away as they waited their turn to bank a train up the steep climb to Miles Platting.

The L&Y's most important main line might be considered to have run from Liverpool to Manchester, and thence via Rochdale and the Calder Valley to Bradford and Leeds, and to Normanton and York, with occasional trains continuing to Hull and Newcastle, but the trains with the most prestige were undoubtedly the 'Residential' trains, which carried Manchester's most prosperous businessmen home nightly to Blackpool and Southport. This traffic grew to such an extent that eventually there were three trains to Blackpool and two to Southport every evening. They were composed of the latest corridor stock, but the Blackpool trains also conveyed the exclusive 'Club' carriages. These were very luxuriously appointed and their use was confined to a limited number of first class season ticket holders, who paid an extra supplement. Membership of the 'Club' was by election.

Above: LNW 'Claughton' class 4-6-0 No 1093 *Sir Guy Calthrop* (LMS 5923) making stately progress through Tamworth on an express from Euston to Manchester London Road c1925. *IAL*

Above right: The famous *Charles Dickens*, LNW 'Precedent' class 2-4-0 No 955 on an express from Euston to Manchester in 1900. It was built at Crewe in 1882 and for many years worked the 8.15am from Manchester London Road to Euston and the 4pm return. It was rebuilt on its existing frames in the 1890s and is reputed to have covered 2,345,107 miles before being broken up in 1912. *IAL*

b) The London & North Western Railway

The LNW had two main stations in Manchester, at London Road and Exchange. It shared London Road with the GC, and owned six dead-ended platforms, which were used for all its southbound expresses, the most important being those to Euston, run in fierce competition with the Midland, the GC and the GN, although the latter was beginning to drop out of the race. By 1910 the LNW had achieved 3hr 30min timings on its fastest London trains, whilst the Midland was almost equal with 3hr 35min.

The LNW's suburban traffic on the lines to Buxton and Crewe and the developing small wealthy towns on the Macclesfield line had grown to such an extent that it could no longer be contained at London Road and a new station, called Mayfield, had opened in 1910 to take the overflow. Mayfield would today be called a satellite station and was never popular with commuters because it entailed a longer walk, but unfortunately

London Road could not be expanded. It might be mentioned here that one of London Road's platforms was given over almost exclusively to the handling of milk churns coming in by train from the dairy farming areas of Cheshire and Staffordshire. Over 1,000 churns a day were dealt with, creating constant comings and goings of horse-drawn milk delivery carts. Milk churns were once part and parcel of the scene at passenger stations the length and breadth of the country, but it was a way of life that has passed into history, and can only be vaguely remembered by older readers.

The LNW's other station at Exchange had opened in 1884, and so was relatively modern. It was not a large station, having only two bay platforms and three through platforms, the main destinations being, westbound (1) Liverpool, (2) Glasgow and Edinburgh via Preston, and (3) North Wales via Warrington; and, eastbound, Leeds, York and Newcastle. However, it also had its 'Club' trains to Llandudno and Windermere.

Below: Layout of London Road passenger station post-World War 1.

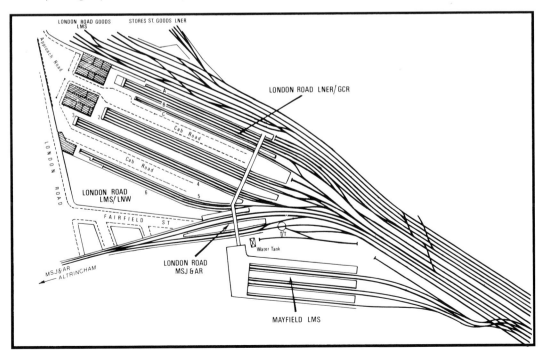

c) Midland Railway

By the turn of the century the Midland had thoroughly established itself at the Central station, and was a one-third partner in the CLC. The Midland's most important trains were its expresses to St Pancras. Although its route had more severe gradients than the LNW, it none the less endeavoured to compete on timings, and whilst it could not always succeed in doing so, it took a pride in running some of the most comfortable trains in Britain.

In order to reduce journey times, the Midland expresses often avoided Derby station and ran via Chaddesden, but E. L. Ahrons, the well-known writer of the time, records the 2pm from St Pancras and other expresses as running via Nottingham, the Erewash Valley as far as Codnor Park, then via Butterley to Ambergate, which must have entertained the passengers somewhat.

The opening of the Dore and Chinley line in 1893 gave the Midland a new route between Sheffield, Manchester and Liverpool which it was quick to exploit, and some of the Manchester–St Pancras expresses were diverted to run via Chinley and Dore South Junction.

Several of the expresses from Manchester Central to St Pancras conveyed through carriages for Birmingham (in competition with the LNW) and for Gloucester and Bristol, and there was a regular through carriage from Blackburn to St Pancras and vice versa, which ran via Victoria, Philips Park, Ancoats Junction and Marple.

The Midland's other main activity was at Victoria. The opening of the Blackburn–Hellifield line in 1880 gave the L&Y a new outlet for its Scottish traffic, and then in 1888 the Midland made an agreement with the L&Y to work all the Scottish trains with Midland engines and coaches, which resulted in further Midland engines appearing in Victoria. These trains also conveyed a second class coach for L&Y passengers to and from intermediate stations between Manchester and Hellifield.

d) Great Central Railway

The GC's main route was over the CLC from Liverpool to Manchester and then to Sheffield via Woodhead, before dividing, with one line continuing eastwards to Grimsby, Immingham Docks (formally opened by King George V in 1912) and Cleethorpes, the other line heading south to Marylebone, via Nottingham, Leicester and Rugby. When the GC opened its London extension in 1899 it inaugurated a series of expresses between Manchester and London, but even though lightly-loaded they could not compete on overall journey time with the LNW and the Midland, taking about

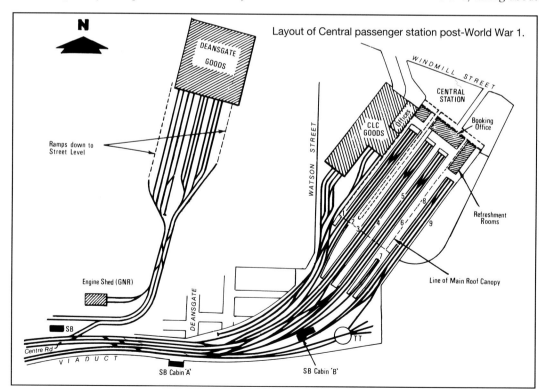

Layout of Central passenger station post-World War 1.

Above: GC 2-4-2T No 731 on a typical turn-of-the-century stopping passenger train. This class of engine was built between 1889 and 1892, and became LNER Class F1. Gorton had quite a large fleet of them. IAL

half an hour longer. However, they provided a competitive service from Manchester to Nottingham and Leicester.

The GC's suburban traffic, mainly at London Road where it had three platforms, was quite heavy, and served both the heavily-industrialised belt out to Guide Bridge and the residential area of Glossop, and also the GC and Midland joint line running to Marple, New Mills and Hayfield. Some years earlier the GC had opened the Fallowfield loop running from Gorton and Fairfield via Levenshulme and Chorlton-cum-Hardy to Manchester Central.

e) Cheshire Lines Committee

The CLC had a network of lines running west and south west from Manchester, and its most important passenger line ran from Manchester Central to Liverpool Central. The CLC operated a very popular hourly service of expresses between the two cities, taking 40min nonstop and 45min with a stop at Warrington They were hauled by Pollitt single-wheelers. Tens of thousands of World War 2 airmen will remember travelling over that route to and from Padgate, which was a main reception centre for recruits to the RAF.

CLC trains were operated by MS&L (later the GC) engines, but the CLC had its own carriages. When the CLC was first established, there was disagreement between the partners (MS&L, GN and Midland) about whose engines should work the traffic, and the question was referred to John

Ramsbottom (then at Crewe) for arbitration. He ruled that the MS&L should provide the engines for local passenger and freight traffic, and the CLC thus became the graveyard for the oldest and most 'scrappable' MS&L (and later the GC and the LNER) engines, as Ramsbottom's award stipulated that if the GN or the Midland wished to overturn it they must purchase the MS&L engines being used, at a valuation, or pay the MS&L compensation for scrapping them. This state of affairs continued until nationalisation, after which LMS 2-6-4Ts began to be used for the passenger traffic. However, two of the three partners in the CLC (the GC and the Midland) operated their own through expresses over the Liverpool line, using the CLC route from Godley Junction, on the GC Sheffield line, then via Stockport Tiviot Dale, Cheadle (where the Midland joined) and Timperley, to a junction with the Manchester–Liverpool line at Glazebrook.

The CLC's other important passenger line ran from Manchester to Chester Northgate via Altrincham and Northwich, although the section from Oxford Road to Altrincham belonged to the MSJ&A, of which the GC and the LNW were joint owners.

Carriage Sheds and Sidings

Although Manchester's main stations had a certain amount of carriage-stabling accommodation, it was quite inadequate for normal day-to-day needs, to say nothing of the stabling of spare carriages. Consequently, each company had laid out siding accommodation and built carriage sheds some distance from the centre in order to obtain the necessary land more easily and more cheaply than city centre prices. Inevitably, this led to the expensive movement of empty trains to and from the carriage sidings for cleaning, servicing and stabling, and an army of tank engines was employed for this work, although train engines sometimes worked direct from or to the carriage sidings.

Manchester's main carriage sidings were located as follows:

a) London and North Western

The main depot was at Longsight, alongside the engine shed, where there were carriage sheds covering 13 sidings. Longsight No 4 signalbox controlled the main line access at the Manchester end, while Longsight No 1 controlled the Crewe end.

To serve Exchange station, there were carriage sidings at Ordsall Lane, and a six-road carriage shed.

b) Lancashire & Yorkshire

The L&Y's intensive train service required so many carriages that they could not all be accommodated in one depot. Consequently, the L&Y had laid out several depots:

i) Newtown, on the down side, between Victoria and Miles Platting. Eight sidings, controlled by Newtown Nos 1 and 2 signalboxes

ii) Red Bank, on the up side, between Cheetham Hill Junction and Victoria, controlled by Footbridge signalbox. Extensive sidings for 180 carriages, and a six-road shed holding 67 carriages

iii) Cheetham Hill, a five-road shed and sidings for 66 carriages

iv) Queens Road (Cheetham Hill), accommodating 94 carriages

v) Monsall Lane, Thorpes Bridge Junction. Extensive sidings and two four-road carriage sheds

vi) Lightbowne, Newton Heath. Nine sidings, giving accommodation for approximately 180 carriages. The Carriage and Wagon Depot was situated alongside the line between here and Monsall Lane.

c) Midland

The Midland shared the CLC sidings and a 12-road carriage shed at Cornbrook, about 1½ miles from Central station.

d) Great Central

The GC's main carriage sidings were at Ardwick, and they shared the CLC shed at Cornbrook.

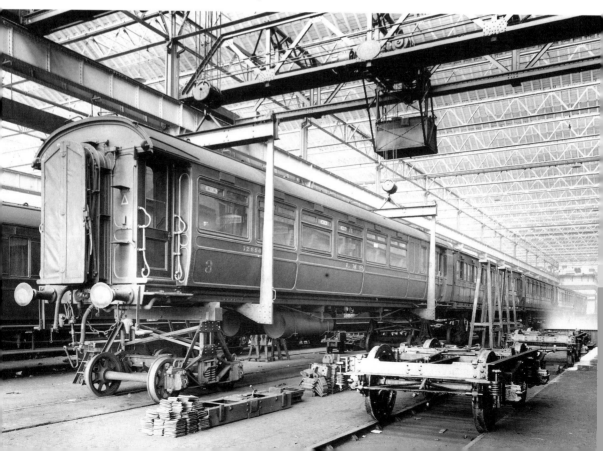

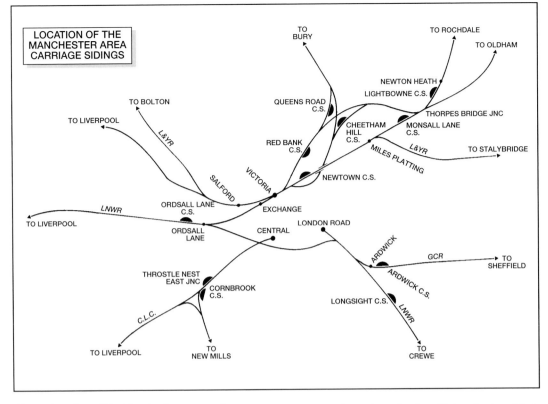

Above: Location of the Manchester area carriage sidings.

Below left: The interior of the L&Y's Newton Heath carriage works lifting shop in early LMS days, showing an ex-L&Y Brake Third Open, LMS No 12856. *National Railway Museum/Crown Copyright Reserved*

Passenger Engines

By the end of the 19th century most railway companies were busily engaged in renewing their fleets of engines to deal more efficiently with the heavier trains, both passenger and freight, which were becoming more common, and to enable higher speeds to be achieved with expresses on competitive routes. The new era in locomotive design was about to introduce 4-6-0s to the scene on the best expresses (except on the Midland), whilst for heavy freight work the ubiquitous 0-6-0, which had moved the nation's goods so cheaply and effectively for half a century, was to be superseded on most lines by the eight-coupled engine, either of 0-8-0 or 2-8-0 design.

The following pages describe the typical engines to be seen at Manchester's main line passenger stations during the years 1900 to 1910. Freight

trains and engine sheds will be dealt with in Chapter 5.

a) Lancashire & Yorkshire Railway

Victoria station was a train-spotter's paradise, with a constant stream of the L&Y's shiny black engines, lined out in red and white. Local passenger trains were mainly in the hands of an excellent class of 2-4-2Ts, introduced by the Chief Mechanical Engineer, J.A.F Aspinall, in 1889, which eventually numbered 330 engines. Although withdrawals started on a small scale in the late 1920s, well over a hundred were still in service after World War 2, by which time they were over half a century old.

Expresses were generally entrusted to 4-4-0s and 4-4-2s. The Atlantics were introduced by John Aspinall in 1899 and 40 were built in 1899/1902. They were spectacular engines, with their high-pitched boilers and 7ft 3in driving wheels, and at the time of their introduction they were said to have the largest boilers of any engine in Britain. They were highly regarded, being fast and free-running, and were mainly shedded at the ends of the system — Leeds, Low Moor, Liverpool (Sandhills), Southport and Blackpool. Withdrawal started in 1926 and they had all gone by 1934.

Left: The pride of the line — L&Y Atlantic No 1403 (LMS 10311) with 7ft 3in driving wheels. It was built at Horwich in 1899 and withdrawn in 1932. There were 40 engines in the class, built in 1899 and 1902, and the last one was withdrawn in 1934. They were known as 'Highflyers', because of their large driving wheels and high-pitched boilers. Newton Heath had several on its allocation. *IAL*

Centre left: Ex-LNW 4-4-2 'Precursor' tank No 1295 (LMS 6783), one of a class of 50 built from 1906 onwards. LMS Class 3P. *IAL*

Below left: Ex-LNW Class 4P 4-6-2T No 6978 (LNW No 1533). One of a class of 47 which came into service from 1910 onwards. *IAL*

Below: LNW 'Jubilee' class compound 4-4-0 No 1905 *Black Diamond* at Manchester London Road. Forty of these engines entered service between 1897 and 1900 but were unsuccessful and were rebuilt as two-cylinder simples from 1908 onwards. The rebuilds were known as 'Renowns'. No 1905 became LMS 5137. *IAL*

Prior to the introduction of the Atlantics, John Aspinall had produced a sizeable fleet of 4-4-0s, starting with a class of 30 with 6ft driving wheels, built by Beyer Peacock in 1888/89 and followed by another 40 with 7ft 3in driving wheels, built in 1891 and 1894. The latter were all withdrawn between 1924 and 1930, but the six-footers lasted until the early 1930s.

As the years passed, trains became even heavier, and George Hughes, the CME from 1904, produced a massive but handsome-looking 4-6-0 in 1908, with 6ft 3in driving wheels and four 16in x 26in cylinders. Twenty of the class were turned out within nine months but they were disappointing, requiring frequent maintenance and repairs and being heavy on coal consumption. Fifteen were rebuilt after the war with superheaters and Walschaerts valve gear, which considerably improved their performance, and many more were built in the early 1920s, but they got short shrift when Stanier's 4-6-0s came along from 1934 onwards.

b) London & North Western Railway

LNW engines were to be seen at both Exchange and London Road. The reign of Francis Webb as Locomotive Superintendent was drawing to its close and he finally retired in 1903, after 32 years at Crewe. LNW engines were painted blackberry black, and the simple (ie non-compound) engines built by Webb throughout his career for passenger work were uncomplicated and rugged. Still at work in the first years of the 20th century were 2-4-2Ts and 0-6-2Ts for suburban work, together with a number of 2-4-0s of various types, such as the improved Precedents with 6ft 6in driving wheels, of which 96 were built between 1887 and 1894, a number surviving to be taken over by the LMS in 1923. Webb also built 90 Whitworths, 2-4-0s with

6ft driving wheels, between 1889 and 1896, and a further 70 Rebuilt Precedents (Jumbos) between 1893 and 1901. They were splendid little engines, but too small for the job.

Also to be seen were many compounds of varying types and wheel arrangements 2-2-2-0, 2-2-2-2 and 4-4-0, some of which were better than others, but they were generally unsatisfactory. Even the later classes, the 10 'John Hicks' of 1894-98, the 40 'Jubilees' of 1897-1900, and the 40 'Alfred the Great' class of 1901-03 were failures. Only Webb's last effort, the 40 'Benbows' from 1903 (rebuilds of Jubilees and Alfreds with extra sets of independent Joy's valve gear for the outside cylinders), were anything like a success.

Top: Ex-LNW 'George the Fifth' class 4-4-0 No 25347 *Elkhound* (LNW No 1706). This engine was built at Crewe in 1911 and survived until World War 2, spending several years at Longsight. *IAL*

Above: Ex-Midland Class 2P 4-4-0 No 422 in its final form. It was built by Sharp, Stewart & Co in 1892 as MR No 2202, and was rebuilt twice, which contributed to its remarkable longevity, a common feature of Midland engines. No 422 survived until 1953, although the last of the class was not withdrawn until 1962. *IAL*

Above right: Ex-Midland compound 4-4-0 Class 4P No 1039, built in 1908/9 and rebuilt in 1920. Behind it stands LMS 10163, an ex-L&Y 4-4-0 (L&Y No 1109), built in 1891 and withdrawn in 1925. *IAL*

Webb was replaced in 1903 by George Whale, who immediately set to work to improve the LNW's parlous situation regarding its express passenger engines. Wholesale scrapping of the compounds began at once and Whale quickly introduced several new classes of simple-cylinder engines, all of which were reliable and uncomplicated, but were heavy on coal. Between 1903-1907, 130 4-4-0 'Precursors' were built, followed a year later by the 4-6-0 'Experiments', with 6ft 3in driving wheels, of which 105 were built between 1905 and 1910. Then from 1908 most of the 'Jubilees' and 'Alfreds', 70 engines in all, were rebuilt as simple two-cylinder machines.

Whale retired in 1909 and was succeeded by C J. Bowen Cooke. Two new classes began to make their appearance in Manchester — the 'George the Fifth' 4-4-0s, of which 90 were built between 1910 and 1915, and the 'Prince of Wales' 4-6-0s, of which 40 were built between 1911 and 1914 (205 more were built later). Both these classes were very capable machines, and appeared to relish being worked hard, but that caused relatively high maintenance costs and high coal consumption, which led to their rapid withdrawal when Stanier produced his 4-6-0s from 1934 onwards.

c) Midland Railway

Midland engines were mainly to be seen at Central, but quite a number found their way to Victoria, on the St Pancras–Blackburn and Hellifield–Manchester trains. At the beginning of the century, the passenger engines were basically of four types:

1) 0-4-4Ts for suburban work, 231 being built from 1869 right up to the end of the century.
2) 2-4-0 tender engines, built by Matthew Kirtley, and dating initially from 1866. Building continued until 1881, by which time up to 300 had been put into service.
3) 4-4-0 tender engines, designed by Samuel Johnson, and put into service from 1876 onwards. Their numbers ran from 300 to 562 (1907 renumbering), the last one appearing in 1901.
4) 4-2-2 tender engines, designed by Samuel Johnson and built between 1887 and 1900, affectionately known as 'Spinners'. They were renumbered 600 to 694 in 1907.

These Midland engines were apparently very long-lived, but most were rebuilt at least once, and some of the 4-4-0 later rebuilds were in effect new engines, merely taking the number of a previous engine. Presumably this was done for accountancy purposes.

Johnson brought out a new class of 4-4-0s in 1900, renumbered 700 to 779 in 1907, with 19½in x 26in cylinders (2) and 6ft 9in driving wheels. They too were rebuilt, but not until after World War 1, with 20½in x 26in cylinders and superheaters.

Finally, Johnson, followed by Deeley, brought out the compound 4-4-0s, the first one appearing in 1901. Johnson built four more, then Deeley built 40 between 1905 and 1909. Their numbers in the 1907 renumbering scheme were 1000 to 1044. In true Midland style, rebuilding of the compounds started as early as 1912. A number were shedded at Trafford Park in 1909 to provide more power for the London expresses.

The Midland never built any passenger engines larger than 4-4-0s, despite the severe gradients on many of its main lines. Its policy was short trains, smartly timed, at intervals as short as the traffic would allow. If longer trains were run, they were double-headed.

The Midland at Central and Victoria will always be remembered for its neat and handsome 4-4-0s, in the colour that became known familiarly as 'Midland Red'. Its carriages, too, were amongst the most luxurious and comfortable of any railway.

d) Great Central Railway

The opening of the London extension to Marylebone in 1899 made the GC a national, rather than a provincial, railway, and brought modern GC express engines and GC London express trains to Manchester.

GC engines were to be seen all over the south side of Manchester. Not only did GC trains use both London Road and Central station, but their engines also hauled all the CLC trains.

The turn of the century was significant for the GC in another way. Pollitt resigned as Locomotive Engineer and was replaced by J. .G. Robinson, who surely ranks as one of the most eminent locomotive engineers of his time. His reign at Gorton lasted throughout the remaining independent life of the GC, and when the LNER was formed in 1923 he was offered the post of Chief Mechanical Engineer, even though he was 66 years old and Gresley of the GN was available. However, he declined the honour.

We must, however, return to the previous locomotive engineer, Harry Pollitt, because it was he who designed the engines for the London extension. These were the Class 11A 4-4-0s, Nos 852 to 881 and 270, with 7ft driving wheels, which appeared in 1898 and 1899.

Other longer-distance passenger work was undertaken by 2-4-0s and 4-4-0s of varying ages, whilst suburban work was mainly entrusted to 2-4-2T and 0-6-2T engines, of which large numbers had been built between 1890 and 1900 (34 2-4-2T and 177 0-6-2T), many of them by Beyer Peacock, whose works were next door to the GC's at Gorton.

Robinson brought out his first 4-4-0s of Class 11B in 1901, Nos 1013 to 1017, with 20 more following in 1902, Nos 1018 to 1037. They were all built by Sharp Stewart and Co. A further class of 4-4-0s, known as 'Directors' and numbered 429 to 438, came out in 1913. However, Robinson recognised the need for larger, more powerful engines and produced his first 4-6-0s in 1902, with 6ft driving wheels, Nos 1067 to 1072 of Class 8, built by Neilson, Reid and Co. These were followed by:

	GC	—LNER	Class			Wheels
180–187	8	B5	Beyer Peacock	1904	6ft 1in
195/6	8C	B18	Beyer Peacock	1904	6ft 9in
1095–1104	8F	B4	Beyer Peacock	1906	6ft 6in
423	1	B2	Gorton	1912	6ft 9in
			named *Sir Sam Fay*			
424–428	11E	B2	Gorton	1913	6ft 9in
4, 279/80}	1A	B8	Gorton	1914	5ft 7in
439–446}					

Robinson also produced a number of Atlantics between 1903 and 1906, with 6ft 9in driving wheels.

For the suburban services, a new series of 4-4-2Ts came out in 1903, with 5ft 7in driving wheels. Fifty-two were built between 1903 and 1907 both by Gorton and outside contractors. Finally, shortly before World War 1, Gorton produced small numbers of 4-6-2T engines.

Mention ought to be made of the single-wheelers used on CLC Manchester–Liverpool trains. These were Pollitt's last design, and he produced six in 1900, numbered 967 to 972, with 7ft 9in driving wheels. They were admirable for the fast, light trains over that easy route, although they had originally been built for the Marylebone–Leicester services.

Parcels Traffic

Before leaving this review of passenger trains and stations, mention must be made of parcels traffic. Who has not been held up, when rushing for a

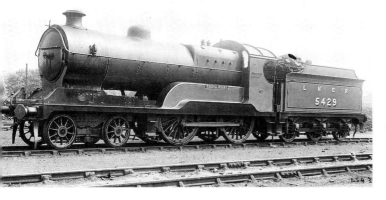

Below opposite: LNER (ex-GC) Class D9 4-4-0 No 6023 (GC No 1023). Built by Sharp, Stewart & Co in 1902, it was allocated to Trafford Park shed in the 1930s and renumbered 2308 in 1946. *IAL*

Above left: The first of the original batch of GC 'Directors', LNER Class D10 4-4-0 No 5429 *Prince Henry,* built in 1913 (GC No 429). It was shedded at Gorton in the 1930s and renumbered 2650 in 1946. *IAL*

Left and centre left: Two fine views of LNER (ex-GC) Class B3 4-6-0 No 6168 *Lord Stuart of Wortley* — (a) in its original form, and (b) after being fitted with Caprotti valve gear in 1929 in a successful endeavour to improve its performance. This engine was shedded at Gorton in the 1930s. Six of these B3s were built by Robinson between 1917 and 1920. *IAL*

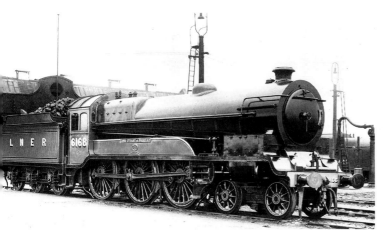

Below: LNER (ex-GC) Class C13 4-4-2T No 6057 at Trafford Park in 1935. This class of engine entered service between 1903 and 1905, and there were nine of them at Trafford Park in the 1930s. This engine became 7402 in the 1946 renumbering. *IAL*

train, by a tractor pulling a seemingly endless line of barrows loaded, sometimes precariously, with all manner of parcels. And if one fell off, as it sometimes did, the whole caravan came to a halt in response to shouts from onlookers, to add to the general exasperation. The L&Y had adopted an ingenious solution at Victoria — a parcels carrier which ran at right angles from the parcels office across all the through platforms. The carrier was suspended from a track which was fixed under the station roof and had a seat for the operator. When the carrier reached the appropriate platform, the operator lowered a basket containing the parcels.

Parcels were originally conveyed in the guard's van, with a waybill for each parcel, checked by the guard, but as the traffic grew a systematic network of parcels trains was introduced. They were not well-known, because they ran mainly during the night in order to give a next-day delivery. Such trains ran at express passenger-train speeds.

The parcels business, now largely gone, was a study in itself. During the afternoon each company's horses and carts, lorries and vans would visit business premises, warehouses, shops, etc to collect the parcels for dispatch, and take them to the parcels office at the station. There, an army of clerks and parcels porters would check them, weigh them and raise the appropriate charges, after which the parcels would be sorted on to barrows for particular trains or vans. The vans themselves would often be sectioned for particular stations, and the trains conveyed vans both for stations *en route*, to be detached there, and for junction stations, where vans would be detached to connect with other parcels trains. The trains would also pick up vans which had been detached from other trains and a very complex interlocking network existed. Punctuality was most important.

Many of the overnight passenger and sleeping-car trains also conveyed vans, in fact some overnight trains conveyed more vans than coaches. These trains were principally used by the General Post Office for conveying mails, which by law the railways were bound to convey, but they were, of course, happy to do so.

The great variety of traffic dealt with under the generic term 'parcels' almost baffles the imagination nowadays. Apart from brown paper parcels, one might see the following:

1. Bags of parcels post. These were carted to and from the station by the GPO, but were then handled by railway parcels porters. They were not individually weighed and checked, but were carried under contract depending on the number of bags scheduled.

2. Bags, trunks and personal items of all descriptions.

3. Theatrical traffic, consisting of the props and scenery of touring companies, often by special trains. The theatrical company also travelled on the same train.

4. Boxes of fish packed in ice.

5. Periodicals and newspapers. Manchester was, and still is to some extent, a regional centre for printing daily newspapers, and trains were run every evening and through the night specially for newspaper traffic.

6. Livestock of every conceivable kind, ranging from horses conveyed in specially constructed horsebox vehicles and carried on passenger trains, to tiny animals in cardboard boxes being sent to livestock shows.

7. Wicker baskets of racing pigeons, and the empty baskets being returned after the pigeons had been released. This traffic was far more extensive than might be expected, and special trains were run at weekends to what were known as 'liberation points', accompanied by the pigeon fanciers to assist railway staff in releasing the pigeons, and generally keep an eye on things.

8. Milk in churns.

9. Foodstuffs. Who can forget Palethorpes sausages, Lyons Cakes, etc?

10. Corpses (in coffins, of course).

Christmas was the busiest period. As it approached, the quantity of parcels, mailbags and bags of parcels post grew day by day until, almost literally, there were mountains of traffic, and passengers had to thread their way through. Extra staff and cartage had to be hired, but by Christmas Eve it had all gone.

Apart from 'Red Star' and some Post Office mails, the parcels business is now but a memory, but we must not forget that it was once an integral part of the life and scene of every large passenger station. And who can forget that curious *mélange* of smells that permeated certain parts of stations, especially from the boxes of fish and from the thousands of horses that were used on collection and delivery duties? Remember *that,* dear passenger, when next you walk across the smart, clean and bright terrazzo tiling at Piccadilly. Passenger stations nowadays are rather more congenial places than they used to be, but the parcels business contributed substantially to the railways' prosperity. Its demise is a separate story that deserves telling.

Right: Manchester Victoria's overhead parcels carrier in action, having just lowered a basket of parcels on to Platform 11 on 15 December 1912. The operator must have had an exciting life, keeping well clear of engine chimneys and safety valves. *National Railway Museum/Crown Copyright Reserved*

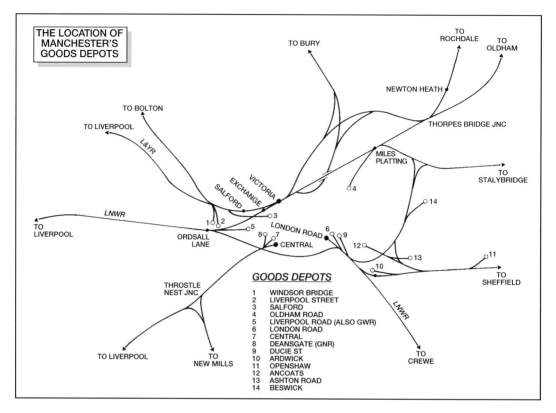

THE LOCATION OF MANCHESTER'S GOODS DEPOTS

TO BURY

TO ROCHDALE
TO OLDHAM

NEWTON HEATH

THORPES BRIDGE JNC

TO BOLTON

TO LIVERPOOL

L&YR

MILES PLATTING

TO STALYBRIDGE

VICTORIA
EXCHANGE
SALFORD

LNWR

TO LIVERPOOL

ORDSALL LANE

1 2
5
8 7
CENTRAL

3

LONDON ROAD
6 9

12 13

14

10

11

TO SHEFFIELD

THROTTLE NEST JNC

GOODS DEPOTS

1	WINDSOR BRIDGE
2	LIVERPOOL STREET
3	SALFORD
4	OLDHAM ROAD
5	LIVERPOOL ROAD (ALSO GWR)
6	LONDON ROAD
7	CENTRAL
8	DEANSGATE (GNR)
9	DUCIE ST
10	ARDWICK
11	OPENSHAW
12	ANCOATS
13	ASHTON ROAD
14	BESWICK

TO LIVERPOOL

TO NEW MILLS

LNWR

TO CREWE

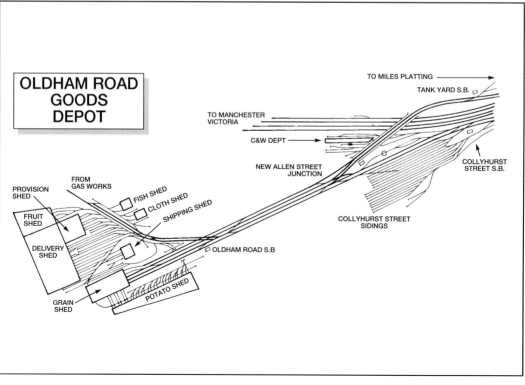

OLDHAM ROAD GOODS DEPOT

TO MILES PLATTING

TANK YARD S.B.

TO MANCHESTER VICTORIA

C&W DEPT

NEW ALLEN STREET JUNCTION

COLLYHURST STREET S.B.

PROVISION SHED

FROM GAS WORKS

FISH SHED

CLOTH SHED

SHIPPING SHED

FRUIT SHED

DELIVERY SHED

COLLYHURST STREET SIDINGS

OLDHAM ROAD S.B

GRAIN SHED

POTATO SHED

5 At the Zenith 1880–1914 (2) Goods Depots, Yards and Engine Sheds

Goods Depots

It is difficult now to remember (if the reader is old enough) or to visualise (if he is not) the bustle and the volume of activity at Manchester's major goods depots before World War 1, with the surrounding streets thronged with horses and carts taking goods to or from the depots. Apart from the traffic which came into Manchester's docks by ship, the city depended almost entirely upon the railways, not only for the means of carrying on its industrial activities, but also for its food and other necessities. It all came and went by train, and the railways were an essential part of Manchester's life.

Goods depots were generally divided into a number of sections. Next to the main line there were sidings for receiving inwards trains and for placing wagons waiting to be taken away. Then there would be a large open area of sidings with roadway access, where goods could be unloaded directly from railway wagons to carts, and vice versa. Finally, there would often be one or more large imposing buildings, usually of several storeys. Goods were warehoused on the upper storeys awaiting customers' instructions, whilst the ground floor would be occupied by a number of platforms with a line of rails on one side and a roadway on the other. Consignments of goods traffic occupying less than a whole wagon — known as smalls or sundries — were dealt with here. As each wagon or van was unloaded, the packages were barrowed to the appropriate delivery cart, of which there were usually quite a number, serving different areas of the city, or were taken to another railway wagon for onward transit. As can be imagined, the amount of to-ing and fro-ing of goods porters pushing two-wheeled barrows was enormous, and the range and variety of traffic dealt with was astonishing.

After the 'inwards' traffic had been dealt with, it was time to rearrange the depot for the 'outwards' traffic. Vans, or wagons which were sheeted before dispatch, would be positioned alongside the platform, and labelled to particular destinations. When the delivery carts returned with the forwarded traffic, the various consignments would be documented and barrowed to the appropriate railway van or wagon. The morning's activity would be repeated in reverse, then at a given time a shunting engine would take the vans away to the outwards sidings, to await collection by a mainline engine. The movement and marshalling of these vans was very carefully planned in advance to ensure that they connected with mainline trains and reached their destinations, as far as possible, next morning. As can be seen, the whole activity was very labour-intensive. Now the remaining warehouses, no longer used for their original purpose, stand like monuments to a bygone age.

Not all goods depots had warehouses. Some dealt only with full wagon loads (ie consignments to or from only one consignor/consignee), which were dealt with in the open. Most depots also had large open areas for dealing with household coal. Merchants generally unloaded the coal directly into sacks, to be delivered straight away; but if there were no immediate orders, and to act as a buffer stock against heavy demand or an interruption of supply, merchants would rent stacking space from the railway company. Here is another everyday scene of earlier years which has completely gone, except from the memory. Imagine a large open area, with lines of often brightly coloured railway trucks, bearing in large distinctive letters the name of the colliery which owned the wagon, or in some cases the name of the individual coal merchant. Around the area are stacks of coal of various grades whose names were once common currency, such as best cobbles, household nuts, Barnsley Hards, and so on. The whole area is filled with horses and carts, and the sound of hooves and cartwheels on the stone setts. In the days when virtually every house in Manchester was warmed by an open coal fire, house coal was big business, both for the trade and the railways, although it entailed costly shunting and tripping to get a particular wagon to a particular merchant's siding.

The more important goods depots in Manchester were:

Above left: Location of Manchester's goods depots.

Below left: Plan of Oldham Road goods depot.

a) Lancashire & Yorkshire Railway

The L&Y's most important depot in Manchester was Oldham Road, the one-time passenger terminus of the Manchester & Leeds Railway. The depot continued to grow throughout the 19th century and was eventually rebuilt in 1916. In its final form it had a number of 'sheds', which were called the Fruit Shed, the Provision Shed, the Delivery Shed, the Fish Shed, the Cloth Shed, the Grain Shed, the Potato Shed and the Shipping Shed, which gives some idea of the range and diversity of traffic handled there.

Access to Oldham Road goods depot was from Miles Platting, via Collyhurst Street. At the latter there was a fan of sidings with capacity for 470 wagons. There was also a flyover bridging the

passenger lines to and from Victoria, and giving access to more sidings on the north side of Miles Platting station. These were known as Tank Yard sidings, with 515 wagons standage, and situated a little further along the line was the Brewery marshalling yard.

The L&Y's other important goods depot was at Salford, reached from Oldfield Road No 2 signalbox. The area was rather neatly bisected by the LNW viaduct on the line between Exchange and Ordsall Lane, and from the train windows the passenger had a good view of the layout of sidings and goods sheds, with small, almost tiny, 0-4-0 'Pug' shunting engines busily shuttling to and fro, placing and withdrawing wagons. The long-lived 0-6-0STs performed the heavier work. These had been built by Barton Wright as 0-6-0 tender engines round

about 1880 and 230 were converted into saddle tank engines in the 1890s. Perhaps more than anything the 0-6-0STs, to be seen in virtually every group of sidings on the L&Y, personified that railway.

There were more sidings nearby at Hope Street, and further along the line, at Pendleton, was situated Brindle Heath marshalling yard, with three separate groups of sidings known as the Up Sidings, the Down Sidings and the Old Sidings. These were served by the adjacent Agecroft engine shed.

b) London & North Western Railway

The LNW had two main goods depots, at London Road and at Liverpool Road.

The workings at London Road are graphically described in Sir William Ackworth's classic work *The Railways of England*, published initially in 1889. The goods depot there was situated under the lines and platforms of the passenger station, and wagons were lowered into the goods depot by means of a wagon hoist. All movements in the depot itself were carried out by rope and hydraulic capstan, using wagon turntables instead of points. Whilst this might appear to be a cumbersome and labour-intensive method of working it was very flexible, and it has to be remembered that in 1900 labour was cheap and readily available. Ackworth describes London Road as one of the busiest goods depots in the world, dealing with up to 2,000 tons of merchandise a day.

In later years a conventional goods shed/warehouse was erected on the north side of London Road passenger station, fronting on to Ducie Street.

Full wagon load traffic was also dealt with at the Ardwick Low Level goods yard, reached by a connection from the London Road–Stockport line at Ardwick Junction, which then passed under the main line to obtain access to the yard.

The sidings used for holding traffic to and from the goods depots were at Longsight, a little further south, and the main marshalling yard was at Edgeley, to the south of Stockport.

Liverpool Road goods depot is famous for including the Manchester passenger terminus of the Liverpool & Manchester Railway, dating from 1830. The building still stands today and is part of the Manchester Museum of Science and Industry. Access to Liverpool Road was obtained from the MSJ&A at Ordsall Lane No 1 signalbox, where lines

Left: Goods depots were rarely inspiring from an architectural viewpoint, and the offices at Oldham Road looked quite shabby in 1967 when this photograph was taken, a few months before their demolition. However, Oldham Road had been the original passenger terminus of the Manchester & Leeds Railway before it was converted to a goods depot, and the title can just be seen below the roof line. *T. A. Fletcher*

Above: A type of engine that symbolised the L&Y for half a century and more. There were 230 of these engines, spread all over the L&Y system, and they dated from the 1890s, when they were converted from Barton Wright's 0-6-0 tender engines originally built between 1876 and 1885. They were extremely long-lived engines, and almost 100 survived into BR days, the last one being withdrawn in 1962, after 82 years' service (67 years as a saddle tank). *IAL*

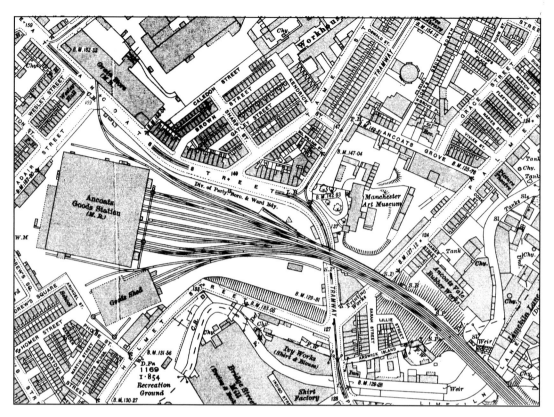

Above: Extract of Manchester (SE) 1915 Ordnance
Survey Map, showing layout of Ancoats goods depot.

led directly to four goods sheds/warehouses, two of
which were used by the Great Western Railway.
(The terms 'shed' and 'warehouse' tend to be used
loosely in railway terminology. At one extreme they
were substantial stone or brick buildings, with
warehouse facilities; at the other they were wooden
structures used only for handling traffic.) The Great
Western's interest in Manchester has already been
mentioned and it was quite considerable. In 1913
the GW employed 217 staff at Liverpool Road goods
depot. Inwards traffic (ie from other parts of the
country) amounted to 45,000 tons, with a similar
amount forwarded. In addition 1,088 wagons of
livestock were handled.

Next to Ordsall Lane No 1 signalbox was No 2
signalbox, which controlled the eastern end of an
extensive group of sidings known as Ordsall Lane.
On the south side of the line there were sidings for
over 400 goods wagons and an extensive coal yard,
whilst on the north side there were the Ordsall Lane
carriage sidings and carriage shed. The western end
of this complex was controlled by Ordsall Lane No 4
signalbox. At Cross Lane, less than a mile away,

there was a large area of sidings and pens for cattle,
known as Cross Lane Cattle Dock sidings.
Railwaymen had to be versatile in those days.

c) Midland Railway

The Midland's goods activities were centred on the
Ancoats/Ashton Road complex, reached initially
from Ashburys West signalbox, on the GC's main
line from Sheffield to London Road, and then, just a
few yards along the branch to Philips Park, from
Ancoats Junction signalbox.

From Ancoats Junction four tracks led directly to
the Midland's major goods depot at Ancoats, with a
separate Scotch shed and large grain warehouse.
The extensive yard at Ashton Road, which was
reached from Ashton Road signalbox on the
Ancoats Branch, had a capacity of over 1,000
wagons, and included a coal yard and a cattle dock.
In 1900 the Midland carted 294,000 tons of
merchandise (forwarded and received) and dealt
with 149,000 tons of non-carted traffic and 86,000
tons of coal, coke and limestone.

d) Great Central Railway

The GC's main goods depots were at London Road
(Ducie Street) and at Central, but there were also

Above: A typical view of industrial Britain in the early 20th century — mill chimneys, terraced houses and railway goods yards thronged with wagons, over all of which hangs the inevitable smoky haze. In this May 1922 scene of the Midland's Ancoats Depot, there are wagons from many railway companies, including MR, GN, LNWR, GC, GE, LBSC, NE, GW, L&Y, SE&C, NB and H&B — an almost incredible array. *National Railway Museum/Crown Copyright Reserved*

Below: The former Great Northern Railway goods warehouse still stands in Deansgate, a monument to the railway age at its zenith. It was built in 1898/99. *P. E. B. Butler*

extensive yards and sidings at Ashburys and Ardwick. Ducie Street was the MS&L's first goods depot, and eventually it extended to several substantial warehouses. The depot at Central was smaller, and was opened in 1877 on the site later occupied by the passenger station, at which time the goods activities were transferred to a site adjoining the Central station, on the north side. This was in effect the Cheshire Lines goods depot.

The GC had large marshalling yards on the Sheffield line in the Guide Bridge area. Apart from the Guide Bridge sidings themselves, known as Liverpool sidings, Cock Lane sidings, Brookside sidings and Dukinfield sidings, there was the extensive Dewsnap marshalling yard, consisting of no fewer than 52 dead-end sidings all facing east.

e) Great Northern Railway

One of the most modern goods depots was that erected in 1898/99 by the GN at Deansgate. This imposing building still stands, together with the remnants of its approach viaducts, a mute testimony to railway competitiveness. It was connected to the main line just outside Central Station at GN Junction signalbox.

Freight Engines

Up to the 1890s freight trains were almost entirely in the hands of an army of 0-6-0s, but as traffic increased and trains became heavier, several railway companies began to introduce more powerful engines. The L&Y also had many hilly routes to contend with, and Aspinall brought out a series of 0-8-0s. The first series, known as the small-boilered 0-8-0s, came out in 1900, and no fewer than 130 were built in the next eight years. Many were subsequently fitted with larger boilers and superheaters, but withdrawal started as early as 1925 and they would probably all have gone by 1940 but for the outbreak of World War 2.

A second series, with larger boilers, came out in 1910. Seventy-eight were built up to 1920, the later ones with superheaters. They were massive-looking engines, with a tractive effort of nearly 30,000lb, and, like the earlier engines, would all have been withdrawn by 1940 but for World War 2. However, they provided the L&Y with a very satisfactory stud of heavy freight engines, ably supported by the 0-6-0s for lighter trains.

The LNW under Francis Webb applied compounding to its heavy freight engines as well as to the passenger engines. His first 3-cylinder 0-8-0s came out in 1892, and 112 were built up to 1900. They were converted to simples by George Whale, mostly to Class G1.

Right and lower right: The L&Y had a large number of heavy freight engines. The small-boilered engines were classified 6F by the LMS, and the large-boilered were classified 7F. Seen here are Class 6F No 12708 (L&Y No 69), built in 1901 and withdrawn in 1934, and L&Y No 67 (LMS Class 7F No 12804), built in 1910 and withdrawn in 1927. A small number survived World War 2, but all had gone by 1951. *IAL*

Webb then produced 170 4-cylinder compound 0-8-0s between 1901 and 1904. Many were converted to two cylinder simples from 1906 onwards, and 60 more of the simple type were built in 1910. Building of simple 0-8-0s continued up to Grouping, and a fleet of over 500 capable machines was handed over to the LMS. Most were converted to Class G2 and almost all survived to be taken over by BR. Indeed, many continued to give good service until the late 1950s/early 1960s and they were ideal for slow, heavy freights.

For mixed goods traffic Whale produced 170 4-6-0s, known as 19in Goods, from 1906 onwards. They were very successful engines, but only a handful survived the slaughter of LNW locomotive stock which occurred under Stanier to live for a few more years.

As is well known, the Midland never went in for big engines, and until the Class 4F 0-6-0s came out in 1911 they relied entirely on an army of well over a thousand 0-6-0s in classes 2F and 3F, some of which were extremely ancient. Double-heading was the rule on the Midland, although it has to be said that the rebuilt Class 3Fs, with Belpaire boilers, were excellent, rugged machines and very long-lived. Even in the early 1960s they could still regularly be seen, and the last ones were not withdrawn until 1964. Nevertheless, it is astonishing that the Midland should have entrusted its enormous coal and mineral traffic to nothing more powerful than a Class 3F 0-6-0 before 1911.

The GC, too, produced a stock of 0-8-0s, starting in 1902. These were the Class 8A outside

Upper right: The LNW had a large fleet of 0-8-0 goods engines, of varying design and development dating from 1892 onwards, and they were the only LNW class of engine which lasted well into BR days in substantial numbers, several hundred receiving BR numbers. There were still well over 100 at work in 1960, and the last ones were not withdrawn until 1964. *IAL*

Bottom right: One of the ubiquitous LNW 'Coal Tanks', of which 300 were built by Francis Webb from 1881 onwards. No 7703 is seen resting at Patricroft shed in 1939. *IAL*

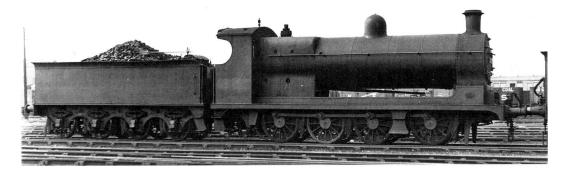

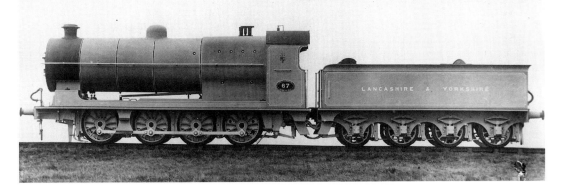

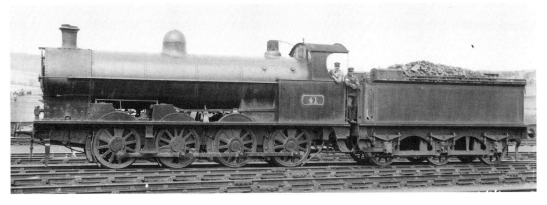

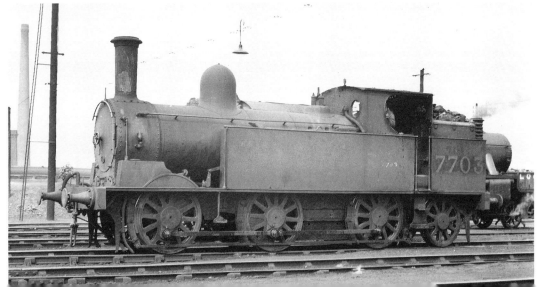

cylinder mineral engines, nicknamed 'Tiny' on account of their massive bulk. Ninety-two were in service by 1911. They were supplemented by a modern fleet of 0-6-0s.

So far as freight working is concerned, Robinson's crowning success must be considered to be his 2-8-0s, of Class 8K, the first of which appeared in 1911. Eight more were built that year, followed by no fewer than 68 in 1912, and 28 in 1913/14. The design was adopted for the official War Department ROD engines built during World War 1 for the Ministry of Munitions, and various contractors and the GC built 521.

Engine Sheds

Whilst Manchester might be described as being surrounded by engine sheds, there was none near the city centre, for which Manchester's citizens must have been mightily thankful, considering the amount of smoke which poured from the chimneys of hundreds of locomotives on shed. Those unfortunates who lived in the row upon row of terraced houses near the sheds just had to put up with it. Many of them worked at the sheds, either as locomen, fitters or labourers and in any case they produced plenty of their own smoke from their domestic hearths.

There were good reasons for not locating engine sheds near city centres. They occupied large areas of land, which was cheaper and more easily obtained further from the centre. Secondly, engine sheds provided engines not just for working trains from the main passenger stations but also for working empty stock to and from the carriage sidings, which were similarly placed some distance from the city centre. Finally, the sheds also provided engines to haul freight trains. Most marshalling yards and sidings were located on the fringe of the city. The main engine sheds were situated as follows:

L&Y	Newton Heath
	Agecroft
LNW	Patricroft (for Exchange and the north side)
	Longsight (for London Road and the south side)
Midland	Belle Vue (to serve Ancoats and Ashton Road)
	Trafford Park (jointly with GC & GN)
GC	Gorton
	Trafford Park
GN	Trafford Park

There were also a number of minor coaling and stabling points, usually within goods yards for the shunting engines employed there.

The Manchester Ship Canal

Despite having three separate railway companies all anxious to convey goods between Liverpool and Manchester, and vice versa, the traders of Manchester laboured under the feeling, perhaps with some justification, that they were the victims of an oppressive railway monopoly, and that they were being held to ransom by high freight rates. The railways, as a means of transport, certainly held a monopoly, and they competed amongst themselves on quality of service rather than on the rates they charged.

The railway companies were generally rigid in their charging systems, and this led to many disputes with traders, which was bad for public relations. Railway rates became extraordinarily complex; in addition to the haulage charge there were extras for cartage, sheeting, roping, terminal costs, wagon demurrage, siding rent, warehousing and others. Lawyers grew fat from settling disputes, yet the railways were the force which had enabled Manchester and other industrial cities to prosper, and no one could say that they were making excessive profits. Possibly the City Fathers thought that the railway companies had become too big and powerful; the LNW, for example, had become the largest joint-stock company in the world. Perhaps the intrigues and squabbles between railway companies had left a nasty taste. For whatever reason, the railway companies did not generally receive the support from municipal authorities that they might reasonably have expected and to which, in fairness, they might be judged to have been entitled.

Thus, rightly or wrongly, there was a search for a means of breaking this monopoly. The answer to the question — 'How can we escape from the twin burdens of high railway rates and high port charges?' — was obvious, even though it might have seemed no more than a pipe-dream — 'Build a canal and bring the ships right into Manchester.' When Manchester Corporation sponsored the idea to the tune of £5 million, equal to a third of the Canal Company's total capital, the pipe-dream became a reality.

Work on this great engineering project started in 1887 and was completed in 1894. The canal was 35 miles long and was dug to the same depth as the Suez Canal. The docks were actually in Salford and a major trading estate grew up at Trafford Park. Engineering especially benefited from the canal, although the original drive to build it had sprung from the cotton industry. As later years showed, the canal did not, and could not, save the cotton industry, nor even postpone its demise.

The impact on the railways was severe. They had to rearrange their freight businesses to reflect the changed importance of Liverpool and Manchester as distributive centres. The Ship Canal Co laid down a considerable network of railway lines to serve the docks, to which the main-line railways were connected. The CLC had a connection from Trafford Park Junction, the L&Y from Windsor Bridge and the LNW from Eccles.

By 1914 the railways had achieved a position of importance in the daily life of Manchester which has never been surpassed. They permeated almost every aspect of industrial, commercial and domestic life in both Manchester and Salford. They were major employers and the railways and their depots and sidings occupied huge areas of land.

Since 1900 their traffic had continued to grow year by year, and in the summer of 1914 it must have seemed that it would continue to do so for ever, and that the sun would never set on the prosperity of the railways. Admittedly, there were signs of more difficult times ahead. The trams had eaten into the railways' short distance passenger traffic. Labour relations in the railway industry were becoming more difficult — there had been serious strikes, and labour costs were bound to rise with higher wages and shorter hours. But, as yet, the railways' main enemies, the car and the lorry, were little more than a slight nuisance, and the car was regarded as something of a rich man's toy.

It seems probable that change would have come only gradually had it not been for events in Europe, where, many hundreds of miles away, the chancelleries of Europe were preparing for war. That fatal pistol shot in Sarajevo on 28 June 1914 signalled the end of the railways' golden age. For almost a century the railways had developed and prospered. After World War 1 not only the railways, but Britain's industries too, would be struggling to survive.

In these two chapters, covering the period from 1880 to 1914, the author has attempted to portray in some detail the everyday scenes in the life of the railways in the years leading up to World War 1. The railways had, in fact, reached maturity, and their physical assets, in terms of stations, depots, tracks, etc would see very little change for the next half century. New engines might appear, and liveries might change, but railway life and railway working methods would continue almost unaltered. The railwayman of 1900, suddenly catapulted forward half a century, would have found no great difficulty in acclimatising himself. In the next chapter we will explore the changes which did take place.

Below: Location of Manchester's engine sheds.

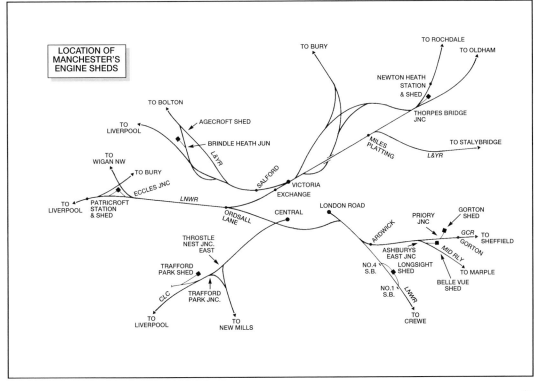

6 Coming To Terms with Change — 1919 to 1939

During World War 1, passenger services were reduced and expresses decelerated, but prewar standards were fairly quickly restored once hostilities had ceased. Railways had suffered very little structural damage and they had no difficulty in replacing those members of their staffs who had failed to return from the battlefield.

However, the government had undergone a major change of attitude towards railway company amalgamations. In the latter part of the 19th century it had consistently set its face against any mergers of the big companies, because it feared that they might exploit the more powerful monopoly positions that would be created. But wartime experience of operating the railways under unified control, plus a realisation that some of the weaker companies might find it difficult to survive in the face of the substantially increased labour costs brought about by the war and the establishment of the eight hour day, together with the increased costs of materials and coal, had persuaded the government that amalgamations were desirable. There was little inkling then of the fierce competition that would soon arise from the motor bus and the motor lorry, despite the fact that the government had flooded the market with surplus army lorries sold off cheaply, which were eagerly snapped up by ex-servicemen who were anxious to work for themselves rather than return to the drudgery of factory and foundry.

The result of government deliberations was the Railways Act of 1921, which created the four main-line companies, known as the 'Big Four':

The London, Midland and Scottish Railway
The London and North Eastern Railway
The Great Western Railway
The Southern Railway

The Act came into effect on 1 January 1923, and as far as Manchester was concerned it grouped the LNW (amalgamated with the L&Y on 1 January 1922 in advance of the Act), the Midland and the North Staffs into the LMS, and the GC and GN into the LNER. The CLC continued to be a joint line, but was henceforth owned two-thirds by the LNER and one third by the LMS. The MSJ&A also continued as a line jointly owned by the LMS and the LNER.

The new company names started to appear on buildings and notice boards, and on locomotives and rolling stock, and new liveries started to appear, although rather slowly. The LNER chose teak for its coaches, green for its express engines and black for others. The LMS extended the colour known as Midland Red to all its coaches and passenger engines, and chose black for its goods engines, but later restricted the red livery to its express passenger engines.

The city corporations, after years of being at the mercy of the railway giants, took advantage of the availability of motor buses and started to develop their fleets and routes, to such an extent that by the mid-1920s they were making serious inroads into the railway companies' suburban traffic.

On the motive power front, the railways continued to turn out locomotives to well-proven designs and this continued for a short time after Grouping, before standard designs started to appear.

Change came very slowly and, apart from the appearance of new liveries and new company names, the railways continued to operate, so far as the casual observer was concerned, very much as they had done before the war, and indeed there was a short honeymoon period before the effects of road competition started to bite. The railway companies found it very difficult to fight back, because their rates and charges had been frozen by Parliament in the old monopoly days. In order to deal with this situation, the Transport Tribunal, created by the 1921 Railways Act, spent five years in devising a new system of charges for goods traffic, and set the rates at a level which they considered would provide a reasonable profit. Unfortunately, the Tribunal failed to foresee and take into account the effects of unrestricted road competition, with the result that the railway companies were not able to achieve the expected profits, and consequently

Above left: The imposing frontage of Manchester Victoria Station in August 1927. *National Railway Museum/Crown Copyright Reserved*

Left: Manchester Central Station frontage in 1927. *National Railway Museum/Crown Copyright Reserved*

could not raise capital as easily as they had done prewar, particularly in the changed economic climate.

Manchester's passenger stations, which had been relatively clean and modern-looking pre-war, began to take on a slightly old-fashioned and shabby appearance. That fatal pistol shot at Sarajevo had triggered off a decline in the railways' fortunes which has continued to the present day. In this chapter, we shall examine how the LMS and LNER dealt with this new situation, so far as Manchester was concerned, under the headings of motive power, electrification, resignalling and miscellaneous.

Motive Power

a) LMS

The LMS inherited a very mixed bag of locomotives. Many were elderly but competent, but many relatively modern types were not very satisfactory in the new cost-conscious era. They had to be worked hard to produce results, which was expensive in coal and maintenance. However, in 1923 new engines were needed and the LMS continued to turn out a number of pre-Grouping designs before embarking on standardisation. Horwich continued to build the four-cylinder 4-6-0s, and over the next two years 42 were put into service, Nos 10433-10474. They were destined to have a very short life, and almost all were withdrawn once sufficient Stanier 4-6-0s became available from 1934 onwards.

During its last decade of independence, the LNWR had been turning out large numbers of engines of the 4-6-0 'Prince of Wales' class and the 'Claughton' class. The 'Prince of Wales' engines were highly thought of from a performance point of view, but suffered from relatively high maintenance and running costs. The 'Claughtons', intended to be the pride of the line, were a disappointment. Crewe produced 130 between 1913 and 1921, renumbered 5900-6029 by the LMS, but they were failures both on costs and performance. A few years later, 10 were fitted with larger boilers, 10 with Caprotti valve gear, and 42 others were 'converted' successfully into 'Patriots' between 1930 and 1933, but the remainder were scrapped. In fact, the conversion took the form of 'scrap and build', with the replacement engine taking merely the name and number of the engine withdrawn.

So far as engines are concerned, one might be forgiven for believing that the Midland had not heard of Grouping, except as a means of flooding the country with Derby products. In the first 10 years of the LMS, its locomotive works, together with a variety of contractors, including Vulcan Foundry, North British Loco, Kerr Stuart, Andrew

Barclay, Bagnall, William Beardmore and Hunslet (a list which indicates the strength and extent of the private locomotive building industry at the time) produced the following engines of former Midland design:

> Class 2P 4-4-0 Nos 563-700
> Class 4P Compound 4-4-0 Nos 1045-1199 and
>   900-939
> Class 4F 0-6-0 Nos 4026-4556
> Class 3F 0-6-0 shunting tanks, Nos 7260-7681

They were mainly quite efficient machines, but the LMS needed more powerful engines. It is ironic that this 'Midlandisation' started under the L&Y's George Hughes, who became the first Chief Mechanical Engineer of the LMS, but he is also credited with producing the highly-regarded 2-6-0s Nos 2700-2944 from 1926 onwards, which had a very Horwich appearance and which were used extensively on the Central Division (mainly the former L&Y).

Before Stanier's arrival, the railway scene had been further enlivened by other new designs, the more notable being:

> 2-6-4T Class 4P, Nos 2300 to 2424. Members of the class were regularly to be seen at London Road and, to a lesser extent, at Victoria.

Above right: LMS (ex-L&Y) Hughes 'Dreadnought' 4-6-0 No 10439, standing at Newton Heath in 1935. These four-cylinder engines dated from 1908, and a number were built in the early years of the LMS, but they were not entirely successful and almost all were withdrawn in the 1930s, some of them only 10 years old, as soon as Stanier replacements became available. A small batch survived at Blackpool into the 1940s, and the last one was withdrawn in 1951. Newton Heath had 10 in 1934, but all had gone by 1938. *IAL*

Centre right: LMS (ex-L&Y) Class 7F 0-8-0 No 12825, of the large-boilered variety, stands at Agecroft shed in 1939. Built at Horwich in 1918, it survived until 1950 owing to wartime and postwar traffic demands. *IAL*

Below right: One of the handsome 'Prince of Wales' class engines, No 25694. They were introduced by the LNWR in 1911 and building continued until after World War 1, the class eventually numbering 245. Although they were efficient engines and could be worked very hard, they suffered from relatively high maintenance and running costs and were rapidly withdrawn in the 1930s as soon as sufficient Stanier replacements became available. In 1934 Longsight shed had four, Newton Heath had five, but Patricroft had no fewer than 22. *IAL*

The 'Royal Scots', Class 6P, Nos 6100-6169, some of which were to be seen at London Road on the Euston expresses.

0-8-0 Class 7F Nos 9500 to 9674. These engines, nicknamed 'Austin Sevens', were widely used on the Central Division, and were often seen at Victoria on through freights.

It is interesting to see the allocation lists for the LMS engine sheds in Manchester, and to note the relatively small extent to which LMS standard types, other than those of Midland design, had been introduced before the arrival of William Stanier as the new CME in 1932 began to affect the railway scene not only in Manchester but throughout the LMS. In fact, apart from Longsight, with 10 2-6-4Ts and six 'Royal Scots', pre-Grouping types vastly predominated, a tribute, so far as the former L&Y was concerned, to the rugged simplicity of the products of Horwich Works.

Stanier revolutionised LMS engine policy, and within a few years, mainly between 1933 and 1938, set about modernising the LMS fleet, with his 2-6-2T and 2-6-4T, his 2-cylinder and 3-cylinder 4-6-0s, his 'Pacifics', and his 2-8-0s. The shed allocation lists for 1938/39 demonstrate the enormous changes which he wrought. Much of the capital needed to finance this prodigious output was provided by government guaranteed loans and grants, intended to relieve unemployment and assist economic recovery. Orders for hundreds of engines were awarded to the North British Locomotive Co, the Vulcan Foundry, and Armstrong–Whitworths. Finally, before leaving this review of LMS motive power development, mention should be made of two

Below: The Hughes/Fowler 2-6-0s were one of the more successful designs turned out by the LMS in pre-Stanier days. Between 1926 and 1932, 245 were built at Horwich and Crewe, and were originally numbered in the 13xxx series, being renumbered from 2700 to 2944 about 1934. No 13018 is seen here on an Up excursion near Miller's Dale that year. They were regularly seen in the Manchester area — in 1938 Longsight had 10 and Newton Heath had 16. *IAL*

Above right: The 'Claughtons' were the LNW's final attempt at a successful express passenger engine, and 130 were built between 1913 and 1921. However, the boiler was not large enough to feed the four cylinders efficiently, and a number of engines were later rebuilt with larger boilers. Forty-two were nominally rebuilt as 'Patriots' between 1930 and 1933, but they were virtually new engines. LNW No 1914, seen here, was built in 1920, and was named *Patriot* in memory of LNWR employees who had given their lives in World War 1. *IAL*

Centre right: After Grouping in 1923, the newly-formed LMS built many hundreds of engines to former Midland Railway designs. The highly successful Midland compounds were turned out in large numbers between 1924 and 1927, from Derby, Horwich, the Vulcan Foundry and the North British Locomotive Co, with five more in 1932. They were known affectionately in some areas as 'Crimson Ramblers' and a few were to be found at both Longsight and Newton Heath (including No 1102 pictured here), whilst they were plentiful on the Midland Division. *IAL*

Below right: LMS (ex-Mid) 0-6-4T No 2007, seen at Trafford Park in 1935. This class of 40 tanks was introduced in 1907 for use on suburban passenger services, and several were stationed at Trafford Park. The class became extinct in 1938. *IAL*

Above: Stanier's 2-6-4Ts were one of his most successful designs and were continued by his successors and by BR. The three-cylinder engines, Nos 2500–2536, were introduced in 1934, and the more numerous two-cylinder engines came out the following year, 520 being built during the next 15 years. No 2458, a Longsight engine, is seen here passing Fairfield Halt on a Buxton to Manchester train. The Stanier tanks were ubiquitous in the Manchester area. *IAL*

Below: One of Mr Stanier's new Class 5XP three-cylinder 4-6-0s, No 5650, built at Crewe in 1934, stands in Manchester Exchange at the head of a parcels train on 4 April 1936. It bears a 10C (Patricroft) shedplate and was named *Blake* in February 1937. *G. Dawson/John Hammond Collection*

'Princess Royal' class Pacifics being transferred to Longsight immediately before World War 2 to work the 'Mancunian', 'Lancastrian' and 'Comet' 3¼hr services to and from London, hauling 500-ton trains unaided, compared with 415 tons for a Royal Scot. The now-preserved No 6201 *Princess Elizabeth* was one of the pair; the other was No 6206 *Princess Marie Louise*. Unfortunately, World War 2 put an end to their brief reign.

b) LNER

It would not be unfair to suggest that the GC entered 1923 with a more modern and capable fleet of engines than its neighbours in Manchester, and the railway scene on the LNER side of London Road, and at Central, changed even less than on the LMS section. The B17 'Sandringham' 4-6-0s began to be allocated to Gorton in the early 1930s, and although they were handsome engines, they were regarded by locomen as rough-riders, and disliked on that account. A few of Gresley's larger engines of the Pacific type and the 'Green Arrow' 2-6-2 class began to appear in Manchester shortly before the outbreak of World War 2.

At Central station the CLC trains continued to be operated by former GC engines, some of them very elderly, and that state of affairs continued right up to World War 2 and beyond.

The LNER's sights were not set on building new steam engines for the Manchester area. They had a more radical idea in mind, which we will explore shortly.

The allocation of engines at the former GC shed at Gorton and at the CLC shed at Trafford Park (LNER section) is shown separately.

The engine shed at Gorton was surrounded by heavy industry, most of it connected with the railway industry and locomotives. The Great Central had established its locomotive building works there, and it was the birthplace of many of J. G. Robinson's finest engines. One of the delights of the Gorton scene was to see engines from 'foreign' sheds out-shopped after maintenance, with their

Below: Extract of Openshaw 1905 Ordnance Survey map, showing extensive layout at Gorton shed and works. Also Ashburys yard and Belle Vue (Mid) shed.

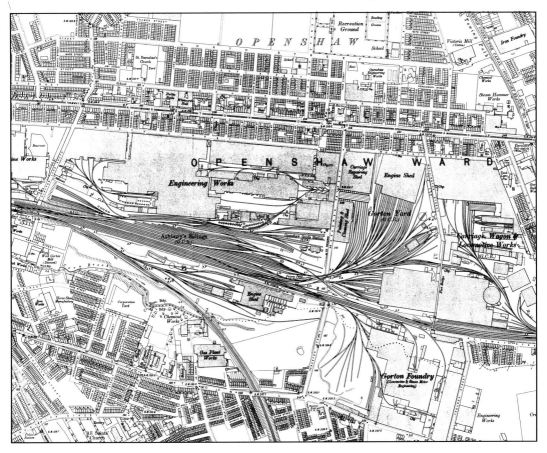

pristine paintwork as yet unsullied by smoke and steam, on running-in turns. The LNER concentrated the building of new engines on the former North Eastern Railway works at Darlington and the former Great Northern Railway works at Doncaster. Contractors were also employed. After 1923, Gorton had mainly to be satisfied with maintenance and repair work.

On the opposite side of the line to the shed and works stood the locomotive works of the renowned firm of Beyer, Peacock & Co, whose products supplied not only the home railways but also most of the world, from China to South America, and most of the British Empire. One particularly famous locomotive built there in 1925 was the LNER's only Garratt locomotive, a huge 2-8-0 + 0-8-2 numbered 2395. Until the electrification of the Woodhead route after World War 2, it spent its working life banking coal trains up the Worsborough incline, between Wath and Penistone.

Yet another famous firm was to be found in the Gorton complex — Armstrong-Whitworth's, who specialised in heavy engineering. And with so much engineering concentrated in such a small area, it is not surprising to find that the whole area was surrounded by row upon row of 19th-century terraced housing. Gorton closed over 30 years ago, in 1963, and little is left today to remind us of this hive of industry. It has gone, to be replaced by a fruit and vegetable market. At least it wasn't turned into a car park or, worse, a scrap yard for old cars.

Left: One of Gorton's Class B17 4-6-0s No 2816 *Fallodon*, of the 'Sandringham' class. They were built by Gresley between 1928 and 1937. *Fallodon* was subsequently rebuilt by Thompson as a two-cylinder engine after World War 2 and placed in Class B2, renumbered 1616. *IAL*

Centre left: Another Gorton engine — ex-GC 4-6-0, LNER Class B7 No 5072, resting at its home depot in 1933. The class of 38 engines was built by Robinson between 1921 and 1924 as a mixed-traffic design, having 5ft 8in wheels. This example was renumbered 1360 in 1946. *IAL*

Below left: LNER Class J39 0-6-0 No 2971, built by Gresley in large numbers between 1926 and 1941. By 1934, Gorton had acquired 16 of these capable machines and Trafford Park had six. It became No 4832 in 1946. *IAL*

Below: Gresley 'Pacifics' continued to be seen in Manchester London Road right up to electrification. No 60107 *Royal Lancer* passes under the wires with an express on 12 May 1954. *John Hammond Collection*

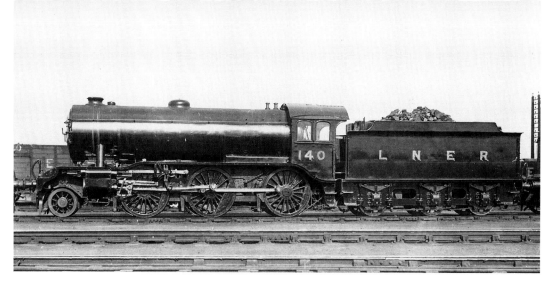

Above: LNER Class K3 2-6-0 No 140. These powerful engines were first built by Gresley for the Great Northern in 1921, and they continued to be built until 1937, being used mainly as mixed traffic engines on fast freight, fish and passenger trains. They were not allocated on a large scale to the Manchester sheds, but were frequently seen working in from other depots. This engine became No 1841 in 1946. *IAL*

Electrification — (in date order)

a) LMS Suburban Electrification

The LMS announced in 1924 that the directors had decided to proceed at once with the electrification of the former L&Y line between Victoria, Oldham and Shaw, including the Royton branch, using the side-contact rail system. The length of line to be dealt with was 12 miles.

A 10min peak service was proposed, with a 20min service off-peak. All-metal open carriages were proposed, and total expenditure was expected to be £600,000, with the work being completed in 12 months' time. The scheme had initially been developed by the L&Y, but ultimately foundered because the money could not be raised.

b) Manchester Underground

Proposals to connect Manchester's terminal stations by an underground link had been made from time to time, although the pre-Grouping companies had little interest in such schemes. However, a £12 million proposal for what was described as an 'Inner Circle' line was discussed before the City Council in 1921. There were to be stations at each of the three main-line termini — London Road, Victoria and Central.

The scheme was not developed, and was resurrected in 1930 only to be shelved again. A cheaper scheme, to link Victoria with Oxford Road at a cost of £700,000, was considered the following year, but had to be suspended owing to what was described as 'financial stress.' Finally, in 1934 the 1921 scheme was again considered, but nothing came of it. In the more optimistic days of 1944, when postwar planning was in full flow, the proposals for an underground railway system were again considered jointly by the LMS and LNER companies and Manchester City Council, but the estimated cost of £38 million was considered to be too expensive. Lancashire's citizens had to endure the nuisance of a change of stations in Manchester for another 50 years.

c) MSJ&A Electrification

This line was jointly owned by the LMS and the LNER as successors to the LNW and GC. It was one of the more prosperous suburban lines but had been badly affected both before and after World War 1 by tramway and, from 1927, express motor bus competition. Electrification was seen as the answer, with faster, more frequent services and reduced operating costs. The scheme was authorised in 1928 and provided for overhead elctrification at 1,500V dc in accordance with the report of the 1927 Railway Electrification Committee. Work commenced in 1929 and the electric trains started to operate in May 1931. The Altrincham tram route ceased to operate the same year.

The carriages provided were of the compartment type, to assist rapid loading and unloading, and were formed into three-car sets (one motor coach and two trailers), providing 40 first-class and 228 third-class seats (later altered to 24 first and 252 third-class). The carriages were

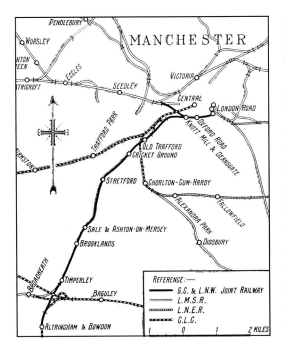

Above: Electrification of the Manchester, South Junction and Altrincham Rly. Map of Railways in the Manchester District, showing the MSJ&A and its connections.

built by Metropolitan-Cammell and the trains had a top speed of 70mph.

Whilst the electrification works were being carried out, motor bus competition increased to such an extent that the railway companies appealed to the Traffic Commissioners for some protection to be given to the high capital costs of electrification. This appeal resulted in bus fares being increased and the municipal express bus services being withdrawn.

It was expected that electrification would double the number of rail passengers, and this figure was achieved some years later.

In view of later developments it is of considerable interest to note that the Regional Town Planning Committee and Manchester Corporation urged the railway companies to adopt electrification in the 1930s. However, the latter's viewpoint was that they could only consider such a step if full protection was given to the capital employed.— with the establishment of a co-ordinated system of road and rail transport, including both municipal and private bus operators, on the lines of the recently-formed London Passenger Transport Board — and if wasteful competition was to be eliminated. World War 2 and nationalisation were to side-track this issue until

Passenger Transport Authorities were created under the 1968 Transport Act, by which time the private car had become the main enemy. These were truly wasted years.

d) Manchester–Sheffield–Wath Electrification

Difficulties in handling its heavy trans-Pennine coal traffic had led the GC to consider electrifying the route, and the matter was re-examined by the LNER in 1926. However, the LNER's financial position did not allow it to undertake such a scheme, until money became available with the assistance of a government-guaranteed loan at a very low rate of interest, under the Railways (Agreement) Act of 1935. The scheme provided for the replacement of 196 steam engines by 121 electric locomotives which would be capable of hauling 1,000-ton mineral trains at an average speed of 27mph, double that which could be achieved by steam. The net cost was put at £1½ million to £2 million.

The contract for the overhead electric line was awarded to BICC in 1937 and erection of the masts was in progress when World War 2 brought the work to a halt. One Bo-Bo electric locomotive was built, and carried out trials on the MSJ&A in 1941. The story of this important project will be told in later chapters.

Modernisation of Signalling

After Grouping in 1923, the LMS considered how the track layout and signalling at Victoria and Exchange could best be altered to take into account the unified ownership of the area, and the plan adopted consisted in joining Platform 11 at Victoria to Platform 3 at Exchange, together with a westwards lengthening of the latter, giving a platform 2,194ft long, hailed by the LMS publicity department, and well-known by every schoolboy, as the longest platform in the world.

At the same time, new running junctions were installed between the former LNW and L&Y lines, so that trains from Exchange could proceed northwestwards on to the L&Y, and trains from Victoria could reach the LNW lines to the west.

Advantage was taken of this remodelling to modernise the signalling, which resulted in two new all-electric signalboxes being constructed, known as Deal Street and Victoria West Junction. The Westinghouse Brake and Saxby Signal Co Ltd was the main contractor.

Six mechanically-operated signalboxes and a ground frame were abolished, these being Salford LNW, Exchange No 2, Exchange No 1, Deal Street, Irwell Bridge and Victoria West Junction

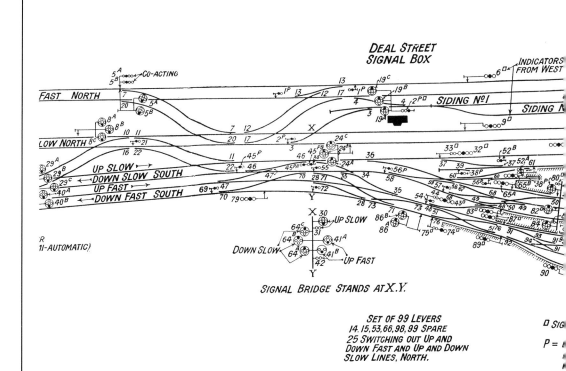

DEAL STREET
SIGNAL BOX

INDICATORS
FROM WEST

FAST NORTH

SLOW NORTH

CO-ACTING

SIDING N°1

SIDING N

UP SLOW
DOWN SLOW SOUTH
UP FAST
DOWN FAST SOUTH

1-AUTOMATIC)

X
Y

UP SLOW

DOWN SLOW

UP FAST

SIGNAL BRIDGE STANDS AT X.Y.

SET OF 99 LEVERS
14. 15, 53, 66, 98, 99 SPARE
25 SWITCHING OUT UP AND
DOWN FAST AND UP AND DOWN
SLOW LINES, NORTH.

D SIG

P =

Above: Signalling plans of resignalling of Victoria West Junction and Deal Street.

Left and below left: Exterior and interior views of the new Victoria West Junction signalbox, showing the large track layout panel and the miniature levers used for operating points and signals. The signalbox commanded a good, clear, all-round view.
Railway Gazette

Right: The approach to Central station, showing the new signalbox and the electric point mechanisms.
Railway Gazette

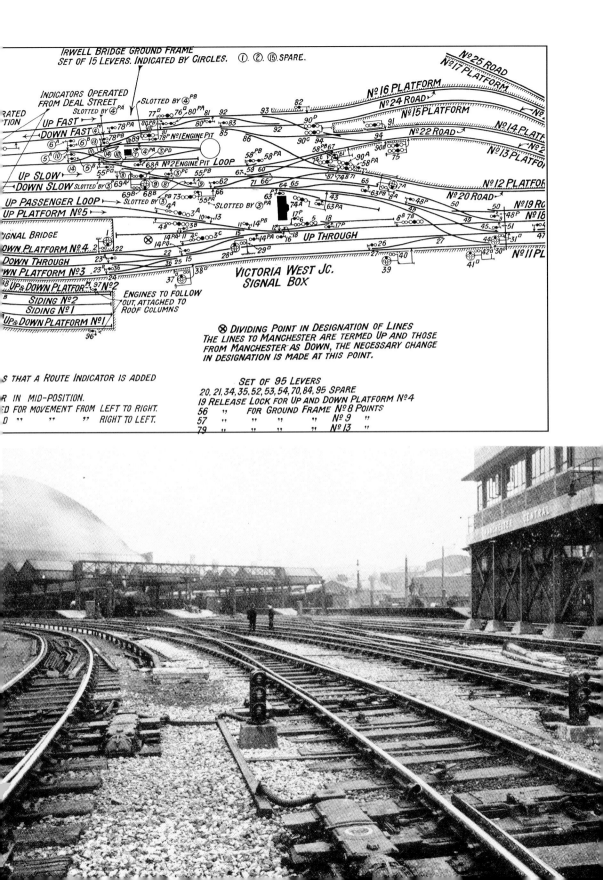

IRWELL BRIDGE GROUND FRAME
SET OF 15 LEVERS. INDICATED BY CIRCLES. ①. ②. ⑮. SPARE.

Nº 25 ROAD
Nº 17 PLATFORM
Nº 16 PLATFORM
Nº 24 ROAD
Nº 15 PLATFORM
Nº 14 PLATF
Nº 22 ROAD
Nº 13 PLATFO
Nº 12 PLATFOR
Nº 20 ROAD
Nº 19 RO
Nº 16
Nº 11 PL

INDICATORS OPERATED
FROM DEAL STREET
SLOTTED BY ④PA
SLOTTED BY ④PB
Up FAST →
← DOWN FAST ④
Nº 1 ENGINE PIT
Nº 2 ENGINE PIT LOOP
Up SLOW →
← DOWN SLOW SLOTTED BY ③
Up PASSENGER LOOP → SLOTTED BY ③
Up PLATFORM Nº 5
SLOTTED BY ③
SIGNAL BRIDGE
DOWN PLATFORM Nº 4
DOWN THROUGH
DOWN PLATFORM Nº 3
Up & Down PLATFORM Nº 2
SIDING Nº 2
SIDING Nº 1
Up & Down PLATFORM Nº 1

Up THROUGH

VICTORIA WEST JC.
SIGNAL BOX

ENGINES TO FOLLOW
OUT, ATTACHED TO
ROOF COLUMNS

⊗ DIVIDING POINT IN DESIGNATION OF LINES
THE LINES TO MANCHESTER ARE TERMED UP AND THOSE
FROM MANCHESTER AS DOWN, THE NECESSARY CHANGE
IN DESIGNATION IS MADE AT THIS POINT.

S THAT A ROUTE INDICATOR IS ADDED

R IN MID-POSITION.
D FOR MOVEMENT FROM LEFT TO RIGHT.
D ''   ''   '' RIGHT TO LEFT.

SET OF 95 LEVERS
20, 21, 34, 35, 52, 53, 54, 70, 84, 95 SPARE
19 RELEASE LOCK FOR Up AND DOWN PLATFORM Nº 4
56   ''   FOR GROUND FRAME Nº 8 POINTS
57   ''   ''   ''   ''   Nº 9   ''
79   ''   ''   ''   ''   Nº 13 ''

signalboxes, and Irwell Bridge ground frame.

Points and signals were worked electrically from the two new signalboxes by miniature levers, and the signals were all of the colour light type, being four-aspect where appropriate. The four aspects — yellow, green, yellow and red — were displayed vertically, except where necessary to give a junction route indication, in which case 'cluster' signals were provided, with the aspects being displayed at yellow (12 o'clock), red (3 o'clock), yellow (6 o'clock) and green (9 o'clock). A cluster was provided for each route except in low-speed areas, where theatre-type route indicators were provided instead of individual clusters.

Calling-on signals were provided where necessary to allow a second train (or an engine) to enter an already occupied platform. These were placed under the main signal and normally exhibited a white light, the 'proceed cautiously' indication being given by a small green light whilst the main red light was still showing.

Illuminated diagrams were provided in both signalboxes, and it is of interest to note that block working was maintained throughout the whole of the area, with the block indicator controlling the release of the last stop signal at the signalbox in rear.

The new signalling was brought into operation in 1929 and lasted for at least 64 years, most of it being taken out of use as recently as 1993.

There were two other important signalling developments in the Manchester area between the wars. It will be recalled that the GC had installed a low-pressure pneumatic signalling system between Ardwick Junction and Hyde Junction in 1905. This was renewed in 1930, using electro-pneumatic equipment, by the contractors, the British Power Railway Signal Co, who had installed the original system.

Across at Central, the LNER and LMS brought into use a power-operated signalbox in 1935, with electrically operated points and colour light signals. The new signalbox, for which the main contractor was the General Railway Signal Co, had 128 levers of the push-pull slide type, and replaced four existing signalboxes:

Central Station A	52 levers
Central Station B	115 levers
Great Northern Junction	24 levers
Viaduct	30 levers
	———
	221

Track circuiting was provided on all lines except the platform middle roads and extended as far as the next signalbox, Cornbrook West Junction. A large illuminated diagram was provided in the signalbox.

The colour light signals were either two-aspect or three-aspect, and subsidiary indications were given as follows:

Shunt	Miniature green light Illuminated letter 'S'
Calling-on, into an occupied platform	Miniature yellow light Illuminated letter 'C'

Modernisation Schemes

a) LNER Ardwick Goods Depot, and other goods developments

The average railway passenger probably knew little

Below: Signalling Plan of the Resignalling of Central station.

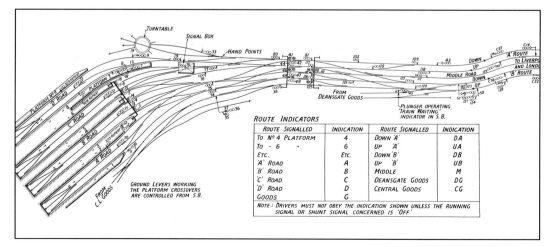

of the railways' very heavy merchandise traffic, apart from seeing row upon row of wagons and vans standing in sidings, and processions of goods trains making their ponderous way across Manchester, but to the railway companies it was of immense importance, as goods traffic provided the bulk of their revenue.

Goods traffic was charged on the principle of 'what the traffic would bear', and the railways' most profitable merchandise traffics were under heavy attack from road haulage contractors, who, because of the rigidity of the railways' charging system, were able to cream off the best-paying traffics.

The LNER therefore considered how it might improve the efficiency of its goods terminal operations in Manchester, in order to give a better service and reduce its costs, thus improving its competitive position. It decided that a new depot was required, to be sited away from the costly city centre where, in any case, land was unavailable, because it was intended that the collection and delivery services of the new depot should be motorised.

Fortunately, a large area at Ardwick had become available, which had formerly been occupied by the works of the Ashburys Railway Carriage & Iron Co. The site extended to 20 acres and had become available because the Ashburys Company's work had been transferred elsewhere. The buildings,

however, were still *in situ*, and although in a dilapidated condition were capable of renovation. It is significant, and an indication of the changes in the railway companies' financial position, that 30 years previously the GNR had thought nothing of spending £1 million to build its Deansgate warehouse, whilst in 1932, and in the very depths of the national trade depression, the LNER had to be content with rehabilitating old factory buildings.

However, the old buildings served their purpose. A triple-span-roofed building was adapted as the main goods shed, to handle traffic in less than wagon loads (known as smalls or sundries) and with accommodation for 78 wagons on three lines. The road side of the platforms was arranged in a saw-toothed fashion, so that road vehicle trailers could be set in echelon manner, allowing more to be accommodated.

The cartage services were completely

Below: An LMS Publicity Dept photograph of Platforms 12 & 13 at Manchester Victoria on 27 August 1927. The clothing fashions of the time make an interesting study, and there is not a bare-headed person in sight. The platform roof in the distance was destroyed during a German air raid in 1940 and not rebuilt. *National Railway Museum/Crown Copyright Reserved*

mechanised by the use of a vehicle which was to become an everyday sight on the streets of Manchester, and was known as the mechanical horse — a 2-ton 'Cob' van tractor, made by Karrier Motors Ltd, which had a single front wheel for greater manoeuvrability. These truly ubiquitous little machines, with an engine rated at only 10hp, could travel at up to 20mph, which was adequate for the streets of Manchester.

Other buildings in the complex were utilised for urgent provision traffic, and as a railhead storage depot.

The new depot was named Ardwick East, and the existing depot became Ardwick West. Some adjustments were made to the function of the LNER's other depots at Ducie Street and Deansgate.

Although the new depot had a fully motorised cartage fleet, the use of horses continued on a diminishing scale until the 1950s at other Manchester goods depots.

One other innovation in the merchandise business in the 1930s was the detachable box-style container, which could be transferred by crane from railway flat wagon to a flat-bed delivery lorry without the contents being touched. This reduced the handling costs at both ends of the journey and reduced the risk of damage or pilferage. Some containers were allocated to specific flows of traffic, and modified internally.

b) Passenger Services

After the war, train services were gradually restored to their prewar pattern, but for some years after Grouping there were no major changes, other than the phasing out of 6-wheeled and gas-lit coaches. However, by the middle 1930s the LMS and LNER had begun to get to grips with the new financial and competitive conditions in which they found themselves, and there was something of a renaissance in express passenger train services, especially on the LMS after the introduction of Stanier's more powerful and more efficient engines — his Class 5XP Jubilee 3-cylinder 4-6-0s and the Class 5P5F mixed traffic 2-cylinder 4-6-0s. Stanier also introduced a large number of new and quite luxurious coaches for longer distance and express services, providing three-a-side compartment seating with arm rests and large picture windows in the third class. For excursion and relief trains the LMS built open-style coaches with tables for four at each side of a central gangway, giving seating for 56 third-class passengers. These also had large picture windows.

With an increasing awareness of the value of publicity and marketing, the LMS decided to name its most important Manchester–St Pancras expresses, and in 1938 the 10.30am from St Pancras

and the 4.25pm return from Central was named the 'Peak Express' whilst the 10am from Manchester and 4.30pm return from St Pancras became the 'Palatine.' The previous year a weak bridge at Chapel-en-le-Frith had been renewed to allow any locomotive up to and including the 'Royal Scots' to use the Derby–Manchester route.

In 1937 the Midland Division embarked upon a series of accelerations, based on the use of Stanier's 4-6-0s, which were now available in large numbers. The best Manchester–St Pancras timings came down to about 3hr 35min in each direction, and whilst it must be admitted that it was not much of an improvement over the pre-World War 1 timings, there were more stops.

By 1939 the timings of the best morning services to London were as follows:

| London Rd | dep | 8.10am | 9.45am | 12.5pm | |
| Euston | arr | 12noon | 1pm | 3.40pm | |

| Central | dep | 7.20am | 8.55am | 10am | 12.25pm |
| St Pancras | arr | 11.20am | 1pm | 1.48pm | 4.10pm |

| London Rd | dep | 8.20am |
| Marylebone | arr | 1.10pm |

The LNER had given up the struggle for the end-to-end traffic, performed so effectively in Great Northern days, and henceforth concentrated on the intermediate traffic, for which it was in a much stronger competitive position.

The daytime Scottish services were:

		via Hellifield	via Shap	via Shap
Manchester Victoria	dep	9.20am	9.35am	12.40pm
Glasgow St. Enoch	arr	3.5pm		
Glasgow Central	arr		2.42pm	5.47pm
Edinburgh Princes St	arr		2.47pm	5.45pm

The Midland route to Scotland had almost been abandoned by this time, apart from seasonal trains, although connections were available at Hellifield on some of the St Pancras to Glasgow St Enoch and

Above right: LNW 'Claughton' class 4-6-0 No 1407 *L/Cpl J A Christie VC* on the 'Sunny South' express, Manchester and Liverpool to Brighton and Ramsgate, composed of comfortable-looking LNW coaches c1920. No 1407 spent some time at Longsight between the wars and became LMS No 5967. *IAL*

Below right: LNER 'Director' class D10 4-4-0 No 5438 *Worsley-Taylor* pilots Class C1 Atlantic No 4420 on an express from Manchester to Sheffield. No 5438 spent some years at Gorton and was renumbered 2659 in 1946. *IAL*

Left: Hughes 4-6-0 No 10435 approaches Preston with an express from Manchester to Windermere in 1924. The train consists of a fine matching rake of L&Y coaches, hardly appropriate for an express to the Lake District. *IAL*

Left: One of the first LMS Standard Compounds, No 1046, on a Manchester to Derby express in pastoral surroundings near Great Longstone in 1934. *IAL*

Left: LNER Class D11 4-4-0 No 5508 *Prince of Wales* on a stopping passenger train. This engine was shedded at Gorton during the 1930s. The D11s were an enlarged version of the Class D10 'Directors', and 11 were built between 1920 and 1922. No 5508 was renumbered 2662 in 1946. *IAL*

Right: A line-up of LMS delivery vans at Manchester Liverpool Road goods depot in 1934. *IAL*

Edinburgh Waverley services.

So far as the Manchester–Liverpool trains were concerned, the best timings were 39min with one stop on the former LNW route, 45min non-stop on the former L&Y route, and 45min with two stops on the CLC.

Diversification

The old, heady days of inter-railway competition had gone and, in the more austere days of the 1930s, co-operation through pooling schemes became the order of the day in order to cut costs. It had to be done to survive; the enemy was now not the other railway company, but the motor lorry, of which there were half a million by 1939. The phenomenal rise of the motor car was 20 years ahead, whilst air competition hardly existed. In any event Railway Air Services Ltd, which operated some routes serving Manchester, was owned by the mainline railways, and if air services had been expanded, the profits, if any, would have gone to the railway companies, although the pre-World War 2 air services ran at a loss.

The railways had adopted a similar diversification strategy so far as buses were concerned. The 1928 Road Transport Acts had enabled the mainline railway companies to operate buses and to invest in existing companies. They chose the latter course, preferring to be sleeping-partners, but they invested to a considerable degree. By the end of 1931 they were associated with almost half of the 41,500 buses in use.

In the northwest they had invested in the following companies at the end of 1935:

- LMSR

Crosville	£358,000
North Western Road Car Co	£246,000
Ribble Motor Services Ltd	£383,000

- LNER

North Western Road Car Co	£123,000

One intriguing thought is the probability that few of the passengers travelling on those buses ever realised that in many cases they were half-owned by the railway companies, who kept very quiet about the fact lest there should be any backlash about a railway-owned monopoly. There were few signs of any attempt at road/rail co-operation, and the railway representatives on the boards of the bus companies were told to regard themselves as busmen during the deliberations. If World War 2 and nationalisation had not come along it seems quite likely that the railway companies would have invested increasingly in bus and road haulage companies and aircraft, and would have abandoned unprofitable railway services sooner than was to be the case under nationalisation. The ultimate tragedy of nationalisation was that it stripped the railways of many of their potentially most profitable assets and left them to struggle, valiantly but mostly in vain, against unequal competition. What Beeching caused to happen, and for which he was unfairly reviled, would in all probability have happened sooner had the railways not been nationalised.

Among the railway companies' ancillary activities was the ownership of a large number of high-class hotels. The Midland Hotel in Manchester was one of the finest in the north of England when it was opened in 1903, and in 1929 the LMS announced that it proposed to have an extension built containing 263 bedrooms, all with private bathrooms, costing £¼ million. One floor was to be allocated to showrooms, exhibition rooms and meeting rooms and there was to be a garage accommodating up to 100 cars underneath the hotel. When completed, the hotel would have been one of the largest in Europe, but the work was postponed for five years 'owing to things being bad, and Manchester particularly in the doldrums.' It was never carried out; the declining cotton industry sounded its death knell.

Left: A Dennis Bros Publicity Dept photograph of an LMS two-ton parcels-delivery van in 1937, once an everyday sight on the streets of Manchester. *IAL*

Below left: A 1934 Ford 5cwt van, used by the LNER Advertising Dept. Photographed at Marylebone. *IAL*

Right: A Cheshire Lines parcels-collecting van, built by Thornycroft Motors Ltd. The chassis bears the inscription 'Speed 20 mph'. *IAL*

So, as Britain went to war again, its main stations in Manchester, so relatively modern in 1914, were beginning to look their age — smoky, grimy and a little old-fashioned. How they were to fare during six years of conflict we shall see in Chapter 7, but before leaving this chapter we will take a look at one of the more typical accidents that occurred in the 1930s.

Accidents

Manchester between the wars was remarkably free from serious accidents, but Miles Platting bank always posed risks in the days of loose-coupled freight trains (see track layout plan in Chapter 7). There was a typical runaway on New Year's Day 1936 involving the 8.35am mineral train from Ashton Moss to Aintree, consisting of 42 loaded coal wagons and a 20T brakevan, hauled by former L&Y 0-8-0 No 12771. The engine had the vacuum brake operating on all wheels but there was only a hand-brake on the tender.

According to instructions, the driver should have stopped at a notice-board near Miles Platting which read 'Goods trains must stop here to pin down brakes', but in practice, when a train stopped there it fouled the junction at Miles Platting, and train crews had adopted an unofficial procedure of drawing past the notice board before coming to a stand, with the front part of the train already on the 1 in 47 falling gradient.

The driver of the train passed through Miles Platting station at what he described as 8–10mph, but as he prepared to stop at the unofficial place beyond the notice board he felt the train pushing him. The fireman jumped off the engine and dropped the hand-brake levers on a few wagons but he was unable to pin them down to provide any retarding effect.

When the driver realised that his train was beginning to run away down the bank he began to 'pop' his whistle, which alerted the signalmen at Newtown No 1 signalbox. They sent the 'Train Running Away Right Line' bell signal to the signalman at Millgate box, who immediately passed it on to the signalmen in Victoria East Junction signalbox.

There was no clear road through Victoria station and the lie of the points would have sent the runaway train into Platform 12, on which a passenger train was standing waiting to leave. The signalman at Victoria East therefore switched the points to divert the runaway into Platform 14, which, although occupied by three coaches, had only just begun to load.

The signalmen at Newtown estimated the speed of the train as 30mph but by the time it reached Millgate it had speeded up to an estimated 60mph. Its speed at Victoria was not recorded but it must have presented a terrifying sight as it clattered over the junction points with the engine whistle shrieking, and thundered into the station. It hit the three non-corridor coaches with an almighty crash and forced them forward over 300 yards, and it is astonishing to learn that the nine passengers on the train were only slightly injured.

Runaways on the hilly L&Y were by no means uncommon in the days of loose-coupled freight trains, and the skills needed by drivers and guards to control their trains, and to judge when sufficient brakes had been pinned down, have passed into history. After the accident it was decided that trains must stop at the notice board, irrespective of other considerations, although it is clear that the local authorities must have connived at the previous unofficial practice. The clanking of the buffers of loose-coupled trains, and the squeaky noise of couplings tightening, are sounds which were common in the Manchester area, and everywhere else on the railways, until the 1960s, but they are to be heard no more except in the memory of those old enough to have lived through those times.

7 War and the Aftermath —
1939 to 1954

The outbreak of World War 2 on 3 September 1939 found the railways of Great Britain well-prepared for wartime conditions, despite the ravages of road competition and industrial depression. The likelihood of war had become increasingly apparent during the last two years of peace, and the role of the railways in wartime had been exercising minds in the Ministry of Transport. Planning began in 1937, and when the Munich crisis arose in September 1938, the Government set up a Railway Executive Committee (REC) to act as the agent of the minister in the control of the railways. The four general managers of the main-line railways formed the REC, together with a representative from the London Passenger Transport Board.

It was obvious that the railways would have to carry two very heavy burdens — (1) a vast new traffic of war material, equipment and ammunition, plus the movement of troops, and (2) the expected very heavy air attacks. The volume of additional traffic was greater than could ever have been imagined, owing to the evacuation of mainland Europe in 1940 and the build-up of troops and material in preparation for the invasion of France in June 1944. On top of that, the strategic bombing of Germany by the Royal Air Force and, later, by the United States Air Force, required the movement of petrol, bombs and other material in prodigious quantities.

The air attacks when they came were heavy and concentrated, but, so far as Manchester was concerned, were fortunately not continuous. Damage to railway installations, though serious, caused only short-lived interruptions to the running of trains, but had Hitler not turned his attention to the Soviet Union in the spring of 1941

Above left: LMS standard Class 8F 2-8-0 No 48500 at home at Longsight in 1950. *IAL*

Below left: The 'Austerity' 2-8-0s were a common sight throughout the northwest during the postwar period until almost the last days of steam. No 90055 is returning a train of empty wagons to the collieries, and is seen coasting through Edale station on the Hope Valley line on 3 October 1959. *M. Mensing*

those air attacks could have become much more severe.

So far as passengers were concerned, it quickly became apparent in September 1939 that we were at war. A strict blackout was imposed at once, vulnerable glass in station roofs was removed, windows were covered with anti-blast protective material, piles of sandbags appeared, and there were uniforms everywhere. Stations became places of tearful goodbyes and joyous welcomes, among the crowds of everyday travellers.

On the trains a speed limit of 45mph was imposed at once, in view of the expected air attacks, but when they did not materialise the speed limit was raised to 60mph, and later to 75mph. Carriage windows were covered with semi-transparent anti-blast material and lights were dimmed. Blinds had to be drawn during darkness.

The number of passenger trains was reduced along with their speed. Timetables were pruned and some restaurant cars were withdrawn. By the winter of 1943, when speed limits had been eased, the morning service of expresses from Manchester to London was as follows:

| Manchester London Rd dep | 8am | 9.45am | 9.52am |
| Euston arr | 12.58pm | 1.50pm | 2.10pm |

The frequency of the service was well below prewar standards, but the 8am and the 9.52am conveyed restaurant cars. Journey times were considerably longer, often due to the inclusion of additional stops. The 8am combined at Crewe with a portion from Liverpool and stopped at Stockport, Wilmslow, Alderley Edge, Crewe, Stafford, Rugby, Bletchley and Watford Junction. In contrast, the 9.45am was non-stop from Stockport. The 9.52am ran via Stoke-on-Trent, and stopped only at Stockport, Macclesfield, Stoke and Watford Junction.

Midland route expresses left Central at 7.20am and 8.55am, due in St Pancras at 12.23pm and 2.28pm respectively. They had been downgraded to semi-fasts and did not convey restaurant cars. The 7.20am had 11 intermediate stops and the 8.55am had 12. The solitary train to Marylebone left London Road at 9.45am and took 5hr 50min. When the German Chancellery was preparing its war strategy it little realised how its actions would affect the Midland main lines. World War 1 resulted in the Grouping, following which the LMS gave priority to the Manchester–Euston services over the former Midland route. World War 2 resulted in further downgrading of Midland services, and nationalisation continued the trend.

The best services to Liverpool took 48min via the L&Y route, 53min via the LNW route and 53min via the CLC.

The railways had entered the war with a relatively modern and capable fleet of locomotives, but it quickly became apparent that more heavy freight engines were needed. This fortuitously resulted in the reappearance of some old friends. Former L&Y Class 6F and Class 7F 0-8-0s had been withdrawn in large numbers in the years before the war but they had not been broken up and were brought back into service, to last for several more years and delight railway enthusiasts congregating at the end of Platform 11 at Victoria (or anywhere else on the old Lanky).

The LMS Standard Class 8F 2-8-0 was selected by the Ministry of Supply as the most suitable type of locomotive for service with the armies overseas, and 240 were ordered from contractors on the outbreak of war. Later, this engine was also built by all four main-line railways for use on their own systems. It had first appeared in 1935, and for several years was virtually confined to the Midland Division in order to eliminate double heading of heavy coal trains by various types of 0-6-0, which had by no means been eliminated by the introduction of 33 Garratt 2-6-0 + 0-6-2 locomotives in 1927/30. 126 2-8-0s had been built by the end of 1939, and building for the LMS continued throughout the war. They spread widely over the Midland and Western Divisions, but very few were ever allocated to Central Division sheds.

In 1943 a simpler design of 2-8-0 was put into production for the Ministry of Supply, and within two or three years contractors built 935 engines of that type, which rapidly became known as Austerities. When the war ended, many of these engines were acquired by the LMS, and almost 200 were allocated to the Central Division, becoming a very common sight at Victoria and Exchange on through freights. The remaining L&Y 0-8-0s were rapidly withdrawn. The LNER, too, acquired a large number of Austerities, which became regular performers on the former GC section.

However, we are carrying our story forward too quickly, and must return to the dark days of 1940.

Heavy night bombing of the British Isles began in the autumn of 1940, and Manchester was an important military target because of the number of factories engaged in war production, especially at Trafford Park. The people of Manchester, and its railwaymen, waited apprehensively for their turn, which they knew was likely to come.

The LMS's valedictory on the railways in wartime, *The LMS at War*, written by George C. Nash and published in 1946, records graphically the events in Manchester just before Christmas 1940. There was a violent onslaught on 22 December, the city's first heavy raid, and there was damage to the railway in 33 places, the most serious being at Exchange, where fires took an extensive hold. The destruction was so bad that the station could not be reopened for passengers until 13 January. There was other damage too. At Ancoats the warehouse was completely destroyed, at London Road, Mayfield was hit, the stables were damaged and a signalbox was burnt out, and at Salford the Divisional Control office telephone circuits were put out of use.

It was the practice of the German Air Force to concentrate its attention on a particular city for several consecutive nights. It was no surprise, therefore, when the drone of bombers' engines was heard the following night. During the very heavy raid which followed, a cluster of bombs fell on Victoria, destroying or extensively damaging all the buildings on Platforms 14 to 17 and bringing down much of the overall roof, to the discomfort of Manchester's passengers for the next 40 years or so. More immediately important, but hidden from the passengers' view and probably unknown to them, was the destruction of the Divisional Control Office and the flooding of the Emergency Control office, which was regarded by the LMS as one of the most serious incidents in the LMS Battle of the Railways.

The Midland Hotel also suffered serious damage. Showers of incendiary bombs fell on the roof, but fortunately all were successfully dealt with. However, 2,000 panes of glass from the windows disappeared overnight.

On the CLC, the large goods warehouse at Central was badly damaged. The whole of the roof was destroyed by incendiaries and the top floor was also damaged. The MSJ&A viaduct was breached between Castlefield and Old Trafford Junctions, and it was several months before the line was restored. In the meantime, the MSJ&A service was diverted to Central station, using steam trains from Warwick Road.

Postwar

The end of hostilities brought little immediate change. The return of a Labour government pledged to the nationalisation of the railways tended to distract railway managements, who had been busily planning their postwar strategies.

Town planning for postwar Britain had started in earnest as early as 1944, and the City of Manchester produced its plan at the end of 1945. It was a very comprehensive document, designed for a 50-year period of fulfilment and, among other matters, gave exhaustive consideration to the subject of present and future railway facilities in the region. The report commented that Manchester had a population of 1¼ million within a five-mile radius of the city centre, and many millions within a 12-mile radius who, if they travelled to the city by train, finished their journeys at one of four main-line stations. Many passengers travelling beyond Manchester had to cross the city because their onward train left from a different station. A historical review included in the plan illustrated how the railway system had developed piecemeal under the pre-Grouping companies.

Right: Ex-LMS rebuilt 'Royal Scot' class No 46151 *The Royal Horse Guardsman* waits to depart from Manchester Exchange. It carries a 6J (Holyhead) shedplate. *Kenneth Field*

Below: Farnley Junction's ex-LMS 'Jubilee' Class 6P5F 4-6-0 No 45581 *Bihar and Orissa* crosses from the through road to the platform at Manchester Exchange with the 9am express Hull to Liverpool Lime St *c*1959. West Junction signalbox can be seen in the top left-hand corner. *Kenneth Field*

Above: Ex-LMS rebuilt 'Patriot' class No 45531 *Sir Frederick Harrison*, allocated to Edge Hill shed, stands in Manchester Exchange at the head of the 9.00am express Liverpool Lime St to Newcastle. Undated, but probably mid-50s. *IAL*

Below: Edge Hill's ex-LMS 'Jubilee' class 4-6-0 No 45673 *Keppel* passes Deal Street signalbox and enters Manchester Exchange station at the head of an eastbound express from Liverpool. Undated, but probably early-50s. *IAL*

The kernel of the plan was the construction of a large new passenger station, to be called Trinity, between Victoria and Salford, with connecting lines from the CLC and London Road to enable trains using Central and London Road to be diverted to Trinity (see plan). The four main stations would no longer be required and the land so occupied could be released to the city for redevelopment.

The report admitted that the proposals had been advanced in tentative form, and it is clear that Trinity would have been a very large station indeed. It would also have been an enormously expensive project, but partly paid for by the large areas of land released at London Road, Central and Victoria. The proposals were not entirely dissimilar to those put forward a century earlier.

The report also drew attention to the number of goods depots near the city centre, seven in all, and suggested that they should be removed to sites outside the central area.

The plan was clearly too radical for the railway companies to adopt and it would have had to be financed by the city. Like many other plans produced in the general euphoria at the end of the war, it sank without trace.

After the war, train services were gradually improved and restaurant cars were restored to important expresses, but it was a slow process. Steel for new engines and rolling stock was severely restricted, and the country's industrial output was directed towards exports, as the only means of economic survival. However, some new coaches began to appear on both the LMS and the LNER, and new locomotives were also to be seen.

On the LMS, building of the highly successful Class 5 mixed traffic 4-6-0 was resumed, with later engines incorporating various modifications, such as self-cleaning smokeboxes, Caprotti valve gear and roller-bearing axleboxes. H. G. Ivatt, CME from 1945, introduced a number of new designs, including Class 2 2-6-0s and 2-6-2Ts for secondary duties, and a Class 4 2-6-0 of somewhat unconventional appearance. The new classes were designed especially with ease of maintenance and servicing in mind. In the postwar world, shortages of labour meant that shed staff were difficult to obtain. Factory work was more congenial than the cold, wet and dirt of a typical engine shed. The LMS also continued to turn out the efficient 2-6-4 taper-boilered tank engine, which ultimately seemed to monopolise the LMS suburban services around Manchester.

The most important steam locomotive development on the LNER in Manchester was probably the introduction of the Class B1 4-6-0, known originally as 'Springboks' or 'Antelopes', after the rather odd-sounding names of the first

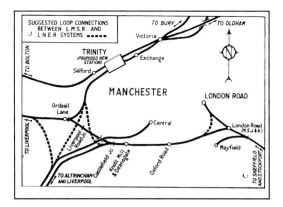

Above: Postwar plan for Manchester's railways, showing the proposed Trinity station.

few engines. They were particularly suitable for GC services and were widely used on a range of passenger and fast freight trains. In any event, the GC line across the Pennines was likely to be an early candidate for electrification. The LNER had reviewed the scheme in December 1944, and although work was resumed in 1946, progress was slow, the Liverpool Street to Shenfield scheme being given priority.

In 1947 the Minister of Transport approved the LNER's scheme to electrify the lines between Sheffield and Manchester, plus Barnsley Junction (Penistone) to Wath, and Fairfield to Trafford Park and Manchester Central, involving a total of 75 route miles. Completion of the work was expected to take four years (it actually took seven) and cost approximately £6 million. The system adopted was to be overhead line at 1,500V dc. It was stated that six out of every 10 trains on the westbound line carried coal and that nearly 100 trains a day passed through Woodhead Tunnel in each direction. Further delay to the Sheffield–Manchester scheme occurred in 1947 when it was decided to renew the Woodhead tunnels after attempts to repair the old tunnels were abandoned. This work started in 1949 and was completed in 1953.

Nationalisation

Any passengers expecting an immediate improvement in services were due for a disappointment. Just as in 1923 following the Grouping, few changes were apparent in 1948. The words BRITISH RAILWAYS appeared on engines, but there was little else to signify the momentous change. For several years it was business as before. The railways became regions, and Manchester found itself firmly in the London Midland Region.

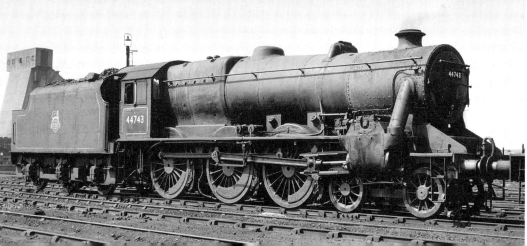

The CLC too, which had retained its separate identity in 1923, became part of the LM Region.

However, railway control organisations were rather too complex to be parcelled out at a politician's whim, and a peculiar dual-organisation was set up to deal with what became known as penetrating lines, of which the GC section of the LNER was one. Operationally it continued to be part of the Eastern Region as successor to the LNER, with its own District Operating Office in Manchester, and this continued for several years, but by 1955 the London Midland Region had taken over all activities.

The newly-formed Railway Executive's policy was to continue producing the former companies' designs of engines and coaches until standard types could be designed, and in the next four years over 600 engines of LMS parentage were produced, 200 of which were for use on other regions. The following types were involved:

Stanier Class 5 mixed traffic 4-6-0
Stanier-derived Class 4 2-6-4T
Ivatt Class 4 2-6-0
Ivatt Class 2 2-6-0
Ivatt Class 2 2-6-2T

Of the new engines produced to former LNER designs, only the 'B1s' were to be seen in Manchester in any quantity.

However, standardisation of engines and coaches was bound to come, although most of the types produced bore signs of LMS influence. Progressively from 1951 BR Standard engines began to be seen in Manchester, and by the beginning of 1954 they were becoming a common sight.

Above left: Ex-LNER Class B1 4-6-0 No 61265 was one of a number of B1s stationed at Gorton during the early years of nationalisation. This mixed-traffic class was introduced by Thompson in 1942 and eventually reached a strength of 409 engines (one was damaged beyond repair at Witham in 1950). *IAL*

Centre left: One of Doncaster's B1s, No 61127, heads for home with an express through Ashburys on 3 June 1954, shortly before the electrification of the line. *John Hammond Collection*

Left: One of the Caprotti valve gear-fitted ex-LMS Class 5 mixed-traffic 4-6-0s, No 44743 stands at Newton Heath between duties in October 1959. This distinctive sub-group of 10 engines was introduced in 1948. *J. E. Wilkinson*

Those allocated to the Manchester sheds were:

Longsight 9A
    'Britannia Class' 7 4-6-2   70031-33/43/44
    Class 4 2-6-4T   80039
Patricroft 10C
    Class 5 4-6-0   73043/4
Newton Heath 26A
    Class 4 2-6-4T   80049-53

BR Standard types were also to be seen working into Manchester from neighbouring sheds, particularly on running-in turns from Crewe to London Road.

BR Mark 1 coaches were also becoming quite common, although they had not been produced in the numbers hoped for. Owing to the steel shortage already referred to, the 1952 freight wagon building programme and the locomotive programme were both cut by 50% and the passenger coach programme was abandoned altogether. However, there was some recovery in 1954 when the building programmes provided for the following new construction:

237 steam locomotives
68 diesel shunting locomotives
1,820 passenger coaches
930 parcels, etc vans
53,000 freight wagons

The most common sight on freight trains had become the Austerity 2-8-0. Newton Heath had 31 of them, and most of the former L&Y sheds had a substantial allocation. The appearance of mineral trains had altered too. Gone was the interesting variety of wording and lettering on private owners' coal wagons, to be replaced by a dull uniformity; indeed the private owners' wagons themselves were rapidly being phased out and replaced by the standard all-steel 16-tonner. In marshalling yards and sidings the elderly, and in some cases ancient, shunting engines were shortly to be replaced by 350hp diesel-electric 0-6-0 shunters but none had yet appeared locally, although the LMS had introduced them prewar at major marshalling yards such as Toton, Crewe and Willesden.

The London Road–Euston services had been restored to prewar standards by 1954, the 8am taking 3hr 45min, and the 9.45am 'Mancunian' a splendid nonstop 3hr 20min. Other Euston expresses took about 3hr 50min. On the Midland side things were not so good. The best train, the 7.20am from Central, took 4hr 14min to St Pancras, whilst the 9am took 5hr. The next departure was at 1.50pm. Marylebone had virtually dropped out of the competition altogether for end-to-end journeys, its through services taking five hours and more.

Left: One of Longsight's 'Britannia' class 'Pacifics', No 70044 *Earl Haig*, backs out of London Road with the empty stock of a train which it has just brought from Euston, and passes under No 2 signalbox. The signalbox still carries its wartime protective roof. No 70044 was built at Crewe in June 1953 and was shedded at Longsight from August that year until the end of 1958. The coaches which are visible are BR Mk 1. This engine was fitted with Westinghouse brake pumps for trials with fitted mineral trains on the Midland main line. *Kenneth Field*

Below left: BR 2-6-4T No 80052 stands in Royton station at the head of the 13.04 stopping passenger train to Manchester Victoria on 18 July 1955. No 80052 was allocated to Newton Heath when new in December 1952, and remained there until May 1955. It was withdrawn in 1964, and its derivation from Stanier's LMS 2-6-4 tanks is readily apparent. *IAL*

Below: A fine action shot of 'Jubilee' class 4-6-0 No 45638 *Zanzibar* being worked hard through Longsight station (adjacent to its home shed) on the 'Mancunian' at the head of a rake of BR Mk 1 coaches in April 1954. The ex-LNWR signal gantry is of interest; the white diamond plate on the left-hand signals indicates that the line is track-circuited. The white 'D' plate on the right-hand signals indicates to the fireman that he must press a plunger fixed on or near the signal post to announce to the signalman the presence of his train when it is detained by the signal being at danger — a simple safety device which avoids the fireman having to walk to the signalbox to do it. *G. Parrish*

The Liverpool trains were taking about 50min nonstop via the L&Y route and 45–50min with one or two stops via the LNW route, although the 8.55am from Newcastle was allowed only 40min with a stop at Earlestown for the Warrington connection. The former CLC route from Central to Liverpool Central had the best service, with a train every hour covering the journey in 45min with two stops. This was very similar to the service which the CLC had introduced in 1877 when the temporary Central station was opened! Until 1930, when the additional stop at Farnworth was introduced, the 45min timing included only the stop at Warrington. Incidentally, the 1954 CLC Liverpool service was worked mainly by LMS 2-6-4Ts.

One should beware of being critical about the failure to restore prewar timings quickly, and then to improve upon them. The railways had been very heavily worked during the war and arrears of maintenance had piled up. After the war, shortages of materials and labour delayed the recovery and priority was given to exports. Nationalisation and reorganisation distracted railway management and led to a lack of positive direction. Finally, most of the rolling stock, locomotives and equipment dated from before World War 2. Stations were fading into an increasingly shabby old age and were badly in need of smartening up.

The railways were still very busy, and summer Saturdays were hectic. One of the special features of

Lancashire was the 'Wakes Week', when whole towns closed down in turn for the annual holiday. Oldham was among the first, and in 1952, 11 special long-distance trains were provided on the Friday evening and 22 on the Saturday. This pattern was repeated throughout the summer holiday period and provided fascinating train-spotting, but it has to be said that Manchester was not a train-spotter's paradise. It was too fragmented, and most through trains avoided the centre. Knowledgeable spotters went to Crewe or Chester or Preston, where almost everything passing through could be seen.

The high spot of 1954 was the opening of the Manchester–Sheffield-Wath electrification scheme. This was performed formally on 14 September by a special train hauled by locomotive No 27000, conveying the Chairman of the British Transport Commission, Sir Brian Robertson, and various civic and railway officials. Woodhead tunnel had been opened on 3 June by the Minister of Transport, Lennox-Boyd. It cost approximately £3 million and was a major civil engineering work.

Seven Co-Co electric locomotives, Nos 27000-06, and 57 Class 76 Bo-Bo locomotives, Nos 26001-57 (following on from the earlier No 26000), were built for the scheme, and a new maintenance depot was constructed at Reddish as the main centre for electric locomotives. The Co-Co locomotives were sold to the Netherlands Railways in 1968/69 following the decision to withdraw passenger services over the Woodhead route.

The major impact of the scheme was felt in the working of heavy westbound coal trains to marshalling yards on the fringe of Manchester and this was the basis of the electrification scheme, but it also enabled passenger trains from Manchester London Road to be electrically hauled as far as Sheffield, and for an accelerated, regular suburban electric service to be introduced on 14 June 1954 from London Road to Hadfield and Glossop, every half-hour, using multiple-unit trains.

Below: Unrebuilt 'Royal Scot' class 4-6-0 No 46148 *The Manchester Regiment* at Longsight shed in July 1951. Its home shed at the time was Crewe North. *Kenneth Field*

Above: Manchester Central station about 50 years ago. *IAL*

Below: A fine view of ex-Midland Belpaire Class 3P 4-4-0 No 40726, built by S. W. Johnson in 1902 and subsequently rebuilt by Fowler, at the head of an SLS/MLS 'Hull and Barnsley' enthusiasts' special at Manchester Central on 24 August 1952. The whole class of 80 engines was extinct shortly afterwards. *E. D. Bruton*

Above: A quiet spell at Manchester Central. The centre line between the two platform lines was provided for the release of engines after they had brought their trains into the terminal, a clever piece of design but it could result in the passengers having a longer walk along the platform. Note the model of an Isle of Man Steam Packet Co's ship in a glass case. There were a number of these models at stations in the northwest, provided by the shipping company as a publicity feature. *IAL*

Centre left: Ex-GC 'Director' Class D10 No 62656 *Sir Clement Royds* at Trafford Park shed in 1951. The D10s were regularly to be seen at Manchester Central until the middle 1950s. *IAL*

Below left: Trafford Park shed in 1952, with a variety of engines, including an ex-GC 0-6-0, ex-LMS compound 4-4-0s, Class 4F 0-6-0s and a Horwich 'Mogul'. The shed roof appears to have lost all its cladding. *IAL*

Above: Ex-GC Class J10 0-6-0 No 5209 trundles a Down Class B goods train near Ashley CLC in 1948. *IAL*

Below: Ex-LMS Class 5 mixed-traffic 4-6-0 No 44906 runs into Miles Platting station with a Blackpool excursion composed of former LMS stock. No 44906 spent most of its working life allocated to Edge Hill (8A). *Kenneth Field*

Above left: Ex-LMS 'Patriot' class 4-6-0 No 45509 *The Derbyshire Yeomanry*, of Newton Heath shed, stands resplendent in Platform 14 at Manchester Victoria, ready to take an excursion train formed of Stanier LMS coaches to Blackpool. Date unknown, but probably late fifties. No 45509 was withdrawn in 1961. 'Patriots' were relatively uncommon on the ex-LMS Central Division; most spent their working lives on the ex-Western Division. *J. Davenport*

Left: A return 'Wakes Week' special, No W652, from Newquay to Oldham, hauled by a pair of Hughes 2-6-0s, and seen near Park Bridge, on the OA & GB Joint line (undated). *J. Davenport/John Hammond Collection*

Above: Co-Co electric locomotive Class EM2 No 27006, built to haul passenger trains over the Woodhead route to Sheffield, at Manchester London Road on 8 April 1955 with the 4.35 departure to Sheffield Victoria. *IAL*

Below: Bo+Bo electric locomotive Class EM1 No 26000 at Dukinfield Depot in September 1953. This locomotive was built by Metropolitan-Vickers in 1941 and was numbered 6701 by the LNER, being renumbered 6000 in 1946. It ran for some time in Holland after the war and was named *Tommy* by Netherlands Railways, after the British soldiers who had liberated their country. *T. K. Widd*

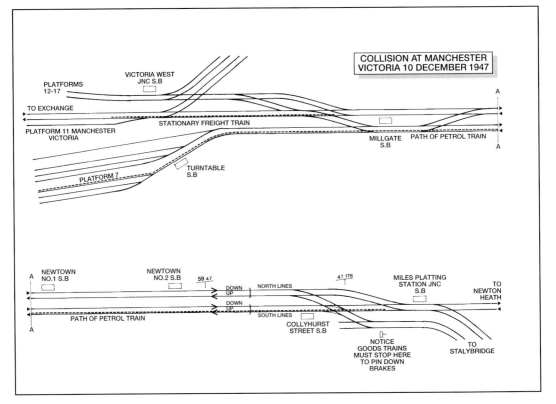

Accidents

Mention has been made in an earlier chapter of the difficulties which drivers sometimes found in controlling their trains when descending Miles Platting bank. Another runaway occurred in the early hours of 10 December 1947 concerning a type of train which older readers will remember — 20 petrol tanks with runner wagons at each end. None of the tanks was fitted with the vacuum brake.

The instructions for descending Miles Platting bank required goods trains to stop near the top of the bank for wagon brakes to be pinned down, so that the descent could be made in safety, with the engine brake being held in reserve. However, the LMS had issued an instruction prohibiting the pinning down of brakes on tank wagons conveying petrol on account of the possible danger from sparks. Therefore to meet that situation it was decided that when trains consisting wholly of petrol tanks required to descend Miles Platting bank they must have a second engine coupled in front to provide additional brake power.

On the night in question the train concerned left Leeds Neville Hill yard at 9.50pm *en route* for Eccles, hauled by an LNW Class 7F 0-8-0 No 8903, with the vacuum brake operating on all the engine and tender wheels. No difficulty had been experienced in descending Micklehurst incline and the driver was confident that he could descend Miles Platting bank without assistance.

There was dense fog when the train arrived at Miles Platting at 3.45am, and after stopping for two minutes the driver gently eased his train on to the bank at about 4mph, but when he reached Newtown No 2 signalbox, after travelling half a mile down the 1 in 47 gradient, the engine wheels began to skid and the application of sand had no effect. In the darkness and fog it was very difficult for the driver to judge his speed, so he began to 'pop' his whistle as a precaution. This was heard by the signalman at Newtown No 1 signalbox, who deduced that the train was out of control and sent the bell signal 'Train running away on right line' to Victoria Millgate box, less than ¼ mile away.

The signalman at Millgate had accepted the train with his points set for No 7 dead-end platform at Victoria, as the through road ahead was occupied by another freight train which had stopped for the purpose of releasing the pinned-down handbrakes. The tank train passed him at an estimated speed of 25mph, continued into the station and crashed into the hydraulic buffers at the end of Platform 7. It overrode them, mounted the concourse and came to rest only a few feet from the booking office. Petrol began

Above left: Track layout — runaway freight train and collision — Manchester Victoria, 10 December 1947.

Above: Ex-LNW 0-8-0 No 49229 at Newton Heath in 1959. An engine of this class was involved in the runaway down Miles Platting bank on 10 December 1947. Although the class numbered several hundred, very few were ever allocated to sheds outside former LNW territory. *J. E. Wilkinson*

to leak from three damaged tanks, but prompt action by the station staff prevented a fire. Unfortunately, the driver's error of judgement cost him his life.

This accident illustrates quite clearly the difficulties which drivers faced in controlling unbraked freight trains in fog, but it is now part of railway history. Unbraked trains have gone. So have the thick fogs which were so common in winter before the Clean Air Act.

One of the most serious accidents in Manchester happened only a few hundred yards away at Irk Valley Junction, some years later, on 15 August 1953. It was one of those nightmarish accidents when two trains crash on a viaduct and one of the coaches plunges into the river below.

Irk Valley Junction was located just over a mile from Victoria on the electrified line to Bury, at the point where a spur diverged to Newton Heath, via Smedley Viaduct. It was a simple double-line junction, with a 20-lever frame signalbox and home and distant signals. There were no track circuits, and no block controls on any of the signals.

The trains concerned were the 7.20am electric from Bury to Victoria, and the 7.36am stopping train from Victoria to Bacup, consisting of four coaches hauled by a Class 4 2-6-4T, travelling chimney-first. Being a Saturday, the trains were lightly loaded, with about 100 passengers in the electric train and only six in the steam train. However, the first coach of the electric train was quite well filled.

The young signalman at Irk Valley Junction had accepted the electric train from the next signalbox at Queens Road, but when he offered it forward to Newtown No 1 signalbox it was refused. He therefore kept his home signal, protecting the junction, at danger.

He was then offered the Bacup train, which he accepted, even though it would have to cross his junction and foul the line from Bury. He was quite entitled to do this, as his junction facing points were set safely towards Bury to give flank protection, and he kept his junction home signal at danger.

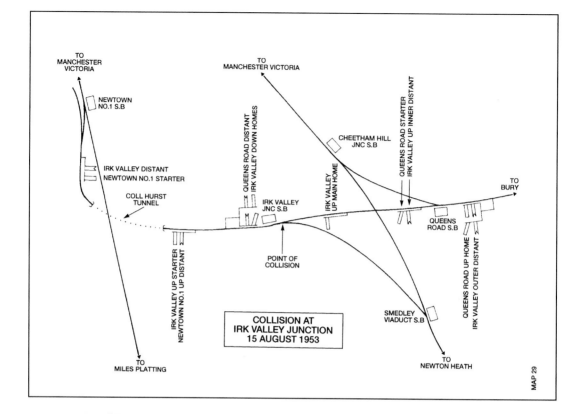

TO
MANCHESTER
VICTORIA

NEWTOWN
NO.1 S.B

IRK VALLEY DISTANT
NEWTOWN NO.1 STARTER

COLL HURST
TUNNEL

TO
MANCHESTER VICTORIA

QUEENS ROAD DISTANT
IRK VALLEY DOWN HOMES

IRK VALLEY
JNC S.B

IRK VALLEY
UP MAIN HOME

CHEETHAM HILL
JNC S.B

QUEENS ROAD STARTER
IRK VALLEY UP INNER DISTANT

TO
BURY

QUEENS
ROAD S.B

POINT OF
COLLISION

IRK VALLEY UP STARTER
NEWTOWN NO.1 UP DISTANT

COLLISION AT
IRK VALLEY JUNCTION
15 AUGUST 1953

SMEDLEY
VIADUCT S.B

QUEENS ROAD UP HOME
IRK VALLEY OUTER DISTANT

TO
MILES PLATTING

TO
NEWTON HEATH

MAP 29

A few minutes later he saw the Bacup train approaching and, anxious to avoid delaying it, he enquired from the signalman at Queens Road of the whereabouts of the electric train. There then ensued a misunderstanding between the signalmen, the upshot being that the Irk Valley signalman thought that the electric train was further away than it really was.

He thereupon decided to run the Bacup train over the junction before the electric train passed, and he reversed his junction points and cleared his junction signal. Just as the steam train started to move forward, the electric train burst into view less than 300yd away, travelling at about 35mph. Its driver should have stopped safely at the home signal but he failed to do so and ran past it without reducing speed. Twenty yards beyond the signal he hit the steam engine of the Bacup train a glancing blow and cannoned off it, the front coach careering over the edge of the viaduct into the valley below. Nine passengers and the driver of the electric train were killed. Twenty-four passengers were badly injured.

It is not known why the driver of the electric train failed to stop at the home signal, as both the inner and the outer distant signals were showing caution. He was 64 years old and was due to retire in three months' time, and had been a driver since 1920. He was also a well-known public figure, being an Alderman and former Mayor of Bury.

The signalling regulations are designed to prevent, or at least mitigate the effects of, collisions at junctions, and signalmen are required to avoid obstructing or fouling the line within ¼ mile of the home signal after they have accepted a train to proceed towards it. This is a second line of defence in case a driver should fail to stop at the home signal when it is at danger. To foul the ¼-mile safety overlap is one of the most serious irregularities that a signalman can commit.

Above left: Track and signalling plan of Irk Valley Junction collision 15 August 1953.

Left: A surprisingly clean ex-L&Y 0-6-0 No 52239 at its home shed, Newton Heath (26A). The photograph is undated, but the engine was withdrawn early in 1956. These engines, dating back to the 19th century and produced in large numbers, were an everyday part of the L&Y and LMS (Central Division) scene, and a reminder of the vast goods and mineral traffic once handled by the railway in Lancashire. *IAL*

Investigations after the accident revealed an alarming state of affairs. Several serious signalling irregularities came to light, involving a number of signalmen, and the standard of supervision was considered to be unsatisfactory. The circumstances of the accident sent a shock wave throughout the railway and there was a long-overdue tightening up. It was a period of chronic staff shortage, and it was often difficult to recruit suitable staff in areas such as Manchester, where there were plenty of better-paid jobs.

To the casual observer of the railway scene in Manchester in 1954 it might have seemed that the railways were gently declining into senility. True, there were some shiny new engines and coaches, but apart from the Manchester–Sheffield electrification there was no sign of urgently needed modernisation, either of equipment or ideas. The nationalised railway management appeared complacent and unconcerned about, or unaware of, the competition soon to arise from car, lorry and plane.

But this was not entirely true. The British Transport Commission had been working away quietly on its plans for the future and they were unveiled with a flourish at the beginning of 1955. They were very radical indeed and forecast major changes in the railway scene, but they had a fundamental, and ultimately almost fatal, flaw. The plans were based on the continuation of 19th-century railway practices, using mid-20th-century technology, on the underlying assumption that competitive conditions would not worsen but would shift in the railway's favour because costs would be cut and efficiency levels would rise. Secondly, the burden of 19th-century anti-monopoly legislation, which had handicapped the railways so severely between the wars, had just been removed. The British Transport Commission rightly expected that these factors would improve the railway's competitive position, but they failed to appreciate that road transport would also cut its costs and become more efficient, and what is more, would ultimately outplay the railways.

The plans also assumed that the nature and scale of economic activity in the country at large would not change. Perhaps that was a reasonable assumption in 1954 but it was to be proved completely wrong. What was lacking were new ideas, new ways of doing things, a new vision of the future. Railway managers had allowed themselves to become hidebound by tradition, but they persuaded the government to part with the money. That was a massive victory but a Pyrrhic one; the Treasury never trusted BR again.

Traffic levels in 1954, and the extent to which they changed over the next 40 years or so, are listed below:

BR Traffic Receipts (£ million)

	1954	1993/94
Passengers	117	2,166
Parcels and Mails	41	78
Merchandise and Livestock	111}	
Minerals	46}	565
Coal and Coke	116}	

In 1954, the receipts from the carriage of coal and coke alone equalled the receipts from passengers. By 1992/93 the receipts from ALL freight traffic had dwindled to less than a third of the passenger receipts.

• BR Statistics (millions)

	1954	1993/94
Passenger journeys (incl. seasons)	991	713
Merchandise (tons)	47}	
Minerals (tons/tonnes)	63}	
Coal and Coke (tons/tonnes)	174}	103
Other (1992/93) tonnes		38}
Total freight (tons/tonnes)	284	103
Train miles — passenger	238	228
— freight	140	21
Passenger miles (billions)	20.7	18.9
Freight net ton miles (billions)	22	8.5
Route miles of line open	19,150	10,275

The decline in the freight business speaks for itself, but the similarity in passenger miles and passenger train miles is astonishing.

Left: No 44172, an ex-LMS Class 4F 0-6-0 of Rowsley shed (17D), stands at Longsight shed between duties in 1950. Whilst the 4Fs were to be found all over the LMS system, the bulk of them were on the Midland Division and they were comparatively rare on the Central Division, where the ex-L&Y 0-6-0s held sway. *IAL*

Left: Manchester Victoria station was never complete without a couple of elderly ex-L&Y 0-6-0s simmering gently at Victoria East Junction waiting to bank eastbound freight trains. Nos 52317 and 52455 are on duty on 19 March 1955. *IAL*

8 Unprecedented Changes and Major Upheavals — 1955 to 1969

Ten years had passed since the end of World War 2, and during that period the railways had struggled to get back on their feet and regain their prewar standards. It was indeed a struggle. Not only were they starved of capital, and unable to obtain adequate supplies of steel, but they were also desperately short of staff. They had, in addition, been subjected to major organisational changes — nationalisation in 1948, and the abolition of the short-lived Railway Executive in 1953. Viewed against such a background it is a wonder that they made any progress at all, and the future appeared to be one of gradual and inevitable decline and decay, faced with the resumption of competition for freight traffic from the newly denationalised road haulage industry.

The 1955 Modernisation Plan

However, the British Transport Commission had been quietly preparing its plans for the future of the railways, and these were announced to an astonished world on 25 January 1955. They were little short of revolutionary, the main points being:

• The building of diesel and electric locomotives on a large scale, to replace steam, at a cost of £345 million
• Multiple units, either diesel or electric, to replace steam-hauled coaches on many services. A fleet of new coaches to be built for loco-hauled trains. Stations to be modernised or rebuilt. Total cost: £285 million

Below: A 'Modernisation Plan' Class 104 diesel multiple unit waits for departure time at Platform 12, Manchester Victoria, forming the 11.45 to Blackpool North on 6 October 1978. The bomb-damaged section of roof at the west end of the platforms was removed and not replaced. *P. J. Howard*

Above: One of the Class AL4 electrics built for the Manchester/Liverpool-Euston service. No E3041 was one of a batch of 10 built by the North British Locomotive Co in conjunction with GEC. Seen at Crewe on 18 September 1961. *Alan H. Bryant*

• Improved track and signalling — £210 million
• Measures to enable freight services to be improved, by modernising freight terminals and marshalling yards, and fitting vacuum brakes to all wagons, at a total cost of £365 million

Total cost approximately £1,200 million.

It was equally astonishing that the government accepted the proposals and underwrote the expenditure, although BR emphasised that half of the expenditure would be required in any case just for normal maintenance and like-for-like renewals. The plan was to be staged over 15 years.

In 1955 steam was still predominant in Manchester, but sweeping changes were forecast. Almost immediately, a new breed of diesel multiple-unit train began to appear in Manchester, replacing steam on suburban and local services, and within five years diesel locomotives started, albeit slowly, to replace steam engines on expresses and freight trains. Typically, steam lingered on until 1968 in the northwest, and it was the last area on BR to become fully dieselised.

For steam enthusiasts the saddest part of the report was the announcement that no more express passenger or suburban steam locomotives were to be built after the 1956 programme and that the building of all steam locomotives would cease

within a few years, but it was envisaged that modern steam locomotives would remain in operation beyond the end of the 15-year plan, ie beyond 1970, although in the event that was not to be. The British Transport Commission initially ordered 170 diesel locomotives of several different types from a number of manufacturers, in order to gain experience and assess their potential before embarking on large-scale orders, but the Commission's financial position worsened in the late 1950s and the government pressed the BTC to go all-out for the replacement of steam by diesels in the shortest practicable timescale in order to achieve economies in day-to-day operation and maintenance.

It might also be mentioned that the Modernisation Plan envisaged the continuing withdrawal of those stopping and local passenger train services which could not be made profitable by the introduction of DMUs, and this was not an idea that Dr Beeching introduced. Indeed, passenger services were withdrawn from over 2,000 miles of route between nationalisation in 1948 and the publication of Dr Beeching's Reshaping Report in 1963. The Modernisation Plan stated 'there will be a marked reduction in the stopping and branch line services which are little used by the public and which, on any dispassionate review of the situation, should be largely handed over to road transport.'

Manchester Piccadilly Electrification

The most significant part of the plan, so far as Manchester was concerned, was the proposal to electrify the line at 25kV from Manchester to Euston, including the rebuilding and resignalling of London Road station. The first stage of this scheme came into operation on 12 September 1960, with the official inauguration of electric traction between Manchester London Road (renamed Piccadilly) and Crewe. Main-line trains were hauled by a new fleet of Bo-Bo electric locomotives, whilst local trains via both Styal and Stockport were worked by four-car electric multiple-units, built by BR with AEI electrical equipment.

Below: One of a series of official photographs produced by the LM Region Publicity Dept. It records the arrival at Piccadilly station of a press trip 1Z50 on 8 September 1960, headed by Class AL3 No E3025.

The initial fleet of 100 ac electric locomotives was as follows:

- Class AL1 (later Class 81)   25 BRCW/AEI (BTH) E3001-23/96/7
- Class AL2 (later Class 82)   10 Beyer Peacock/AEI (MV) E3046-55
- Class AL3 (later Class 83)   15 Vulcan/EE E3024-35 E3098-3100
- Class AL4 (later Class 84)   10 NBL/GEC E3036-45
- Class AL5 (later Class 85)   40 BR/AEI (MV) E3056-95

All five classes are now completely withdrawn. Abbreviations used for main contractors:
BRCW—Birmingham Railway Carriage and Wagon Co
Vulcan — Vulcan Foundry
NBL — North British Locomotive Co

These locomotives were all of 3,000 to 3,300hp and had to be capable of hauling a 475-ton express passenger train from Manchester to Euston at an average speed of 67mph, with a maximum running speed of 100mph. However, the full benefits of eletrification were not to be realised until the system was commissioned throughout to Euston, which was not achieved until 1966. In the meantime, many of the Euston trains were diverted to St Pancras to relieve the pressure on the West Coast main line during the modernisation period.

One of the early 'Modernisation Plan' Type 4 main-line diesels, No D231, passes through Manchester Exchange station *en route* to Ordsall Lane carriage sidings with the empty stock of the Down 'Comet' during the rebuilding of London Road station. No D231 was built by English Electric and entered service in P10/59. For a time it carried the name *Sylvania*. The English Electric Type 4s were regularly to be seen at London Road/Piccadilly, several being allocated to Longsight, and North Eastern Region examples could be seen at Victoria/Exchange on the Newcastle–Liverpool trains. *J. R. Carter*

Central dep	07.25	07.45		08.25	09.25		10.25	12.25
Piccadilly dep			08.00			09.40		
St Pancras arr	11.20	10.55		12.20	13.13		14.13	16.00
Euston arr			11.40			13.20		

The morning service from Manchester to London during the summer of 1963 was as above:

The 07.45 from Central was the Midland Pullman introduced in 1960, an all first-class train, calling only at Cheadle Heath to pick up. The timing of 3hr 10min for the journey was quite exceptional, and the best ever achieved on the Midland route. The return train left St Pancras at 18.10 and was due in Central at 21.20. The Midland Pullman was made up of six cars, providing 132 seats, and about half of the passengers joined at Cheadle Heath. The fare from Manchester was £3 9s plus £1 Pullman supplement.

Reverting to developments at Piccadilly, a new, intensified, suburban electric service was introduced on 12 June 1961 between Oxford Road, Piccadilly and Crewe (via both Stockport and Styal) after a winter of working mainly to the previous steam schedule. The effect of this was to give Alderley Edge a half-hourly all-stations service to Oxford Road via Stockport, and a complementary half-hourly service via the Styal line, with additional fast trains during the peak hours providing 18min journeys to Piccadilly and 20min journeys to Oxford Road, a considerable improvement over the steam service.

By this time, DMUs had been introduced on the services from Piccadilly to both Buxton and Macclesfield, and few steam locomotives were henceforth to be seen at Piccadilly in normal circumstances.

Manchester Piccadilly Resignalling

The operation of these intensified train services was facilitated by the commissioning in stages of a new power-operated signalbox at Piccadilly in 1960, the work being completed on 28 August. The new signalbox controlled all the platforms at Piccadilly, together with all the signalling on the lines from Oxford Road through Piccadilly to Heaton Chapel (on the Stockport line), to Gatley (on the Styal line), to Ashburys (on the Guide Bridge line) and to Midland Junction (on the Philips Park line). This area was formerly operated by 13 signalboxes with a total of 848 levers. Eleven were abolished and two were converted to ground frames.

Left: Another BR Publicity Dept photograph, showing the renewal of Piccadilly station roof. This interesting photograph also shows the MSJ&A platforms under reconstruction, and (top right) the rather grim and bulky frontage of Mayfield station. A trolleybus completes the scene. *IAL*

Above: Piccadilly station — the new tower block and the station buildings. Motor car enthusiasts will find this a fascinating photograph. *IAL*

Right: A quiet concourse at Piccadilly. Compare this uncluttered scene with the photograph of the station in Chapter 10. *IAL*

Above: Platforms 6 & 7 at the new Piccadilly. *IAL*

Left: Why was Longsight's 'Britannia' No 70043 *Lord Kitchener* running into Victoria with a main-line express? The answer is that some of the London Road expresses were diverted to Victoria/Exchange during the rebuilding of London Road station. This photograph is particularly interesting because it shows the old Victoria East Junction signalbox and its semaphore signal gantry. *Kenneth Field*

Above: Here, the same photographer has retreated a few yards down the platform and included the framework of the new East Junction power signalbox, opened in 1962. An early English Electric Type 4 diesel, No D214 of 1959, heads the Down 'Comet'. *Kenneth Field*

Below: The MSJ&A platform at London Road on 23 August 1958, with one of the original 1931 electric sets. This service terminated at Oxford Road station from the following month. Ten 4-wheeled platform barrows are lined up ready for use. Was there really so much parcels traffic on the MSJ&A platforms? *T. K. Widd*

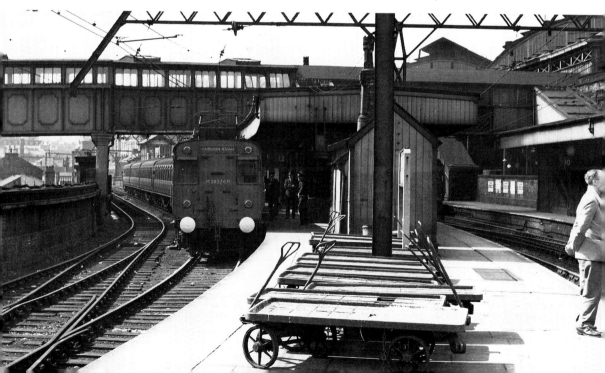

The new signalbox was part of a large, imposing glass and panel structure on the west side of the line just outside Piccadilly station. The operating room housed a console 47ft long, on which were mounted 491 route switches and 121 individual point switches and ground frame releases. A large, illuminated track diagram, incorporating four-character train description headcodes in 'windows' at signals, was mounted above the console.

Each route switch operated a point and its associated signal, on what was at that time the standard 'OCS' (one control switch) system. All the points were operated electro-pneumatically and the signals were of the now-familiar multiple-aspect colour light type, with position light subsidiary signals where necessary. All the signalling equipment in the Piccadilly station area was operated directly from the new signalbox, but remote equipment was operated from satellite relay interlockings, of which there were five. The signalbox was manned by a regulator and three signalmen on each shift.

Although Piccadilly had opened in 1960, the rebuilding of the station had not been completed at that date. The whole financial basis of the Manchester/Liverpool–Euston electrification was then under examination, as was the larger question of BR's finances, and what became known as stage 2 of the rebuilding was deferred. It was subsequently authorised in 1963, with demolition of the remaining portion of the old station buildings due to start in February 1964, followed by the erection of the new passenger station buildings, including a cafeteria, waiting-rooms, bar, seat reservation and enquiry office and four shops. Ominously, it was officially disclosed that when building work was complete it was planned to divert more services to Piccadilly, which might lead to the closure of Central.

The new Piccadilly station was officially opened by the Lord Mayor on 11 May 1966, seven years after the start of work, but there was a final phase still to complete. This consisted of the demolition of the former LNW goods warehouse on the approach to the station, after which a consortium of companies built a row of 17 shops surmounted by a seven-storey office block on the site of the warehouse, the new building being called Gateway House. As part of this phase, the station approach road was remodelled into a dual carriageway.

Below: Gateshead's English Electric Type 4 No D274 descends the bank from Miles Platting into Manchester Victoria and passes East Junction signalbox on its way to Exchange with the 9.50am Newcastle to Liverpool Lime Street. *John Clarke*

A few weeks earlier, on 18 April 1966, the long-awaited new electrified services to Euston were introduced. From Piccadilly there were 10 expresses to Euston, the basic service being two-hourly, with an increased frequency during the morning and evening peaks, including two first class Pullman trains. The fastest trains took 2hr 30min. From March 1967 the morning timetable was a follows:

Piccadilly dep	07.20	07.35	09.00	09.30
Euston arr	10.18	10.05	11.36	12.15
Piccadilly dep	10.30	11.30	13.30	
Euston arr	13.15	14.10	16.10	

The 07.35 was named the 'Manchester Pullman' and called only at Stockport and Wilmslow to take up. The 09.00 had the same stopping pattern, but all the other trains ran via Stoke-on-Trent. Electrification was a great success. In the first year the number of passenger journeys increased by 54% on London–Manchester services. The locomotives built for these services will be dealt with later in this chapter.

Comparison with the 1994 timetable is interesting:

Piccadilly dep	05.20	06.00	06.45	07.10
Euston arr	08.13	08.40	09.16	09.44
Piccadilly dep	07.30	08.30	and then hourly	
Euston arr	10.11	11.08		

The 10 expresses in 1967 had grown to 17 in 1994, with a remarkable emphasis on early morning departures. In 1967 there were only two departures before 09.00; in 1994 there were six, illustrating a considerable shift in the business travel pattern and its intensity. As before, most trains run via Stoke-on-Trent, and the overall journey times are virtually unchanged. The latter factor is important; without changes in track or traction, acceleration can hardly be expected, indeed, with ageing track and locomotives BR has done well to maintain the 1967 timings, but in a competitive arena the need for speeded-up timings is self-evident, a fact fully appreciated by BR, which is currently unable to deliver because of lack of investment (although there are now promising developments involving private capital).

The improved service following electrification led, sadly but understandably, to the complete withdrawal of services via the Midland route to St Pancras. The sight of 'Jubilees', 'Royal Scots' and 'Britannias' pounding up to Peak Forest and through Monsal Dale will forever be a cherished memory for those who were fortunate enough to

have been around at the time. Ruskin's famous diatribe protesting at the proposal to build a railway line through Monsal Dale and the Peak District: 'There was a rocky valley between Buxton and Bakewell ... divine as the temple of Tempe; you might have seen the gods there morning and evening ... you enterprised a railroad ... you blasted its rocks away ... and now every fool in Buxton can be at Bakewell in half-an-hour, and every fool in Bakewell at Buxton' comes inevitably to mind. Apollo and the Muses can enjoy the peace of Monsal Dale once more, but in the company of the ghosts of those engine drivers who loved it and those passengers who gazed out of the train windows with awe. Buxton and Bakewell fools are away on the A6.

The Cinderella of the London Midland Region, the old L&Y, was not without a certain amount of modernisation by 1960. Diesel multiple units had been introduced on suburban services from Victoria, but main-line diesel locomotives were still in the minority. However, the North Eastern Region came to the rescue, by providing Type 4 English Electric 2,000hp diesels for the Newcastle–Leeds–Manchester–Liverpool trains, with a reduction in the overall journey time of more than half an hour. The North Eastern Region had also been developing an InterCity DMU for the Hull–Liverpool via Leeds service. These six-coach trains were built at Swindon, with four of the six coaches being powered in view of the heavy gradients between Huddersfield and Stalybridge, and the desire for accelerated timings. The trains were recognisable by their rounded ends and wrap-around windscreens. Seating, mainly in open saloons, was provided for 60 first-class and 232 second-class passengers, and there was a buffet section. The introduction of these trains enabled 40min to be cut from the Liverpool–Hull timings, almost half of which was between Leeds and Manchester. Finally, new electric multiple units were introduced on the Bury service, replacing the L&Y stock which had been put into service when the line was first electrified during World War 1. The Bury services were eventually transferred to Platforms 4 and 5 at Victoria, and Platforms 1 to 3, previously used, were taken out of use.

Victoria Resignalling

Hard on the heels of the Modernisation Programme, the London Midland Region prepared a scheme for a new power-operated signalbox at Victoria East Junction, but it could not be developed at the time (1955) because all the available technical resources were engaged on the Manchester–Crewe and Liverpool–Crewe resignalling schemes. When those schemes were

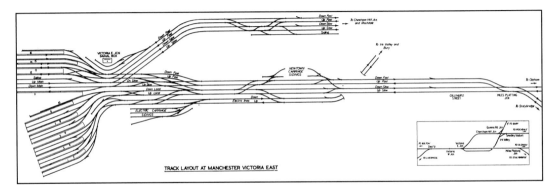

TRACK LAYOUT AT MANCHESTER VICTORIA EAST

Above: Plan of Victoria resignalling 1962.

finally completed and brought into use, planning started for the Victoria East Junction scheme, which was commissioned in 1962.

The new signalbox controlled the Cheetham Hill line as far as Cheetham Hill Junction signalbox and the Miles Platting line as far as Collyhurst Street signalbox, enabling six mechanical signalboxes to be closed, including Newtown Nos 1 and 2, Millgate, Turntable and Footbridge.

Westinghouse were the main contractors, and both the signalling equipment and the controls were similar to those installed at Piccadilly. The signals were of the standard three or four-aspect colour light type, with position light subsidiary signals where necessary. The standard 'first-wheel replacement to red' applied to all running signals except for those signals applicable to trains climbing Miles Platting bank. 'Last wheel replacement' applied here, so that the bank engine driver would receive the same indication at a signal as the one received by the train engine driver. Points were operated electro-pneumatically, and the whole area was track-circuited throughout.

A special feature at the new signalbox catered for the problem, referred to in previous pages, of freight trains running away out of control on the banks approaching Victoria station from the east. With no signalman available on those banks to observe passing trains and take immediate emergency action if a train was seen to be running away, it was necessary to have an alternative automatic system to cover such an eventuality. This took the form of an audible and visual warning which operated in the new signalbox as soon as a train passed a signal at danger and occupied the overlap track circuit beyond it.

The points and signals were operated by thumb switches, set in rows on a console. Each thumb switch, when turned, set the points for a particular route and cleared the applicable signal. Above the console there was a large illuminated diagram showing the track layout of the whole area. When the signalman set a route for a train it was indicated on the diagram by a row of white lights, and the

presence of a train was indicated by red lights. Train describers were provided, which indicated the description of a train at any particular signal and stepped along automatically from signal to signal on the illuminated diagram as the train progressed.

The new signalbox was located at the east junction and was provided with large windows, giving the signalmen an excellent view over the whole area.

The Beeching Report
(more properly called 'The Reshaping of British Railways Report 1963')

The Modernisation Report of 1955 had ushered in a period of euphoric optimism after 15 years of under-investment, but this was destined to be short-lived. The road haulage industry began to expand vigorously following denationalisation in 1953, and more and more cars appeared on the roads, as a result of which the financial position of the railways worsened during the later fifties. This caused considerable concern to the government, even though a similar Conservative government had approved the Modernisation Plan only two or three years earlier. That document had made it quite clear that the financial benefits of the Modernisation Plan would take several years to be realised, but the Government were impatient for results and were presumably hoping that a miracle would occur. Committees were appointed to study the problem, and reports and white papers were issued, culminating eventually in the Transport Act of 1962, which abolished the ill-fated British Transport Commission and established the British Railways Board. A new chairman was appointed, whose name was to become a household word — Dr Richard Beeching.

BR's Reshaping Report, issued in 1963, stunned the nation by the sweeping nature of its proposals for withdrawing passenger services which were judged to be unremunerative. They were very extensive and contained some quite doubtful cases, but the Report has to be judged in the context of 1963. The remit given to the Railways Board by the government (who were in effect both its shareholders and its Board of Directors) was that it must balance its books. If a line, or a passenger service, did not pay it should be discarded. The government's philosophy, with which one cannot quarrel, was that if there were non-financial reasons why a service should be retained, it was properly a matter for the Government to adjudicate upon, as public money was involved. It was not the duty of the BRB to make social decisions. Fortunately, as matters have turned out, the Government refused to allow a substantial number of closure proposals, some of which were quite significant.

It might also be said that Dr Beeching did not thrust his closure policy down the throats of an unwilling Railways Board. Its mouth was already open. When the railways were nationalised in 1948, passenger services were operated on approximately 15,000 route miles. By 1963 that mileage had fallen to 12,631, and many senior railwaymen felt that the key to financial success and the railway's survival was to be found in disposing of all those passenger services which did not pay. The tragedy of the situation was that insufficient endeavour was made to reorganise and modernise working methods, practices and equipment, with a view to providing a better service at less cost. If as much effort had been directed into those positive channels as went into closures, many lines might have been saved or might not even have been submitted for closure.

As might be expected, the list of proposed withdrawals affecting Manchester was considerable:

1. All passenger services to be withdrawn:
> Central–Chinley–Hope–Sheffield Midland
> Exchange–Stalybridge–Greenfield
> Piccadilly–Buxton
> Piccadilly–Hadfield/Glossop
> Piccadilly–Romiley–Hayfield/Macclesfield
> Victoria–Bury–Bacup
> Victoria–Bury–Accrington–Colne
> Victoria–Newton Heath–Middleton
> Victoria–Horwich

Below: Local passenger services were under threat in the 1960s. Fowler 2-6-4T No 42343 draws into Castleton station with the 5.15pm Rochdale-Southport train, formed rather generously of BR Mk 1 corridor stock, on 1 June 1965. *R. S. Greenwood*

Above: Electrification and the advent of diesels meant that former pride-of-the-line express engines found themselves demoted to more mundane duties in the 1960s. Longsight's 'Royal Scot' class No 46115 *Scots Guardsman* finds itself at Manchester Central at the head of the 17.30 commuters' train to Buxton, formed of BR Mk 1 corridor stock, on 4 May 1964. The train ran via Cheadle Heath and Chinley and it must have been worth an hour of anyone's time to travel over such a route in comfort behind a 'Royal Scot'. No such luxury for Buxton passengers from Piccadilly, but at least their service survived Beeching. *IAL*

2. Local passenger services to be withdrawn
    Central–Chinley–Derby Midland
    Exchange–Tyldesley–Wigan North
      Western
      Exchange–Warrington Bank
      Quay–Chester General
    Exchange–Patricroft–Tyldesley–Liverpool
      Lime St
    Exchange–Huddersfield
3. Passenger services to be modified
    Central–Liverpool Central
    Oxford Road–Piccadilly
    Piccadilly–Macclesfield–Stoke-on-Trent
    Victoria–Rochdale–Todmorden

Victoria–Wigan Wallgate–Southport
    Chapel Street
Victoria–Blackpool
Victoria–Rochdale/Oldham

4. Passenger stations within a few miles of Manchester, on routes from Manchester, to be closed

    Ardwick*
    Ashburys*
    Chorlton-cum-Hardy
    Clayton Bridge
    Crumpsall*
    Droylsden
    Eccles*
    Fairfield*
    Gorton and Openshaw*
    Heaton Park*
    Miles Platting*
    Newton Heath
    Park*
    Pendleton*
    Woodlands Road*

Of the 15 stations listed, no fewer than the 11 asterisked survived and are still open. The closure and withdrawal proposals aroused intense opposition. What the Railways Board had done (perhaps mischievously in some cases) was to list all those lines and stations that lost money. It was for the government to decide, following a report from the Transport Users Consultative Committee, which of the proposals should be allowed to proceed and which should be refused. Fortuitously, before decision-time arrived in many cases, a Labour government had come into power and there was an emerging feeling that the unfettered use of cars and buses was incompatible with a decent environment in a city. Some of the closure proposals, eg Manchester to Buxton and to Bury, concerned heavily-used suburban routes, and to have closed them would have been politically unacceptable, apart from any other considerations. So, most of Manchester's local stations and services survived, and were developed in later years, as we shall see.

Below: The Major Trunk Route Report assumed that the Woodhead route would be one of the two cross-Pennine routes to be developed, although the authors of the report may have felt that they would have exposed themselves to ridicule had they suggested closing a line which had been electrified at considerable cost only 10 years or so earlier. E26000, the original 1941 locomotive, stands at Reddish on 21 July 1969. *David L. Percival*

The Duplicate Trunk Route Problem

Hot on the heels of the Reshaping Report, and in some ways more fundamental, was the publication of another report, entitled 'The Development of the Major Railway Trunk Routes.' It appeared in February 1965, and was a logical successor to the Reshaping Report. The new report sought to address the problem of what became known, somewhat spuriously, as duplicate routes. Manchester was involved in several, eg

- to London
  - via Crewe to Euston
  - via Derby to St Pancras
  - via the former GC route to Marylebone
- Cross-Pennine
  - via Rochdale (L&Y route)
  - via Diggle (LNW route)
  - via Woodhead (GC route)
  - via Hope Valley (Midland route)
  - via Peak Forest (Midland route)
- to Liverpool
  - to Exchange (L&Y route)
  - to Lime St (LNW route)
  - to Central (CLC route)

The report was a complete non-event so far as press and public were concerned, in complete contrast to the Reshaping Report, yet its effects

were to be more far-reaching. It recognised that much bigger savings were to be made by closing complete routes and major terminal stations than by withdrawing local passenger trains and closing small stations. It is interesting to see what was proposed in 1965 and what was the outcome, the moral of which is — take great care when attempting to predict the future 20 years ahead and then don't do it. For example, the report forecast that steel production in 1984 would be 41 million tons. It was 15.1 million tons. It forecast coal output as 170 million tons. It was actually 110 million tons, and falling. It suggested that nuclear power stations would provide a third of the nation's electricity. They provided 19%. Finally it assumed that there would be 21 million cars on our roads by 1984. On this they were nearer the mark. There were actually 16 million.

The report was intended to be positive. It was based upon selecting the best duplicate route, taking all factors into consideration, and then abandoning the others. It also aimed to get to grips with the problem of over-provision of routes arising from 19th-century inter-railway competition. It was also positive in the sense that it suggested that it was wrong to spread the available investment funds thinly over all duplicate lines, but that it would be more beneficial to concentrate such funds on routes with the best potential, a philosophy with

which one can hardly disagree. However, it had one fundamental flaw — it thought mainly in terms of end-to-end traffic, ignoring the potential of intermediate travel, which has become of greater importance on several long-distance routes, where air competition has eaten into the end-to-end traffic. This factor was already evident when the report was written.

However, reverting to our list of Manchester's duplicate routes, the report proposed the development of the following routes:

- to London   via Crewe to Euston
- Cross-Pennine via Woodhead (GC route)
                          via Rochdale (L&Y route)
- to Liverpool   via St Helens Junction (LNW route)
                          via Warrington (CLC route)

The subsequent unexpectedly calamitous fall in coal and steel production, and the effects of the

Below: BR/Sulzer Type 4 No D38, built in 1961, stands in the doomed Manchester Central station at the head of train No 1C93, the 6.10pm to Nottingham, on 27 September 1967. The train shed has now been reborn as the celebrated G-Mex Exhibition Centre. J. M. Cooper-Smith

later 1968 Transport Act, invalidated some of these proposals, but they were revised as time went by. The Woodhead route was closed, and as a consequence the case for the retention of the Hope Valley route became stronger. Equally, the Diggle route has taken on a new lease of life.

The Closure of Central and Exchange

The closure of the Peak Forest route led in turn to the closure of Central station, which took place on 5 May 1969. It then suffered the ultimate humiliation of being turned into a car park, a fate which it had to endure through the dark ages of Manchester's railways, until it re-emerged as the G-Mex Exhibition Centre in 1986. The closure of Central station was approved by the Minister of Transport in 1967, together with the withdrawal of all passenger services over the following lines:

Central station to Cornbrook West Junction
Fairfield Junction to Chorlton Junction
Old Trafford Junction to Cornbrook West Junction
Throstle Nest East Junction to New Mills South
       Junction (via Cheadle Heath)
Heaton Mersey Station Junction to Romiley
       Junction

It was the death knell for the Midland's services to Manchester. About 130 trains a day were using Central and the Minister stipulated that the transfer of these to Oxford Road and Piccadilly must not be accompanied by any reduction in the number of trains using those two stations nor in the number to be diverted to them. It was planned to divert to Piccadilly the trains from the former Midland line to Central via Romiley, and for the CLC trains from Liverpool and Chester to be diverted into Oxford Road or Piccadilly. The minister also specified improvements at Oxford Road to facilitate the more intensive movement of passengers, including the widening of the footbridge and stairs.

The Midland-line trains were diverted at the beginning of 1968, and the CLC services in May 1969. The Liverpool DMU service ran to Piccadilly and used Platforms 13 and 14. Oxford Road was used by 118 additional trains on weekdays, and there were no fewer than 168 additional trains at Piccadilly, using Platforms 13 and 14. The track layout at Oxford Road was modified to provide an extra platform, and some improvements were made at Piccadilly to facilitate passenger movement.

Below: Trafford Park's Class 5 4-6-0 No 44929 draws a couple of parcels vans out of Platform 2 at Manchester Central on 2 November 1967. *John H. Bird*

Left: The metamorphosis of Oxford Road station. A 'before' photograph, taken in 1948, shows a dingy station with an MSJ&A set at the platform. *IAL*

Centre left: There is no doubt that this is an 'after' photograph. The rather futuristic architectural style was not repeated, and it certainly clashed with the drab surroundings. Reconstruction work is not quite complete in this late-1968 BR Publicity Dept photograph, taken looking towards Deansgate. *IAL*

Below: June 1969. An original MSJ&A 1931 set stands in the bay platform on the left, whilst a 25kv AC EMU waits to depart to Alderley Edge via Piccadilly. *N. D. Griffiths*

Right: A commendably clean Class 5, No 45285 of Llandudno Junction, is impatient for departure at the head of the 16.30 Manchester Exchange-Llandudno 'Club' train on 7 April 1965. *D. S. Frith*

The whole of the area was resignalled, with control being transferred to Piccadilly powerbox, which then controlled the routes via Oxford Road to Ordsall Lane No 1, Trafford Park Junction and Warwick Road. Some track alterations were made, and a new 50mph junction was installed at Cornbrook, together with a new bridge. The following signalboxes were abolished:

Manchester Central
Cornbrook West Junction
Cornbrook East Junction
Old Trafford Junction
Cornbrook Sidings
Throstle Nest East Junction
Oxford Road
Castlefield

Exchange station also closed its doors on 5 May 1969. Its most important passenger services were the trans-Pennine trains between Liverpool Lime Street, Manchester Exchange, Leeds and Newcastle, and trains to Chester, Llandudno and Holyhead. Most of the through services between Manchester and Glasgow/Edinburgh already used Victoria, and the reduction in the number of local trains at Victoria enabled that station to accept Exchange's traffic with little difficulty.

Freight

It has to be emphasised that the Reshaping Report was not simply concerned with closures, although that is how it became established in the public mind. The report also addressed the problem of losses incurred in dealing with merchandise traffic and enthusiastically proposed the development of the liner train concept. A similar service of road/rail container transport known as the 'Condor' — container door-to-door — had started in 1959 between London and Glasgow, and its success had led to the introduction of a similar service, known as 'Speedfreight', between London and Manchester in April 1963. Comprehensive studies of the freight market led to the planned development of a nationwide liner train container service, and Freightliner was born. It was rapidly developed under BR management from 1965, and by the close of this chapter the national network had been established. Manchester's terminal was at Longsight, and it received its first train on 28 February 1966, from York Way, London. A Glasgow service was subsequently introduced, together with a second London service. The Longsight depot had three 1,000ft-long tracks, served by two Drott Travelift gantry cranes. Road transport equipment consisted of 12 haulage units

Below: In July 1968 BR established a special overnight parcels service with a money-back guarantee. It was launched by the dispatch of parcels from London to the Manchester department store of Kendal, Milne on the 22nd. The first batch of parcels were sucessfully delivered by 9am the following day. *Fox Photos*

and 24 trailers.

Eventually, the Longsight depot proved to be too small and it was decided to seek a more spacious site. BR's Manchester people were firmly in favour of Ashton Moss, but Regional HQ were not convinced and to settle the issue the general manager himself carried out a survey by helicopter. He chose Trafford Park, where there was plenty of vacant railway-owned land following the closure of the engine shed and the marshalling yard.

For some years after nationalisation, BR continued to handle its sundries traffic at a large number of depots, based largely on pre-Grouping practices. These were:

- Ex-LNW London Road (both below the
         passenger station and at the warehouse)
         Liverpool Road
- Ex-L&Y Oldham Road
         Salford
- Ex-Mid Ancoats
- Ex-GC   Ducie Street
         Ashburys
- Ex-GN   Deansgate
- Ex-CLC Central

Handling sundries traffic at so many depots imposed enormous costs, particularly in cartage, shunting and tripping, the provision of wagons, and in train working. The traffic was carried at a considerable loss, and closures began as BR struggled to reduce its costs. The handling of sundries traffic was reorganised and concentrated on fewer depots, but this was often less successful than had been hoped. The remaining depots were often swamped with traffic beyond their capacity to handle it efficiently, resulting in delay and damage. Dissatisfied traders simply took their traffic away from the railways and put it on the roads. Further closures of goods depots were inevitable in the circumstances — Deansgate had closed as early as 1954, the CLC at Central was closed in 1964, and both Salford and Ducie St closed in 1967. Deansgate was subsequently used as a parcels depot for some years and finally closed in 1970. It is still standing, derelict and mute, a monument to the Great Railway Age. Ducie Street became, inevitably, a car park, but part of the site was used for BR's new divisional headquarters, called Rail House.

Full wagonload traffic was concentrated on the depots at Ardwick South (ex LNW) and Ardwick (ex GC), whilst steel traffic was handled mainly at Bolton for the whole area. Concentrations and closures enabled many of the marshalling yards and sidings in the Manchester area to be closed, and ultimately only Brewery and Dewsnap remained. Even their reprieve was to be short-lived.

The 1968 Transport Act — Passenger Transport Authorities and Executives

The expected improvement in BR's financial position, arising from the changes made in the 1962 Transport Act, failed to materialise, and losses mounted. Yet another reorganisation was inevitable, and it came in 1968 with the passage of yet another Transport Act, which was to have a marked effect on Manchester.

The public uproar over the withdrawal of passenger trains and the closure of stations continued during the 1960s, and was revived each time BR put forward a new proposal. It was therefore decided by the Government that those services which were to be retained in the public interest, but which did not pay their way, should be supported by public funds. Even more important was the proposal to establish Passenger Transport Authorities in all the major conurbations, including Manchester, whose duty would be to plan, co-ordinate and develop public passenger transport within their areas, or, as set out in the immortal words of the Act, 'to secure or promote the provision of a properly integrated and efficient system of public passenger transport to meet the needs of the area.'

In future the PTAs, appointed partly by local authorities and partly by the Minister of Transport, would be responsible for deciding which services would run, and the timetable, together with the fares to be charged. BR became contractors, and any losses on the operation were recouped from central government through the PTAs. The PTAs also became responsible for local stations, but not the main-line termini.

This part of the Act was a lifeline for BR and has been highly successful. BR's loss of autonomy was a small price to pay. A later Conservative government was to upset these far-sighted proposals of the 1968 Act by deregulating buses in the mid-1980s, but that is a separate story.

However, we must step back in time for a short while to the years before the establishment of the PTAs/PTEs. Mention has already been made in these pages, of proposals for cross-city lines, underground services, etc which had always previously foundered on the twin rocks of cost and lack of real municipal interest. However, Manchester City Corporation began to show a real interest in the mid-1960s.

In 1965 Taylor Woodrow Construction Ltd proposed a full-scale feasibility study on the application of the Safège monorail system to a suggested route from Ringway Airport to the city centre and northwards to the overspill estate at

Langley, a distance of 16 miles. This corridor was chosen because it coincided with the heaviest demand on the bus services and gave direct access to the airport.

However, the Minister of Transport felt that a more widely-based rapid transit survey was desirable, and early in 1966 Manchester City Corporation and the Ministry jointly initiated a detailed investigation, based on the same route, to compare the relative merits of all forms of urban rapid transport. Consulting engineers were appointed to evaluate available systems, under the overall direction of a steering group representing Manchester Corporation, BR and the Ministry.

The consultants' report was published at the end of 1967. Six systems had been investigated — two monorail systems, two systems using guided rubber-tyred vehicles, the use of ordinary buses operating on exclusive bus roadways, and orthodox railways. On all counts an orthodox rail solution was found to be the most favourable.

Accordingly, a further study was made of possible improvements to existing BR lines, under three headings:
• Intensification of services within the limits of the existing signalling and terminal facilities
• Improvement of the signalling system and the lengthening of platforms to permit greater density of services and longer trains
• As scheme 2, plus an underground link between Oxford Road station and Victoria to allow through running between Bury and Altrincham, with an underground station in the heart of the city.

In the meantime, a major land use/transportation study was taking place for southeast Lancashire and northeast Cheshire (SELNEC), with the object of producing a comprehensive plan for highways and public transport. Therefore action on the Rapid Transit Study was deferred until the SELNEC report was available. The SELNEC report was published in November 1968 and recommended a new 11-mile-long electric railway from Higher Blackley in the north to Northenden in the south, passing through central Manchester in tunnels. Central area stations were proposed at University, Oxford Road, St Peter's Square, Market Street and Victoria, with the total cost being in the region of £50 million. Richard Marsh, the new Minister of Transport (and later the Chairman of the British Railways Board), supported a recommendation that the study should be carried a stage further, and that a full financial and economic evaluation should be made.

Various schemes for rapid transit had been discussed previously, and the justification for the current proposals was based on the need to find an effective answer to the congestion caused by the increasing use of the private car, which made bus services less reliable and added to the congestion. The space that could be provided for roads and parking without destroying the character of the city centre would not allow more than 30% of people to commute by car, according to the report.

The dusty pile of reports dealing with the question of some form of metro system, partly underground, for the Manchester area continued to grow. Whether this latest report was any more fortunate than its predecessors in actually producing tangible results in the form of new track and trains we shall see in the next chapter, but we must leave the story for the time being at the end of 1969, with reports being pored over and earnest discussions being held. It is time to turn our thoughts once more to the freight problem, where major organisational changes were imminent.

The 1968 Transport Act — Freight

Barbara Castle, as Minister of Transport in 1967, was equally radical in her proposals for freight. Much faith was placed in the development of the Freightliner network, and it was proposed to introduce both quality licensing and quantity licensing to the road haulage industry, in order to encourage the carriage of merchandise by the Freightliner service. This would undoubtedly have resulted in a succession of disputes concerning the interpretation and operation of the Act's provisions, but it was well-intentioned. However, the proposals were never put to the test; the quantity licensing provisions were quickly dropped by the new Conservative government in 1970. The Freightliner service became the joint child of BR and another body created by the 1968 Act — the National Freight Corporation, and never achieved the high hopes of its early days.

In an attempt to solve the problem of the losses incurred in handling sundries traffic, BR created a new organisation to handle both sundries and cartage. Initially called the Sundries Division, it became National Carriers Ltd, and a year later the 1968 Transport Act transferred it, lock, stock and barrel, to the ownership of the National Freight Corporation. BR had to decide exactly which assets were to be transferred to National Carriers Ltd, and to do so quickly. The job was done almost on the back of a cigarette packet. Only warehouse buildings handling sundries traffic were transferred, together with the land on which the warehouses stood. Everything else in the goods yards remained with BR — the track, sidings, land and full wagon-load facilities. Sundries warehouses became an island of NCL/NFC property surrounded by a large area of BR property. This may not have been a vital factor when it was all Crown property, but when the NFC was privatised it became a matter of some consequence, especially when the BR facilities became redundant and BR sought to redevelop the land or sell it off, with a little piece of someone else's land slap bang in the middle of it.

The duty of the NFC as laid down in the Act deserves recording:

'... in conjunction with the Railways Board :-
  i) to provide, or secure or promote the provision of, properly integrated services for the carriage of goods ... by road or rail, and
  ii) to secure that ... goods are carried by rail whenever such carriage is efficient and economic.'

There is a saying that fine words butter no parsnips. The good intentions of the Act were rapidly forgotten, and disputes quickly arose as to what was efficient and economic. National Carriers Ltd, created by BR to take over the sundries business and the warehouses together with the associated cartage, quickly gave up the struggle to make the carriage of sundries by rail economic and put the traffic entirely on the roads. It was probably the most effective way of dealing with the problem, but it spelt the death of BR's splendid network of fast, overnight, fully-fitted freight trains and led to the closure of Ancoats in July 1972. Those who drafted the 1968 Act failed to achieve their aims for freight, but if a Labour government had been re-elected in 1970 the future might have been different. On the other hand, it is difficult to see how railway sundries could ever have been made to pay in the developing industrial scene, and BR were glad to get rid of the problem.

Motive Power

It is now time to look at the motive power scene. When this chapter started, in 1955, BR had 18,420 steam locomotives, 320 diesels (of which 309 were shunting engines) and 71 electrics; and steam locomotives were still being built. Thirteen years later steam on BR was extinct. It lingered on in the northwest until the very end, in August 1968; especially to the north of Manchester. Belle Vue shed closed as early as 1956, but ten years were to elapse before the next closure, Agecroft, in 1966. Newton Heath, Trafford Park and Patricroft all survived to the end, Newton Heath then becoming a diesel depot.

Changes in the motive power scene were dramatic and on a major scale. When this chapter opened, the Manchester-Sheffield-Wath electrification had just been commissioned. Elsewhere, steam reigned supreme and unchallenged. Pacifics, 'Royal Scots', 'Jubilees' and 'Patriots' handled nearly all the expresses, with the now ubiquitous Class 5 4-6-0s in support.

As the 1950s progressed, BR Standard types began to appear. Longsight received 'Britannia' Pacifics Nos 70031/34 when new in 1952 and

Below: One of Stanier's prewar 2-6-4Ts, No 42472, takes over the Harwich-Liverpool Central boat train from one of the Woodhead electrics, at Guide Bridge. An undated photograph, but probably from the late 1950s. The engine bears a shed plate 9G, which at that time was Gorton. The ex-LMS 2-6-4T engines were an integral part of the everyday scene in the Manchester area for 30 years. *Kenneth Field*

Left: One of the prestige cross-country trains, the 9am restaurant car express from Liverpool Lime Street to Newcastle via Leeds, passes Threlfalls Brewery and Deal Street signalbox, and runs into Manchester Exchange, in charge of rebuilt 'Patriot' No 45535 *Sir Herbert Walker KCB*, in July 1960. This was almost the end of an era — soon the train would be diesel-hauled and the stock would gradually cease to be front-rank. *J. R. Carter*

Below left: Another prestige service — the 9.30am Manchester to Glasgow Central restaurant car express, seen passing Threlfalls Brewery in July 1960 behind rebuilt 'Royal Scot' class No 46107 *Argyll and Sutherland Highlander*. Today there is no through morning service from Manchester to Scotland's largest city. *J. R. Carter*

Above right: Lightweight BR 2-6-0 No 78056, of Chester Northgate shed (6D), stands quietly at the buffers having brought a train from Chester to Manchester Central via Northwich. Undated, but *c*1957. No 78056 entered service in August 1956. *IAL*

Centre right: One of Newton Heath's stalwarts, 'Jubilee' class No 45701 *Conqueror*, rests at its home depot in 1960. Most steam engines tended to be moved from shed to shed during their lifetimes, but *Conqueror* spent almost all its 27-year life at Newton Heath. *IAL*

Below right:
An elderly Fowler 2-6-2T No 40009 rests at its home depot Trafford Park (9E) in 1960. *IAL*

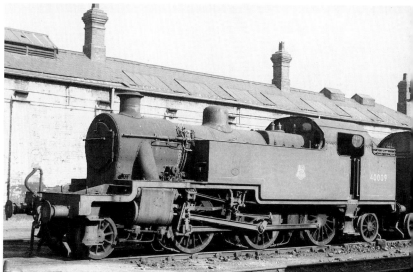

Left: BR Standard engine, Class 4 4-6-0 No 75012, draws the 1.35pm to Llandudno out of Manchester Exchange on 27 July 1955, and works back to its home shed (6G). The argument as to whether BR should have built large numbers of steam engines to standard designs in the 1950s continues. *W. Garth*

Below left: As the new diesels and electrics displaced steam engines on express duties, the latter found themselves relegated to more mundane duties, and nothing could be more mundane than a train-load of coal empties. Upperby's 'Jubilee' No 45555 *Quebec* has been commandeered to work such a train from the Manchester Ship Canal to Ellenbrook Colliery, through Eccles, in August 1960. *J. R. Carter*

Right: It seems altogether fitting that one of Stanier's most successful designs, his Class 5 mixed-traffic 4-6-0, should survive until the very end of steam in 1968. Thirty-one-year-old No 45305 stands at the head of a 'Steam Tour of N W Lines' at Manchester Victoria on 4 August 1968. It is also fitting that this engine should have been preserved, and named *Alderman Draper* after the man who saved it from the scrapheap. Now 58 years old, No 45305 can still be seen in service on preserved lines. *M. Shackleton*

Nos 70043/4 the following year, and kept them until displaced by diesels and electrics in 1959/60/61. Trafford Park received Nos 70014/5/7/21/42 in 1958 for the St Pancras services, and kept them until displaced by diesels in 1961. Even Newton Heath had some for a short while in 1960/61 — Nos 70014/5, 70045/8/9. Patricroft had to be content with BR Standard Class 5 4-6-0s.

As soon as the dieselisation programme got under way, diesel-electric locomotives began to appear in Manchester. BR/Sulzer 2,500hp locos, known as the 'Peak' class and numbered D1 onwards, first appeared on the scene in 1959, and no fewer than 123 were allocated to the Midland line between 1960 and 1962, numbered D43 to D165. They were mainly to be seen in Central station, on the Derby and St Pancras services, but North Eastern Region locomotives of that type worked through Exchange on the Newcastle-Leeds-Manchester-Liverpool Lime Street trains.

The Western lines (former LNW) received a different class of diesel-electric locomotive — the English Electric Type 4 of 2000hp. They were numbered from D200, and the Western lines initial allocation in 1959 was D210-D236. They bore the names of famous passenger liners. The following year further deliveries started, from D287 to D344, and D369 to D384, the programme being completed by early 1962.

For secondary duties, Derby and Crewe Works began to turn out Type 2 diesel-electrics in 1958. They had Sulzer 1,160hp engines, and were numbered from D5000 upwards. Early deliveries were to the Western lines, but the Midland lines did

not receive them until 1962. The Type 2s were turned out in very large numbers, D5000-D5299 and D7500-D7677. Later machines were of 1,250hp.

Finally, one of the most successful designs, the Brush Type 4 diesel-electric, with Sulzer engines rated at 2,750hp, began to appear in 1962, although they were not widely seen in Manchester until the later 1960s. They were numbered D1100-1111 and D1500-D1999.

With the entry into service of the new diesels, those fine steam engines which had been the pride of the line began to find themselves transferred to sheds of lower prestige, to be employed on freight and secondary passenger duties, which was rather a sad end.

For the new West Coast main line electrified services, a new class of electric locomotives was built, known as Class 86. They were built by BR/AEI and BR/English Electric, and were numbered E3101-E3200. These 100 locomotives proved consistently more reliable in service than the earlier classes and included a number of technical advances, such as 2,000kW rheostatic braking. A visual difference was the fitting of one pantograph instead of two. It had been decided to incorporate axle-hung traction motors on the Class 86 locomotives, but service experience proved that this arrangement created excessive dynamic loading on the track. In plain English they bashed the track to bits, and the fleet was subsequently divided into freight locomotives, with a limited maximum speed to reduce track damage, and passenger locomotives (Class 86/2), which were fitted with flexicoil secondary suspension to reduce dynamic loading on the track.

1969 — Manchester — The Wider Scene

The decline in Manchester's industrial base since World War 2 had been dramatic, and indeed it continued beyond the end of the period covered by this chapter. There were some indications that newer industries, such as electrical engineering, with Metropolitan-Vickers and Ferranti, pharmaceuticals (ICI), and synthetic fabrics (Courtaulds and ICI), might make up the deficiency, but it was not to be. By 1969 job losses were mounting, and between 1966 and 1972 one in every three jobs in manual employment in manufacturing was lost, and a quarter of all factories and workshops closed.

The Manchester Ship Canal, which only a few years earlier had been thriving, also fell on hard times. Rising costs, falling productivity, and disruptive strikes caused shipping lines to withdraw their services and, by 1980, shipping traffic had virtually ceased at the Manchester end of the canal. The withdrawal of shipping services by the Prince Line, the Furness Withy Line and Manchester Liners was the final blow. The docks, which for almost a century had been thronged with ships, fell silent. By 1985 the canal was, to all intents and purposes, closed.

The malaise of decay was clearly not confined to the railways. Those industries, factories and workshops, together with their associated rows of Victorian terraced housing, which developed around the commercial, shopping and business centre of Manchester, withered and created a new feature of the built-up landscape — inner-city decay, to which the railways themselves contributed. They occupied huge areas of land around the inner core, on which stood, or had stood, engine sheds, goods depots, carriage sidings, marshalling yards, and works which had built and repaired locomotives, carriages and wagons. To an increasing degree, these facilities were no longer required for railway purposes.

The reduction in inner suburban housing was balanced by a population move to the more salubrious outskirts. Manchester's population after the war was in the region of 700,000; it fell by a third in the next 30 years. In one way this was good news for BR, because the increase in service employment led to a potentially healthy commuter traffic.

1969 — The Railway Scene

The changes which had taken place in the 10 years since 1959 were of an extent unparalleled in railway history. No activity escaped, but there was a definite north/south split in the nature of some of the changes. Piccadilly had become a fine modern station, with excellent electrified services and a range of diesel multiple units on non-electrified services. Its rolling stock and locomotives were comparatively new and the whole area was equipped with modern signalling.

The decision to close the Central station was inevitable, given the decline in its services and the ability of Piccadilly and Oxford Road to absorb those remaining. The economic case was overwhelming. None the less, one could not look upon that marvellous overall roof in the years that followed without a tinge of sadness and regret, but nostalgia did not pay the wages and the heritage industry was in its infancy.

The decline was most noticeable at Victoria. No one seemed to know what to do with the old Lanky and its headquarters. The station, still bearing its wartime scars, slipped further into decay. Well-established services disappeared. The Colne to Euston through carriage had gone some years previously, and in 1966 the old 'Windermere Club Train', five coaches with an open first, was withdrawn in one of the periodic 'revisions' (ie reductions) of services. It had left Exchange at 17.22 and arrived at Windermere at 19.39. The routeing of the evening Windermere Club train, originally via Tyldesley and the Whelley line, then later via Dobbs Brow Junction and Chorley, and later still via Hindley and the Whelley line (because it got in the way of the Blackpool Club trains) is a story in itself. The morning train left Windermere at 08.10, arriving in Manchester at 10.20.

Even the refreshment rooms, welcome as they were, had an old-fashioned feel. Only the gantries of semaphore signals had gone; at least the signalling had been modernised. However, Victoria continued to be busy with its non-passenger business. The newspaper trains were a very important nightly feature (see separate list), and there was plenty of parcels post and letter mail traffic.

The most encouraging development towards the end of the sixties was the establishment of the Passenger Transport Authority and its Executive, with a clear remit so far as the railways were concerned; and the most difficult and pressing problem with which they and BR had to grapple was the lack of a north/south railway line through Manchester. The solution to that problem was a novel one, probably undreamt of in Manchester except in the minds of those who had studied the German and Dutch answer to the problem of urban public transport. Could such a Continental solution be applied in Manchester? It must have seemed unlikely in 1969.

9 Laboured Progress — 1970 to 1985

The Year 1970 opened to find BR struggling to adapt to the fundamental changes introduced by the 1968 Transport Act. It was becoming increasingly a passenger and parcels railway. Its sundries traffic had been transferred to a separate, publicly-owned company known as National Carriers Ltd, whose bosses were far more ruthless than ever the railway bosses had been, or so popular opinion has it. Wagonload freight traffic had a large question mark over its future. Even Freightliner, once referred to as the brightest jewel in the railways' crown, was half-owned by the road-based National Freight Corporation.

BR's freedom of action in the handling of its passenger business had been further curtailed by the 1968 Act, and whilst it must be emphasised that the establishment of Passenger Transport Authorities saved many local passenger services from almost certain oblivion, it also meant that BR was no longer the decision maker. It had become a contractor, and its job was to provide the services that the PTAs required.

Few can now doubt that surrendering commercial freedom was a small price for BR to pay, for the PTA concept has been a resounding success in all the conurbations where PTAs have been created. One might add — better late than never. It might with advantage have been done in 1948 when the railways were nationalised, but politically it was not achievable then, although the logic of the concept of local planning and control of all forms of passenger transport, whether rail, bus, or private car, together with all associated town-planning issues, has strong support. The London Passenger Transport Board, formed in 1933, showed what could be achieved in this respect. However, central government, as ever, has been unwilling to surrender overall control and this has had a damaging effect. Neither party in government is free from criticism in this respect, despite the fact that governments exercise very little influence or control over the provision and use of lorries and private cars.

The North–South Connection

The history of Manchester's north–south railway link is a case in point. Over many decades up to 1970 this issue had been examined and plans had been prepared, but to no avail. However, as described in Chapter 8, matters were reaching the stage where decisions had to be taken if any further progress was to be made. The springboard for decision was the publication in late 1970 of the report of the SELNEC Transportation Study, which set out a 'Recommended Broad Transportation Plan for 1984.' Its main features were:

• An underground line linking Victoria and Piccadilly stations, with intermediate stations at Princess Street/Whitworth Street, St Peter's Square/Albert Square and Market Street
• Upgrading of 13 radial suburban lines
• Feeder bus services to suburban stations
• Modernisation of suburban stations and provision of car parking
• Conversion of the Bury line to 25kV
• Manchester-Bolton services to be routed via Radcliffe (on the Bury line), and the section between Radcliffe and Bolton to be electrified
• Track and signalling to be improved where necessary to deal satisfactorily with the new and intensified train services.

The cost of the tunnel section, which became known as Picc-Vic, was estimated to be approximately £20 million, which was less than a tenth of the sum allocated to highway construction in the area and quite modest by comparison.

The Picc-Vicc line was planned to diverge from the BR Bury line near Cheetham Hill carriage sidings, then descend into tunnel, passing under the River Irk, Collingham Street and Red Bank to a new station under Victoria Station (near the Bury line platforms). After passing under the central area and through a new underground (or low-level) station at Piccadilly BR station, the line was planned to resurface and join the main Manchester–Crewe line about a mile south of Piccadilly, near Ardwick Junction. The new line would had been 2¾ miles long, of which 2.18 miles would have been in tunnel.

The Picc-Vic proposals were in line with the city's plans for pedestrianising large parts of the central area, and the locations of the new underground stations had been carefully selected to dovetail with the city's development plans.

Above left and left: Two views of the new order at Piccadilly. Class 86 No E3199 has brought the 10.00 from Euston, whilst sister engine No E3143 prepares to leave with the 13.30 to Euston, on 30 March 1971.
J. H. Cooper-Smith

Above: On 2 November 1974, Class 40 diesel No 40015 *Aquitania* pulls out of Piccadilly with a southbound excursion, past the power signalbox, whilst Class 87 electric No 87027 waits for the rightaway with the 10.10 to Euston. *David A. Flitcroft*

Right: A Bury electric set heads for Manchester Victoria past Queens Road signalbox on 3 July 1982. The Metrolink depot now occupies the site of the former Queens Road carriage sidings and the route itself has been sold to Metrolink. *Dr L. A. Nixon*

Below: SELNEC plans for Manchester

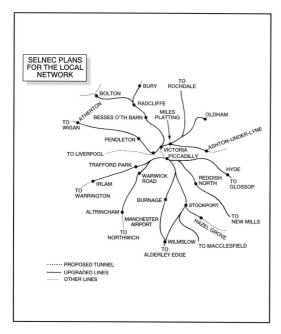

SELNEC PLANS FOR THE LOCAL NETWORK

TO ROCHDALE
BURY
BOLTON
RADCLIFFE
ATHERTON
MILES PLATTING
BESSES O'TH BARN
TO WIGAN
OLDHAM
PENDLETON
ASHTON-UNDER-LYNE
TO LIVERPOOL
VICTORIA
PICCADILLY
TRAFFORD PARK
HYDE
WARWICK ROAD
REDDISH NORTH
TO GLOSSOP
IRLAM
TO WARRINGTON
BURNAGE
STOCKPORT
ALTRINCHAM
TO NEW MILLS
MANCHESTER AIRPORT
HAZEL GROVE
TO NORTHWICH
WILMSLOW
TO MACCLESFIELD
TO ALDERLEY EDGE

······ PROPOSED TUNNEL
—— UPGRADED LINES
—— OTHER LINES

In order to make progress, SELNEC Passenger Transport Authority announced early in 1971 that it was preparing to promote a Bill in Parliament in conjunction with BR and the City of Manchester for the underground rail link, with a commissioning date of 1977. Trial borings were carried out by Cementation Ground Engineering Ltd to examine the sub-surface strata. The promoters of the Bill expected no delay in obtaining a government grant towards the costs of construction.

By the international standards of the 1990s the Picc-Vic scheme was quite modest, but 20 years earlier it was regarded in government quarters as rather too ambitious. Perhaps eyebrows had been raised at the prospect of a phase 2 tunnel, recommended in the SELNEC Report, which was to run from Knott Mill to Piccadilly station via Deansgate, Market Street and Piccadilly Gardens. There was also provision in the report for the building of two moving pavements, one from Oxford Street station to St Peter's Square and the other from Piccadilly station to Piccadilly Gardens.

SELNEC PTE then applied for a 75% infrastructure grant towards the £72 million cost of these proposals, but this was refused by the government, who told SELNEC to consider cheaper alternatives, owing to the need to reduce public expenditure. However, after some lobbying, John Peyton, the Minister for Transport Industries, gave qualified approval to the Picc-Vic tunnel scheme, but said that the project would have to be reconsidered by the new Greater Manchester

Council (GMC), and in any event could not start before 1975/76. The GMC took over the mantle of the City Council and a large surrounding area as part of the 1974 Local Government Reorganisation, and at the same time SELNEC PTE became the Greater Manchester PTE. One might question whether it was the job of the Government or the City Fathers to decide whether Manchester should have an underground railway and a decent public transport system but the Government held the purse strings and that was that. Most of the money available for metro-type schemes had already gone to Liverpool and Newcastle, and Manchester had to live with the consequences of its rather absurd courtship of monorail systems in the 1960s. It had lost its place in the queue for funds, but the real villain of the piece was Manchester's awful legacy of four railway terminals, whilst Liverpool already had a well-developed suburban rail system, and Newcastle benefited from its history of being served by only one pre-Grouping railway, the North Eastern, which had resulted in a sensible, non-duplicated, network and one main through station.

The Labour government which came into power in 1974 soon found itself in serious financial difficulties and proved to be no more generous than the previous Conservative administration. It informed the Greater Manchester PTE that it could have £1 million for the Picc-Vic scheme in order to keep planning work alive, but no indication was given as to when, or even whether, a grant towards construction costs would be made. The Government's financial plight worsened in 1976, and Peter Shore, the Environment Secretary, demanded that local government reduce its costs. Greater Manchester Council realised that it was unlikely to make any progress with the Picc-Vic scheme and formally abandoned it in 1976.

However, the need for a north-south rail link was as strong as ever, and the GMC Transport Committee was asked to look for a cheaper alternative. Early in 1978 the Committee produced a report, approved by the Council in February, for a new curve linking Salford station with Deansgate station, to allow through-running between Victoria and Piccadilly. Overhead electrification at 25kV would be installed between Victoria and Castlefield Junction, near Deansgate, and dual voltage rolling stock was proposed so that trains could run through from Bury at 1,200V dc and change to 25kV overhead at Victoria. The ultimate goal, so far as BR was concerned, was the closure of Victoria and the concentration of all passenger services at Piccadilly, but that remained a dream, only partially realised years later when Metrolink and the Windsor Link came on the scene. The Castlefield Curve could have been a useful addition to the Manchester rail network in former times, but its need had gone.

Below: The Picc-Vic rail tunnel proposal.

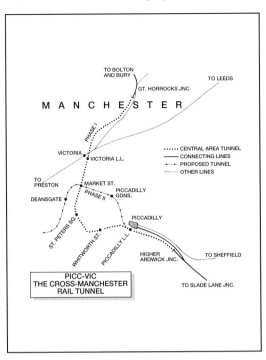

PICC-VIC
THE CROSS-MANCHESTER
RAIL TUNNEL

Below: Near Newtown, a DMU for Leeds climbs the
bank to Miles Platting, whilst a Bury electric set coasts
down to Victoria, on 12 September 1978.
Graham Williams

The major flaw in the Castlefield Curve proposal
was its failure to serve the city centre, and its
inability to provide for through-running between
Preston, Bolton and the north, and former LNW
lines to the south. It merely enabled trains from
Bury to be extended to Piccadilly and the south,
which missed most of the benefits of the Picc-Vic
scheme and was, for that reason, opposed by the
City Council, who wanted rail access to the central
area business and shopping centres. It also
indicated that the planners were becoming
desperate in their search for an affordable solution
to the north-south problem, and the proposals
made no progress. None the less, the search
continued, but nothing fruitful emerged for several
years, until into the eighties. They were 15 wasted
years, a tragedy for the public transport system of a
great city.

BR had also been pondering over possible
solutions, and proposed a new chord line, which
became known as the 'Windsor Link.' The link,
which was eventually built, is 780yd long, and runs
from a junction off the former L&Y line at Windsor
Bridge to a junction with the former LNW line at
Ordsall Lane, giving trains from Bolton, Preston and
the north direct running facilities to Piccadilly. BR
obtained parliamentary powers in the 1980/81
session, but obtaining Department of Transport
approval turned out to be more difficult and
protracted. It was not given until 1985 and the
scheme will be examined in more detail in the next
chapter.

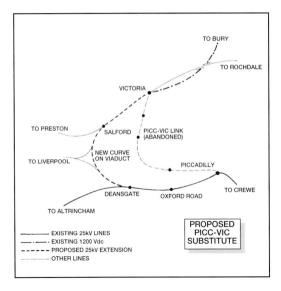

Above: The 'Castlefield Curve' proposal.

Below: The 'Windsor Link', and track layout plan for Salford Crescent area.

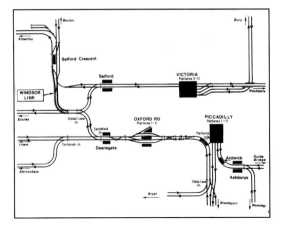

Local Passenger Services — The PTA/PTE Involvement

SELNEC Passenger Transport Authority took over responsibility for local rail services in its area on New Year's Day 1972 as a result of an order made by John Peyton, Minister for Transport Industries, that Section 20 of the 1968 Transport Act should come into effect. This required the PTA to review local passenger services and to decide which were necessary as part of the local transport system of the area.

The review took nearly two years to complete, since there were some 26 local services then operating. Various options were considered, including:

- Replacing a train service with a bus service, and using express bus services where appropriate
- Cutting back bus services and developing an extensive network of bus/rail interchanges.

A considerable amount of planning and evaluation was undertaken, and a number of train services were not recommended for support. These were:

Bury (Bolton Street)–Rawtenstall
Rochdale–Bury (Knowsley Street)–Bolton
Manchester Victoria–Radcliffe–Bolton
Manchester Victoria–Clifton Junction–Bury
Piccadilly–High Lane–Macclesfield
Piccadilly–Hayfield.

These closures had been proposed in the Reshaping Report (The Beeching Plan) but had not yet been put into effect, unlike the closure of the Middleton and Royton branches.

The PTA set the fares on the services which it wished to support, and was responsible for meeting the deficits on those services, but the Government undertook to pay a grant of 90% for 1972, tapering off by 10% each year in 1973–75. The arrangement was to be reviewed in 1975 with the creation of the new Metropolitan County Council for Greater Manchester.

During the previous year (1971) the overhead electrification system of the MSJ&A had been converted to 25kV, allowing through-running between Crewe and Altrincham via Piccadilly and Oxford Road, and leading to the withdrawal of the elderly but well-liked original LMS sets, dating from the introduction of electrification in 1931.

The system of government grants to cover losses on individual train services was altered in 1974 as a result of Britain's membership of the European Economic Community. Fred Mulley, Minister of Transport in the new Labour administration, put forward a bill to bring the grant system into line with EEC regulations, the main effect of which was to replace the individual grant system with a block grant to cover BR's entire passenger operations. It was comforting for rail passengers to hear that a substantial programme of line closures had been ruled out. The individual grants for 1974, the last year of that system, were as follows:

Right and overleaf: Two views at Piccadilly of PTE-supported services. On 13 May 1978 Class 304 EMUs wait to depart to Altrincham (left) and Alderley Edge (centre), whilst on 2 June 1981 a variety of EMUs and DMUs 'sit' on the buffers. The trans-Pennine set on the extreme right, with curved windscreen, worked the (unsupported) Hull services for many years.
Philip Edwards/Gary Grafton

1968 Transport Act

	Payments by the Secretary of State under Sec 39(1) £000s	Payments by PTE under Sec 20 £000s	Total £000s
Liverpool–Patricroft–Manchester	140	172	312
Liverpool–Warrington–Manchester	471	593	1064
Manchester to:			
Altrincham		430	430
Blackburn	266	327	593
Blackpool	1121	351	1472
Bolton/Wigan/			
Southport	464	716	1180
Bury		504	504
Buxton	314	490	804
Glossop/Hadfield		484	484
Huddersfield	55	116	171
Northwich/Chester	469	123	592
Oldham		451	451
Romiley/Rose Hill	35	607	642
Stockport/Crewe	450	261	711
Stoke/Stafford	734	161	895
Styal/Crewe	193	302	495
Warrington/Chester	422		422
Leeds–Liverpool	606	115	721
Stockport–Stalybridge	85		85

Pacers and Sprinters

Right from the start of the PTE's relationship with BR through the Section 20 Agreement, it pressed BR for its proposals to replace the first-generation DMUs, which were beginning to show their age, but neither proposals nor ideas were forthcoming, and it appeared to the PTE that BR was concentrating its efforts on InterCity developments. This situation lasted almost throughout the 1970s, then, in 1979, BR workshops produced a new model DMU, which became known as Class 210. It was similar to the electric multiple units then being produced, and had sliding doors. The diesel engines were mounted above the floor for ease of maintenance, because mechanical engineers had always complained bitterly and with some justification about the difficulties of maintaining the under-floor mounted engines on the Modernisation Plan DMUs, and their wishes were granted so far as the Class 210 units were concerned. Two prototypes were built: one a three-car set and the other a four-car set.

However, the PTE took the view that the Class 210s were rather better than they wanted for local commuter work and suggested that BR look for a cheaper alternative. By coincidence, BR, under pressure from the Department of Transport to design a cheap, lightweight railcar, had just produced a unit consisting of a bus body on a two-axle chassis for use on light-traffic rural branches, which was expected to be less expensive than a conventional unit. The PTE, which had considered the Class 210s to be over-specified and expensive, took the opposite view with the two-axle vehicles, which had not been designed for busy commuter routes.

There are two schools of thought about these lightweight vehicles, which became known as 'Pacers.' On the one hand, business managers thought they were a good buy, providing plenty of seats, quick acceleration, a creditable top speed and a reasonable ride on well-maintained track (although bouncy on jointed track). They were also thought to be cheaper than anything else available, and it was availability which was the key. At the time, there was little else on the market.

But there was another school of thought. Whilst 'Pacers' may have been suitable for commuters with only a newspaper to carry, there were others, such as mothers with small children and a pushchair, retired people with luggage, students with cycles and rucksacks, etc who thought that the trains were inadequate, cramped and uncomfortable. Engineers found them a nightmare to maintain. Operators found it difficult to provide a satisfactory service with breakdowns and vehicles out of service. Relations with the PTE deteriorated.

Below left: A BRCW Class 104/1 DMU approaches Victoria East Junction from the Cheetham Hill loop with a Blackpool service on 22 September 1976. The Miles Platting route, with its complicated track layout, is on the right. *Brian Morrison*

Right: Before the advent of 'Sprinters', the Blackpool services were worked by 'Modernisation Plan' DMUs. A Class 120 stands under the roofless portion of Manchester Victoria's Platform 13 with the 13.15 to Blackpool North on 3 September 1982.
John E. Oxley

Centre right: Two of BR's 'Pacer' DMUs, Class 142 built by BREL, stand in all their shiny new Greater Manchester PTE livery at Manchester Victoria, betraying no sign of mechanical problems to come. *Gary Grafton*

Below right: The second-generation bogie DMU, Class 150 set No 150207, takes the new Windsor Link at Ordsall Lane with the diverted 14.20 Manchester Victoria to Southport on 15 April 1988.
Paul D. Shannon

When the two-axle vehicles were first being considered, warnings were sounded that they might not operate track circuits reliably, and that the design ought not to be proceeded with unless a solution to that problem could be found, because vital questions of safety were involved. However, the warnings were ignored, with the result that special measures have had to be taken by operators and technical departments alike in order to maintain safety.

Was the right decision taken to buy lots of 'Pacers'? Published figures indicate that there was not a great deal of difference in the cost per passenger seat — £4,450 for a Class 210, £3,725 for a Class 141 two-axle unit (which was achieved only by cramming in as many seats as possible and leaving no space for anything else). Secondly, the conventional Class 210 could have been expected to be more reliable in day-to-day operation. Thirdly, the Class 210 would have been a far more comfortable train for the passengers than the spartan Class 141s and their derivatives. Fourthly, the Class 210s could have been expected to last for at least 20-25 years, whereas 'Pacers' are likely to be on the scrapheap long before that.

'Pacers', with their bus bodies and bus-type bench seating are suitable only for bus-type journeys, ie short journeys without prams, bicycles, luggage, etc. In their early years, at least, they were an operating and maintenance nightmare, the main problem being the gear boxes; and BR's failure to produce a reliable service with 'Pacers' was the cause of repeated complaints from the PTE and passengers. With the benefit of hindsight, it would probably have been cheaper overall, and certainly more satisfactory, to have opted for volume production of Class 210s, after a satisfactory trial period. Unfortunately, the 'Pacers' were rushed into production before their faults had become apparent. This whole saga is a sad comment on the lack of well-organised forward planning which afflicted the BRB before the Businesses were created.

The first 'Pacers' were known as Class 141, and 20 were authorised in 1982 at a cost of £7 million. They had modified Leyland bus bodies on a two-axle chassis, and were powered by Leyland engines, giving a maximum speed of 75mph. Deliveries began in 1983, and were completed the following year.

Volume production began in 1985 of a modified Class 141. British Rail Engineering Ltd, Derby (known as BREL) built 50 similar vehicles, of Class 142, followed quickly by a further batch of 50, whilst Andrew Barclay and Sons, in conjunction with Walter Alexander (Coachbuilders) of Falkirk, built 25, of Class 143. The majority of the Class 142 units are based on Newton Heath for maintenance and are used on Manchester area train services.

Whilst the 'Pacers' were being developed, BR was considering designs for a bogie-wheeled DMU, to operate medium and longer distance secondary and suburban services. In 1983, two three-car prototype sets were ordered from Metro-Cammell Ltd of Birmingham (Class 151) and two sets from BREL (Class 150). The general specifications included a seating capacity of 250, power-operated doors, and a maximum speed of 75mph, but the builders were encouraged to incorporate their own ideas and equipment.

On 12 February 1984, the Secretary of State for Transport authorised the building of 50 bogie-wheeled two-car DMUs at a cost of £24.5 million, and on 7 June that year BREL produced its two prototypes, which used the same bodyshell as the Class 317 and Class 455 electric multiple-units. Evaluation of the two prototype designs then commenced, and in December, one of the Class 150 units was used on a demonstration run to Blackpool. These units became known as 'Sprinters'.

BREL won the contract, and delivered 50 units, Class 150/1, from their York Works, commencing in 1985. A further batch was turned out in 1987, Class 150/2. Newton Heath's allocation is 18 Class 150/1 and 11 Class 150/2. Although the Class 150 series suffers from poor seating layout, the wide doorways located away from the vehicle ends are a good design feature and allow quick exit and entry for passengers.

Electrification

Throughout the period covered by this chapter there had been calls, supported by the PTE, for electrification of the Manchester–Bolton–Preston–Blackpool route. A glance at a map of BR's electrified routes clearly indicates how valuable such a link would be if it were electrified, especially between Euxton Junction (south of Preston) and Manchester, but the calls for it to be done have always fallen on deaf ears. The Department of Transport has consistently turned down all such proposals, the excuse in the early eighties being that the new Class 150 DMUs would suffice. In fact they were unsatisfactory for such a route as Manchester to Blackpool and now only work the stopping service between Blackpool and Buxton. The express service between Blackpool and Manchester Airport is worked by Class 156 units. The next excuse was the cost of installing overhead electrification in Victoria, and the immunisation of the signalling, but those factors have become invalid following the rebuilding of Victoria, the construction of the Windsor Link allowing several services to be diverted to Piccadilly, and the extension (immunised) of the control of Piccadilly power signalbox along the Preston line as far as Blackrod. For some reason, which probably has its roots in the trade depression which haunted the area between the wars, and which has continued to do so to some extent since, the area once served by the old Lanky is always at the end of the queue when money is being handed out.

Another unhappy story came to an end in 1980 with the closure of the Woodhead route, whose electrification and modernisation had been completed with such a fanfare of trumpets only 26 years earlier and whose works included a new three-mile-long tunnel. Two factors contributed to its closure — the lack of satisfactory feeder routes after rationalisation at the Sheffield end, which had led to the withdrawal of passenger services over the route in 1970, and the severe fall in cross-Pennine freight traffic. At the time of closure, only 25 freight trains per day used the route, and they were diverted to other routes. Annual savings were estimated at £2.5 million. The Woodhead route remained open between Piccadilly and Glossop/Hadfield, and in 1984 the original Class 506 EMU sets were finally withdrawn, being replaced by the only slightly younger Class 303s from the Glasgow area. The service is now worked by Class 305 units.

A rather happier event was the extension of electrification from Stockport (Edgeley Junction) to Hazel Grove on the former LNW Buxton line, a distance of 2¼ miles, on 1 June 1981. The station was spruced up and became a railhead for commuters to Manchester from a wide area. This scheme was paid for by the PTE, and was a remnant from the ill-fated Picc-Vic proposals.

The previous year, 1980, overhead electrification had been extended for 1¼ miles from Cornbrook Junction to the freightliner depot at Trafford Park, allowing the depot at Longsight to be closed. One side-effect was the new ability to run EMUs to the station serving Manchester United's football ground.

Freight and Parcels

In 1970 the Glasgow Freightliner service was transferred to Trafford Park in order to provide additional capacity at Longsight for the growth of London container traffic. Freightliner was now under the dual parentage of BR and the National Freight Corporation and was still making a slight loss (less than £1 million). New services were planned from Manchester for 1971, and by 1973 the loss had been turned into a £1 million profit, but it was quite clear that the expected influx of new business arising from joint ownership with the road-based NFC had not materialised. BR lobbied for the return of Freightliner to 100% BR ownership, and success was finally achieved in 1978 when William Rodgers, remembered perhaps as one of the 'Gang of Four' who founded the Social Democratic Party, was Labour Transport Secretary.

National Carriers Ltd, which had been formed from BR's Sundries Division, continued to rationalise its operations, and further goods depot closures followed — Ancoats in 1972 and Liverpool

Right: Passenger services over the Woodhead route to Sheffield had been withdrawn in 1970, and the route itself was closed in 1980. Electric locomotive No 76006 is being used for a commemorative railtour run by the Locomotive Club of Great Britain and is seen ready to leave Piccadilly on 30 December 1980. *Steve Turner*

Road in 1975. The CLC warehouses at Central were demolished in 1978.

The same story of unprofitability and decline dogged the Collected and Delivered (C&D) Parcels Business. BR had rationalised the arrangements for dealing with parcels in Manchester, and had concentrated its activities on Mayfield, Bolton and Oldham, building a new parcels concentration depot at the latter. A mechanical sorting device, known as a carousel, was installed at Mayfield. Bolton and Oldham were chosen because large mail-order companies had located themselves there to take advantage of redundant cotton mills, and for a number of years both depots were very busy, handling up to 30,000 parcels a day. However, the costs of running the parcels business were more than the revenue could sustain, and the situation was not helped by the terms of the contract which BR was required to make with National Carriers Ltd for the daily provision of C&D vehicles and drivers, which virtually guaranteed NCL a profit on the operation. Ultimately BR had little option but to abandon the C&D parcels business, which it did in 1981, preferring to concentrate instead on the profitable, premium-priced Red Star station-to-station service.

BR had converted Mayfield into a parcels-concentration depot in 1971, in conjunction with the development of a major GPO depot on the other side of Piccadilly station, but after the abandonment of the C&D parcels business it became a Royal Mail depot for a time. It was ultimately closed in 1986, and it ceased to be rail-served in 1987. Mayfield had truly had a chequered career.

Newspaper traffic, once such a feature of the late evening scene, particularly at Victoria but also to a lesser extent at London Road, declined rapidly and was gone. A combination of internal changes in the industry, the expansion of the motorway network, the desire of newspaper proprietors to be in charge of their own transport arrangements, coupled with delays to trains and the periodical threats of industrial action by the railway trade unions, brought about the transfer of the traffic to road. To some extent, the same has been true of parcels post and letter mail traffic.

One other aspect of the freight business ought to be mentioned. John Peyton (now Lord Peyton) was a Conservative Minister of Transport who became quite rail-minded, and in 1974 he piloted a Bill through Parliament to give 50% grants to the owners of private sidings towards expenditure of a capital nature incurred in the provision of sidings, depots, access roads and equipment for use in connection with the loading or unloading of freight by rail, provided it would be in the public interest, defined as giving relief to local roads. This provision

Below left: Class 45 diesel No 45052 passes Deal Street signalbox on its way into Manchester Victoria at the head of a parcels service on 31 May 1984. *Brian Morrison*

Victoria still sees a number of through freight trains. Here are three eastbound examples:

Right: Class 56 diesel No 56058 takes a train of merry-go-round empties on 10 December 1985. *T. W. Rowley*

Centre right: An earlier generation of diesel locomotive, Class 40 No 40007 restarts a heavy train of loaded oil tanks, whilst Class 25 diesel No 25194 waits to provide banking assistance for it to Miles Platting. *David A. Flitcroft*

Below right: Another train of loaded 100-ton oil tanks, with Class 47 power, No 47287, on 11 August 1978. *J. C. Hillmer*

These views of Manchester Victoria and its signalling have passed into history, but freight trains are still operated through the new Victoria.

was set out in Section 8 of the 1974 Railways Act, and the grants have accordingly become known as 'Section 8 Grants.' In 1976 such a grant was awarded to Shell Chemicals (UK) for rail freight developments at its Carrington Works.

Passenger Developments

Although properly belonging to the next chapter, mention might be made of BR's application at the end of 1982 for parliamentary powers to construct a 3½-mile-long loop line from the Styal line to serve Manchester Airport. The provision of a loop, rather than a dead-end line, was chosen to enable InterCity trains to be routed via the airport.

At the same time, BR sought powers for the construction of a 600yd chord line at Hazel Grove to connect the former Midland Railway New Mills–Cheadle Heath line (freight only since the closure of Central station in 1969) with the former LNWR line from Buxton to Piccadilly via Stockport. This would allow Sheffield–Manchester trains via the Hope Valley to serve Stockport and provide connections there with trains on the Piccadilly–Crewe/Stoke lines.

Newton Heath DMU depot was refurbished in the mid-1980s, equipping it to service the growing fleet of second-generation DMUs more efficiently. At the same time, the reduction in the number of locomotive-hauled passenger trains allowed a number of carriage sidings to be closed, including Red Bank, Cheetham Hill and Lightbowne.

At Victoria the old, but imposing, L&Y Hunts Bank offices were demolished in 1978. They had

Below: The Manchester airport link.

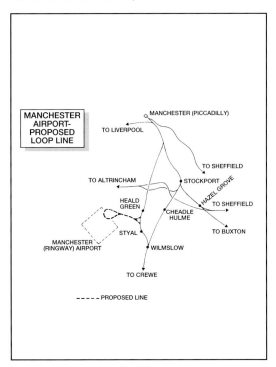

Edwardian railway prosperity and grandeur stamped all over them, but were unsuitable for modern office use. Another link with a past way of life, and perhaps regretted by some, was the abolition of 'Ladies Only' compartments and waiting rooms. This was an unforeseen result of the Sex Discrimination Act and was done on the advice of BR's legal department to avoid challenge in the courts, or possibly a demand for 'Gentlemen Only' compartments. This might have caused some difficulties in interpretation!

Accidents

A few miles west of Manchester the M602 motorway and the former LNWR line from Liverpool Lime Street to Manchester Exchange run side by side. On the morning of 4 December 1984 drivers on the motorway were suddenly confronted by a ball of flame spreading across from the railway line, and were showered with burning debris. The 10.05 loco-hauled express from Liverpool Lime Street to Scarborough had plunged into the back of an almost-stationary loaded oil-tank train at 45/50mph. Fortunately the front two coaches, which were engulfed in flames, were almost empty and only two passengers were killed. The driver also lost his life.

The cause of the disaster was clear. The driver had run past the Eccles distant signal, which was at

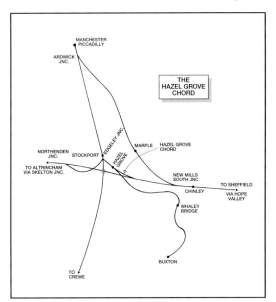

Above: The Hazel Grove chord.

caution, at undiminished speed and had then passed the home signal, which was at danger to protect the oil-tank train.

Since the late 1950s BR had been carrying out a programme of installing an automatic warning system at distant signals on its main and suburban lines to prevent such an accident, but there was no such equipment at Eccles, despite its location on a busy main line, and despite the use of that line by freight trains conveying inflammable liquids. The line was a victim of the planning blight which affected much of the non-electrified area around Manchester; caused by uncertainties regarding the future. It had been expected for years that the signalling in the area would be modernised, leading to the abolition of mechanical signalboxes such as Eccles, but it had not happened. It was typical of the indecision that afflicted the non-electrified railways in the Manchester area during much of the period covered by this chapter, the causes of which were four-fold:

• BR was no longer in sole control of policy. The PTE was a prominent, perhaps even dominant, partner in the planning process
• The inordinate length of time taken to resolve the question of a north–south through route.

• Constant interference by the Department of Transport in railway policy and investment, in unsuccessful attempts to solve the problem of the railway deficit
• BR's lack of a firm policy for the area, including the trans-Pennine routes. The PTE was dismayed by what it regarded as a lack of initiative on the part of BR management, and particularly so when the PTE felt that its ideas for improving the local rail network were being met with a negative or over-priced response.

However, it is fair to say that 1985 ended on a note of optimism. There were several exciting new developments in the offing, including not one, but two, north–south routes; second generation DMUs were beginning to appear; and BR's Business Sectorisation Policy was beginning to develop under a new Chairman, Robert Reid.

Below: Trafford Park is a busy area of rail freight activity. Class 47 diesel No 47056 is seen leaving the Freightliner terminal with the 15.54 to Holyhead on 28 August 1985. *Paul D. Shannon*

Above: Another historic scene. Class 45 diesel No 45134 passes the now-demolished West Junction signalbox on its way into Victoria with the 09.05 from Liverpool Lime Street to Scarborough on 30 August 1985. *Paul D. Shannon*

Left: The unmodernised part of the Manchester area — the old 'Lanky'. Class 47 diesel No 47538 passes Philips Park No 1 signalbox with the 09.15 from Bangor to Scarborough on 26 April 1984. This signalbox lies at the Manchester end of the triangle leading to Stalybridge and to Ashburys, and the triangle, with its complex of sidings, was a major interchange point for freight in former days. *Paul D. Shannon*

Below left: Eccles, site of the disastrous collision on 4 December 1984. Class 31 diesel No 31417 runs alongside the M602 motorway with the 12.27 from Liverpool Lime Street to Manchester Victoria on 23 February 1990. *Paul D. Shannon*

10 A New Era is Born —
1986 to 1995

The previous chapter was characterised by difficulty and doubt, delay and stagnation. Or so it must have seemed to the citizens of Greater Manchester, who wanted to see tangible signs of improvement. One of the more significant events of 1986 was the abolition by government of the metropolitan counties, including Greater Manchester itself, but fortunately for the future well-being of passenger rail services in the area the Greater Manchester PTA/PTE was retained, although the PTA lost its overall control of public passenger transport owing to the loss of bus operation powers in the Act for the deregulation of buses the same year.

However, behind the scenes a lot of plans were being developed which came to fruition in the period covered by this chapter, and Network NorthWest was born in 1989, a child with three parents — BR's Provincial Sector North West (now Regional Railways North West); Greater Manchester PTE and Lancashire County Council, a springboard for many developments, some now achieved, others still to be fought for.

The Hazel Grove Chord

The year 1986 started well, with work under way on the £1.4 million Hazel Grove chord (see map in Chapter 9), a new section of line ⅓ mile in length, which linked the former Midland Railway Sheffield–Hope Valley–Manchester line with the former LNWR Buxton–Stockport–Piccadilly line and enabled the Sheffield–Manchester trains to be rerouted from New Mills South Junction to run via Stockport, an important industrial centre with good connecting rail services. An hourly service was introduced when the chord was opened in May 1986, and most of the expresses were extended to Liverpool via Warrington Central. Manchester was reached from Sheffield in under an hour, including the Stockport stop, and Liverpool in well under two hours, the best service ever between Sheffield and Liverpool.

The Windsor Link

Another new chord line of considerable importance in the Greater Manchester rail network is the 'Windsor Link', 780yd long, between Windsor Bridge Junction on the former L&Y, and Ordsall Lane Junction on the former LNWR (see layout plan in Chapter 9). It was by no means a new idea, having been considered many years earlier as part of a scheme to close Victoria, but it was not pressed forward at the time, probably for financial reasons. The proposal was then resurrected, and BR obtained powers in its 1980/81 Bill to build the link. However, it took five years to persuade the Department to give the go-ahead. Relations between BR and the Department had been rather strained in the early 1980s — the Government had been stung by Sir Peter Parker's famous and apt phrase 'the crumbling edge of quality', and it had fallen to his successor, the quiet but determined Robert (later Sir Robert) Reid, to mend fences and ease the passage of investment submissions. Eventually, David Mitchell, Parliamentary Under-Secretary of State for Transport, announced in 1985 that the £12.5-million scheme had received Department of Transport approval.

Work on the link was completed in April 1988, but its full utilisation had to wait for the completion of resignalling and the transfer of control to Piccadilly power signalbox. The original submission for the Windsor Link had included the possible electrification of the Manchester–Bolton–Preston–Blackpool line, but this appears to have been too much for the Department of Transport to swallow, and several years were wasted until BR 'discovered' that the new Sprinter DMUs could give quite a satisfactory service, whereupon they abandoned the electrification part of the scheme in order to enable progress to be made. Had BR not done so it is possible that the BR/DTp argument would still have been rumbling on. Manchester–Blackpool electrification must surely come some day. Its benefits are obvious to almost everyone, but the Department of Transport and the Treasury remain unconvinced. A clear case for regional government, perhaps.

The Windsor Link enabled the dream of a through north-south route to be achieved. Whilst the link does not pass through the city centre, it is hoped that Oxford Road station will develop in this respect, but it does allow through communication between the Blackpool–Preston–Bolton–Manchester line and Oxford Road, Deansgate,

Left: Now a very busy piece of railway, the former MSJ&A between Oxford Road and Piccadilly stations. On 25 July 1990, Class 47 diesel No 47517 *Andrew Carnegie*, on the 07.22 from Edinburgh to Birmingham, passes a Class 142 DMU.
J. C. Hillmer

A few days earlier,
Below left: Class 37 No 37517 draws a train of empty 100-ton tankers, forming the 08.46 from Glazebrook to Haverton Hill, past the same spot. *Paul D. Shannon*

Above right: Manchester's new airport station, with a smart-looking Class 101 DMU on a pre-opening special party service on 24 April 1993. The 'exposed skeleton' style of station architecture has been in vogue for several years. It has a superficial functional appeal, but is not to everyone's taste.
Author

Centre right: Regional Railways Unit 305515 leaves Manchester Piccadilly on a shuttle service to the airport on 30 June 1994.
Author

Below right: The busy concourse at Piccadilly with the usual array of shops. Will the desire of the new station-owners to maximise shopping rental, adversely affect the space allotted to the facilities required by railway passengers in what is already a quite congested area? *Author*

Piccadilly and the south, which is a major improvement and gives passengers from the northwest of Manchester access to a range of long-distance services at either Piccadilly or Stockport without a change of stations in Manchester. The layout at Piccadilly is not perfect, and passengers changing trains there have to face the long trek from the through-island platform to the terminal platforms, but it is clearly the best that could be achieved and a great improvement over the previous arrangements. In many cases a change of trains at Stockport may be an acceptable and more convenient alternative. These new train services came into effect in May 1989.

The Manchester Airport Link

In 1982 a proposal had been made for the construction of a single line link from the Wilmslow–Piccadilly 'Styal' line to Manchester Airport, but this was overtaken by a later scheme for a double-track, electrified line. This later scheme, estimated to cost £25 million, was approved by the Government in 1989, and was funded jointly by BR (55%) and the Greater Manchester PTE (45%). The new line consists of a 1½-mile electrified spur from the Styal line to the airport terminal station, and came into operation on 17 May 1993.

When the new airport station opened, it was served by hourly trains from Blackpool (via Preston and Bolton), and from Scarborough (via York and Leeds). In the half-hourly interval between these two services there was a shuttle service from Piccadilly, providing four trains an hour from Manchester. Four Class 323 EMUs have been provided for the airport shuttle service from Piccadilly since July 1994 and are painted in GMPTE colours. They have storage areas for luggage.

The new station was an immediate success, with 200,000 people using it in the first 10 weeks of operation, therefore the service was increased from four trains per hour to six from May 1994, with additional trains from Barrow-in-Furness, Windermere, Edinburgh, Liverpool and Sheffield. The inwards train service is currently as shown below, but may be modified in May 1995:

From Manchester Piccadilly	Every 30min
From Blackpool	Hourly
From Liverpool	Hourly
From Middlesbrough	Hourly
(replacing the service from Scarborough)	
From Windermere	Two-hourly
From Barrow-in-Furness	Two-hourly
(two trains convey a portion from Edinburgh, attached at Preston)	
From Edinburgh	Two per day
From Sheffield & beyond	Three per day

These additional trains, together with the diverted trans-Pennine services, have made the Piccadilly–Slade Lane Junction four-track section very busy indeed, with the consequent risk of overloading its practical capacity. The flat junctions at Ardwick and Slade Lane are the main problem, which can be cured only by flyovers or dive-unders, but the funds are not available for such desirable improvements. It is interesting to recall that a flyover at Slade Lane Junction was one of BR's requirements in the original Picc-Vic scheme.

Here is a nice little problem now for Railtrack, which naturally wishes to maximise its track occupation, but will face heated complaints from train operators when delays occur through congestion. This is a classic railway conundrum, and it will be interesting to see what the reorganised railways make of it, and whether the expertise still exists to provide a classic railway solution.

The success of the airport station has prompted plans for the construction of a south-facing chord from the airport branch to the Styal line, which will then provide a triangular junction with the main line and enable trains from Crewe and south thereof to run directly to the airport station.

This 500m chord is expected to cost £5.6 million, and construction work has already started. Regional Railways had initially committed itself to a £1.5-million contribution, but it withdrew its offer in October 1992 amid some controversy. Fortunately, Manchester Airport plc has increased its offer to £3.5 million, and contributions are to be made by Cheshire County Council and the Greater Manchester PTE.

Manchester airport ranks 18th in size in the world, and is the fastest growing airport in Europe. It is the first European airport to form itself into a private sector company, 55% of its equity being held by Manchester Corporation and 5% each by the nine Metropolitan authorities.

The airport station is located between Terminals 1 and 2, and is on three levels. At basement level there is an island platform with buffet and waiting rooms. The main concourse and ticket office, etc are at ground level, whilst at the upper level there is a concourse area giving access to a travelator link with Terminal 1. At present the access to the new Terminal 2 is via a bus link.

The six trains an hour each way now using the airport station have swallowed up the room for expansion that was allowed for in the station's original design, and the GMPTE has ordered a £25,000 feasibility study into increasing the size of the station, regarded as an essential feature before the opening of the southern chord.

The airport rail link has been a great success, particularly so far as longer-distance traffic is concerned, and the ability of BR to provide feeder services to the airport has been greatly helped by the Windsor Link.

Train Services — InterCity

a) London

The current Euston service has shown little change for some years. It runs basically at hourly intervals, with extras in the morning peak from Manchester and in the evening peak from Euston. Most of the trains are routed via Stoke-on-Trent and the standard journey time southbound is about 2hr 35min. The timings have varied little since electrification through to Euston in 1966, and in the absence of route improvements are unlikely to do so. Steady, albeit slight, deceleration, rather than acceleration, is likely to occur unless the West Coast main line is upgraded for 125/140mph running and unless new traction is introduced. The West Coast main line and its expresses need considerable investment, but that is a story outside the confines of this book.

A comparison with the best journey times over the years reveals the following:

Manchester London Road/Piccadilly to Euston

1910	3hr 30min
1939	3hr 15min
1954	3hr 20min
1966	2hr 30min
1995	2hr 31min

b) Southeast/Southwest

There is a basic hourly service at 17min past the hour from Piccadilly to Birmingham New Street, with trains going forward from there as follows:

	per day
To Oxford, Reading, Southampton, Bournemouth & Poole	4 trains
To Oxford, Reading, Gatwick Airport and Brighton	2 trains
To Oxford, Reading and Paddington	2 trains
To Bristol and Plymouth	1 train

The service via Oxford, with eight trains per day (two of which are through trains from Glasgow), is excellent, but to Gloucester, Bristol and the Southwest it is very meagre, with only one through train per day, and it relies heavily on connections at Birmingham New Street. Services on the Northwest/Northeast to Southwest route have cried out for improvement for years, and suffer by comparison with other cross-country services from Manchester to Leeds and the Northeast, to Peterborough and Norwich, and to South Wales, but those services belong to Regional Railways. Ten through trains a day from Manchester to Cardiff

(Regional Railways), but only one to Bristol (InterCity), and that one not until 14.04, certainly seems out of balance. Does it accurately reflect the market or is it rather an indication of over-emphasis on the London hub by InterCity? Either way, it will be interesting to see what passenger train service franchisees make of it.

c) Scotland

Today's through train service between Manchester and Glasgow is probably the worst in its history. The hapless Manchester passenger wanting a through train to Glasgow has to wait until 15.25, which is useless for the businessman (who will probably fly anyway) and not much better for the optional or leisure market. Edinburgh is rather better served with an 11.25 departure (a train which starts at Bournemouth) and a $3\frac{1}{2}$ hour journey time, and three Class 158 services which originate at Manchester Airport. There are some reasonable connections for Glasgow at Carlisle for those who don't mind a change of trains, but many passengers in the optional/leisure market do mind, especially older people, or those with young families, or those who are cluttered with luggage, ie the typical passenger on any long-distance train not serving London. The older railways knew the value of through carriages, but they are operationally inconvenient and costly today. This inevitably prompts the question of whether the railways are being run for the benefit of the operators or the benefit of the passengers, but the main problem is the lack of an overhead electric wire between Manchester and Preston. Perhaps Railtrack and the Train Operating Companies will between them achieve what BR has been unable to.

Train Services — Regional Railways

Many would argue that Regional Railways marks the finest flowering of Sir Robert Reid's 'Business Railway' concept. The improvement in cross-country services in the Northwest is little short of astonishing, and has provided Manchester with the most frequent and the fastest service ever to many provincial cities. The major change took place in 1989 with the opening of the Windsor Link, and has been subject to several changes of pattern in the intervening five years as a result of experience. The following are examples of some of the current services:

a) Trans-Pennine

The introduction of Class 158 Sprinter Express diesel multiple-units, air-conditioned, fast and smooth-riding, has enabled this service to be

Above: 'Sprinter' express unit 158796 leaves Piccadilly on the next stage of its journey to Norwich with the 10.51 from Liverpool Lime Street on 30 June 1994. *Author*

Right: A historic photograph in several ways. Platform 11 at Victoria holds the 10.25 to Glasgow, composed of air-conditioned main-line stock, in charge of Class 47 diesel No 47471, on 24 February 1988. The train no longer runs, and the platform and West Junction signalbox (seen top left) have been swept away.
Peter Marsh

Below right: Class 37 diesel No 37430 approaches the new Salford Crescent station with the 17.06 from Manchester Victoria to Southport on 3 June 1991.
Paul D. Shannon

Far right: Were the passengers pleased to find a Class 37 plus conventional coaches acting as a substitute for a 'Sprinter' on the 10.00 from Piccadilly to Cardiff on 25 March 1989? At least they would have had a better view of the countryside, but they might have missed the air-conditioning and the quiet, smooth ride.
Paul D. Shannon

revolutionised. The Class 158s, excellent in so many respects, are not perfect — the seating arrangements leave a lot to be desired and the coaches can easily become very congested, especially near the doorways. Loading and unloading can be slow at major intermediate stations. Comment has been made that the accountants have crammed in too many seats and have failed to consider the merits of one or two fewer banks of seats, which would give ALL passengers a more comfortable journey on the 90% of train journeys when the train is less than completely full. Even on the other 10% of journeys, the extra seats benefit only a handful of passengers. However, having made that comment, one cannot fail to be impressed by the train service, which provides trains every 20min to Leeds, going forward from there every hour to Hull and to Middlesbrough, and every two hours to Newcastle and to Scarborough. One hopes that there will be sufficient units to avoid the overcrowding that has marred this route in recent years.

b) East Midlands/East Anglia

This is another success story for the Regional Railways concept, providing an hourly service to Sheffield, Nottingham, Peterborough and Norwich,

with a connection at Ely for Cambridge. Cross-country services of this nature, with so many conflicting junctions to traverse, were always difficult to arrange under the old regional structure of railway organisation, which inevitably created and nurtured an iron curtain regional boundary mentality — witness the sad decline of the former Midland Railway's main line services since 1948, as a result of running through the territory of no fewer than four regions.

c) Preston and Blackpool

An hourly Buxton to Blackpool service and an hourly Manchester Airport to Blackpool service give Piccadilly a half-hourly service to Bolton, Preston and Blackpool via Oxford Road and the Windsor Link. There are now hardly any Blackpool trains at Victoria, an enormous break with tradition, but there is still a single example of the old 'Club' trains, the 07.06 from Blackpool, due in Victoria at 08.31 with eight intermediate stops, and the 17.28 return, due in Blackpool at 18.47, which is similar to prewar standards, or even pre-World War 1 standards, but those were crack trains with few stops, full of wealthy and influential businessmen, which today's trains are not. They are, however, loco-hauled by Class 37s, to provide

Left: Heritage DMU 101685, painted in the 1950s green livery, enters Hattersley station *en route* to Manchester Piccadilly on 30 June 1994. *Author*

sufficient accommodation. Mk2 coaches are used, which some passengers find preferable to the stock normally in use on the Blackpool trains.

The Passenger Transport Authority

Probably the most significant development in the period covered by this chapter has been the Metrolink concept, and this will be dealt with in Chapter 11. It is sufficient now to comment that the existing Metrolink service will not be affected by the privatisation of BR, but future extensions using former BR track now owned by Railtrack could result in some interesting negotiations.

a) New Stations

The PTE-supported local train service pattern had already become established by 1986, but in the following years strange-sounding station names began to appear in the railway timetable index. The PTE had developed a policy of opening new stations, following a wide-ranging study of the local rail network. The new stations programme was agreed by the Greater Manchester Council in 1983-84, and 28 potential sites were incorporated into the Greater Manchester structure plan. The sites were identified on grounds of both traffic potential and accessibility, and the catchment sizes (ie households within walking distance) varied between 1,500 and 3,000 plus. The new stations cost in the region of £100,000 each, and the following have been opened in the Manchester area:

Atherton & Hag Fold	between Swinton and Wigan
Derker	between Oldham and Rochdale
Flowery Field	between Guide Bridge and Godley
Godley (Mottram Road)	west of the former Godley station
Hattersley	between Godley and Glossop
Humphrey Park	between Trafford Park and Urmston
Mills Hill	between Moston and Castleton
Ryder Brow	between Belle Vue and Reddish
Salford Crescent	between Salford and Pendleton
Smithy Bridge	between Rochdale and Littleborough (originally closed in 1960)
Woodsmoor	between Stockport and Hazel Grove

Improvements were also made at Oxford Road and Deansgate to deal with increased traffic. One other opening must be mentioned — the conversion of the former Central station train shed into the G-Mex centre (the Greater Manchester Exhibition and Event Centre), officially opened by HM The Queen on 21 March 1986. It is served by an adjacent Metrolink station, and by BR at Deansgate.

Finally, there are three imminent closures — in February 1994 BR gave the notice required under

Right: One tends to think of Piccadilly as new, but in this photograph, taken on 14 June 1988, we see the 28-year-old station, with a Class 304 EMU of similar vintage, and an even older first generation DMU. Nor is the electric train behind the EMU reasonably new — the coaches are Mk 2 of 15–20 years earlier, and the electric loco is likely to be well over 20 years old. *John Glover*

Section 52 of the 1962 Transport Act of its intention to close Miles Platting and Park stations, on the line from Victoria to Stalybridge, and Godley East on the line to Glossop. Godley East (the former junction station) has in effect been replaced by the more conveniently located and recently-built Godley (Mottram Road) station, now known simply as Godley.

b) Funding and Policy

To put it bluntly, the Government has rarely if ever made sufficient funds available to enable the PTE to do all that it would wish to do, and the situation is no different at the time of writing. The problem has been exacerbated by changes in local authority funding which were introduced at the time of the change from local rates to the community charge. Prior to that, the PTA made a direct precept upon the ratepayers in its area to cover the costs of the Section 20 support, but now it levies the Metropolitan borough councils, who decide for themselves how much they will pay, based upon their views on the importance of public passenger transport, their other commitments and, ultimately, how much money they have got. They may also raise political objections to the amounts they are called upon to pay, and in any case, all the sums concerned are 'capped'. This creates considerable problems, both financial and political, for the PTA,

and inevitably leads to difficulties in relationships with BR as the latter attempts to live within its budget.

In 1990/91 the estimated Section 20 support grant by the PTE for the operation by BR of local rail services was £20 million, but the actual grant required turned out to be £27.9 million owing to an increase by BR of £6 million in its costs. The PTE responded by withholding £9.5 million of its support grant, including £3.5 million for poor performance, but privately this was judged to be a political posture, intended to put pressure on the borough councils to increase their contributions. The Section 20 grant figure for 1991/92 was estimated to be £26.3 million, but this was exceeded in practice by £4 million.

These difficulties would appear to pale into insignificance when viewed against the emerging situation created by BR's pre-privatisation restructuring, which has resulted in the new organisation Railtrack, demanding dramatically increased track access charges (up by 147%) for PTE-supported services. The PTE initially refused to pay the increase, but a compromise was eventually reached under which the Department of Transport has agreed to meet the increase for the next two years, until April 1996, under a new mechanism known as the Metropolitan Railway Grant. After that, the monies would be paid directly to the

Metropolitan borough councils by the Department of the Environment as part of the block grant, raising fears again that it may be hijacked by the boroughs for other purposes. The Government has succeeded in weaving a very tangled web.

One problem is a fall in the number of passengers using PTE-supported services, with a consequent loss of revenue, despite the opening of new stations and the use of newer rolling stock. Perhaps passengers do not like 'Pacer' DMUs and perhaps they were disillusioned by their unreliability. So far as the PTE is concerned, the reasons for the loss of rail passengers stem from what it regards as a run-down, under-invested rail infrastructure, especially on the north side of Manchester, typified by the continuing use of ageing first-generation DMUs, the uncomfortable and unreliable 'Pacers', and capacity problems between Castlefield Junction and Piccadilly resulting in train delays.

The PTE, considerably disillusioned, has complained vigorously and repeatedly over several years to BR about the standard of service given, and is still doing so. In fact, the PTA is again considering withholding the Section 20 grant because of the alleged failure by BR to meet performance targets. It was said that for 1993 the standard of service given was 'totally unacceptable', and that performance was steadily worsening. The chairman of the PTA said that he did not want to impose financial penalties on BR but was not prepared to part with local taxpayers' money for a sub-standard service. BR has tried to give the service that the PTE requires, but has not had sufficient, nor sufficiently reliable, resources to do so. Unwisely, it tried to do too much with too little, and it would have been more prudent not to have attempted to do more than it could reasonably have hoped to achieve. It is hardly surprising, therefore, that the PTE promoted Metrolink, hoping to control it better than it felt BR could.

The lost passengers have not deserted BR in favour of the buses, or so it would seem. Over a period of six years following bus deregulation in 1986, the number of bus passenger journeys fell from 355 million to 254 million, a decrease of 28%. During the same period, bus fares increased by two-thirds, after taking inflation into account. It seems likely that there has been a transfer from

Below: EMUs are noted for their long lives. A Class 303 EMU, introduced in 1959, passes Castlefield Junction with the 16.55 Hazel Grove-Altrincham service on 11 May 1990. At least the designers had the foresight to incorporate sliding doors. The other route leads to Ordsall Lane. The castellated viaduct (top right) used to carry the main lines into Central; after many years of disuse it now carries the Metrolink Altrincham service. *Paul D. Shannon*

public transport to the private car, despite all the efforts of the PTE, not helped by the generous provision of car parking spaces. There are indications of continual structural decline in the employment pattern in the city centre, and new developments are often at sites not very well served by either heavy rail or by bus. Perhaps Metrolink will halt the decline, but that can occur only on the routes it serves.

Whilst it is wrong to heap all the blame on BR, which is no longer the master in its own house, BR should not have promised more than it could hope to achieve efficiently. Yet, in the past BR has been accused of demanding over-engineered solutions. It cannot win in such a situation. On the one hand the Government demands a cheaper railway; on the other the PTE expects a better service; the two requirements are irreconcilable. 'Pacers' still have reliability problems, and the original Leyland engines on the Class 142 fleet are being replaced by Cummins engines. The braking systems are also being completely re-engineered, and these two measures are at last enabling a significant improvement in reliability and performance to be achieved.

The Channel Tunnel

By the time this book appears in print it is to be hoped that Sir Edward Watkin's dream of through trains from Manchester to Paris via a tunnel under the Channel will have become a reality. The starting date for this new service has not yet been set, but work started at Longsight in January 1994 on the construction of a £9.5 million servicing and maintenance depot for Eurostar trains, due for completion in March 1995. The start of work ceremony was performed by Graham Stringer, leader of Manchester City Council, when he took control of a piling rig to bore the first pile. The building will be nearly 400yd long and will house two 16-car Eurostar train sets overnight. These trains are expected to enter service on the daily Manchester to Paris and Brussels routes by the end of 1995.

The Rebuilding of Victoria

After many years, decades even, of decline and decay, major changes are at last taking place at Victoria, but the fine turn-of-the-century frontage will be preserved. There have been occasional attempts to improve Victoria, by cleaning the stonework of the frontage and by resurfacing some of the flooring with marble terrazzo, but there has

Below: Plan and track layout of the rebuilt Victoria station.

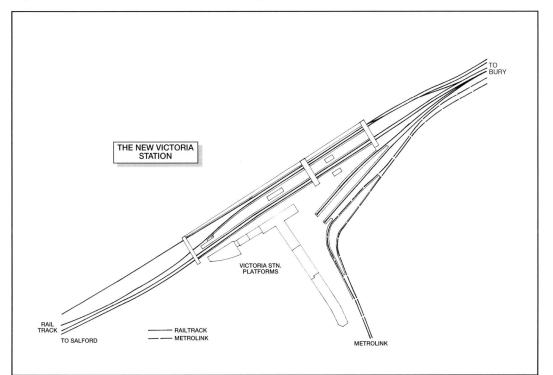

165

been nothing approaching the present scale, which is virtually that of a new station.

The present scheme has its roots in a number of factors:

• The reduction in the number of trains using Victoria caused by the diversion of services to Piccadilly, including Manchester–Blackpool, and trans-Pennine via Huddersfield

• The transfer of the Bury line electric service to Metrolink
• The planned transfer of the Rochdale via Oldham service to Metrolink
• Manchester's bid to host the Olympic Games in the year 2000, a bid that was ultimately unsuccessful
• The need to do something about Victoria in any event

Preparatory work started at the end of 1992, when demolition experts removed the 90-year-old roof from Platforms 12 to 16 during the Christmas break. Contractors also removed the through lines between Platforms 11 and 12 in order to clear an area where a new island platform was subsequently built.

Stage 2 of the scheme began in mid-1993, when Platform 11 and one side of the new island platform came into use. At the same time, the developers moved on to Platforms 12 and 13, and Victoria West signalbox was taken out of use. Track circuit block working with train describers is now in operation between Victoria East and Deal Street signalboxes.

Stage 3 began in 1994, with the opening of the whole of the new island platform and the re-opening of Platform 12, whilst the developers took over the area occupied by Platforms 13 and 16, although work was severely hampered when a 1,600-ton coal train became derailed on 9 March and virtually wrecked the east junction.

Ultimately, the scheme has given Victoria four through platform lines, served by an island platform and two single-sided platforms, together with the retention of two dead-end bay platforms. All the platforms have been renumbered to conform with the new layout, and the rebuilt station, expected to be opened formally by Sir Robert Reid, Chairman of British Rail, was, in the end, opened without ceremony. Actually, the station now belongs to Railtrack, a quite separate state-owned body, which is an intriguing situation.

Regional Railways North West Train Operating Unit is the main user of the station, and one can foresee conflicts arising between that body and Railtrack over the preparation of the platforming plan for trains, and over day-to-day adjustments to cater for alterations to the train service and late running. Railwaymen will no doubt use their commonsense, but the question is not entirely academic, and could become a real issue if and when those separate organisations become privately owned. The complexity of the organisation at Victoria is as nothing compared to that at Piccadilly, where the station is now a separate and free-standing organisational unit, which will have dealings with a number of train operating units and with Railtrack.

However, reverting to the Victoria redevelopment, there are very ambitious plans for an Olympic-size sports arena, which is currently under construction and due to open in 1995, and there will be a multi-storey car park. The main entrance to the arena will be from the concourse at Victoria, where the beginnings of a 'City Room', complete with shops, will be built. Whether the City Room concept will develop to its planned extent, with more shops, restaurants, etc will depend upon private funding. The original development plans for the area also envisaged the erection of a 46-storey 'crystal tower block' of commercial premises, offices and an hotel, designed to support Manchester's bid to stage the Olympic Games in

Left: The preserved concourse at Manchester Victoria, with its terrazzo tiling looking very spick and span. *Author*

Right: The new Victoria takes shape, seen from the former Platform 11 on 24 April 1993. West Junction signalbox has also now been demolished.
Author

Centre right: Platform 11 at Victoria was still in use when this photograph was taken of the 12.42 stopping service to Chester via Warrington Bank Quay, formed by a Class 142 Pacer, set No 142028, on 7 November 1986.
Alex Dasi-Sutton

Below: The old part of the new Victoria, but the trains are modern. From left to right a Piccadilly-bound Metrolink service, a Class 142 Pacer to Wakefield, and a Class 158 Sprinter Express set No 158908 for York via Bradford.
Paul D. Shannon

Above: The very much simplified track layout at the west end of the new Victoria, over which Class 31 diesel No 31432 brings the 10.00 (SO) from Blackpool North into Victoria station on 16 July 1994. The site of the former Exchange station can be seen on the left. *Paul D. Shannon*

Left: The new through platforms at Manchester Victoria, clinically clean and uncluttered, but lacking the homely feel of the old Victoria. A good thing too, some may say! *Author*

Below left: The new sports arena takes shape above the new Victoria station, whilst a Class 142 Pacer, set No 142046 passes by with the 11.13 Rochdale–Bolton service on 16 July 1994. This was part of Manchester's bid to stage the Olympic Games in the year 2000 and stimulate the city's economy. *Paul D. Shannon*

Above right: Victoria East Junction before the recent simplification of the track layout. No 47424 runs down Miles Platting bank and into the station with the 10.17 Newcastle to Liverpool Lime Street on 14 February 1989.
 Paul D. Shannon

the year 2000, but with the failure of that bid the tower block, if it is actually built, is likely to be on a less ambitious scale.

Electrification

Both BR and the PTE see two routes as top priority for electrification:

• Manchester–Bolton–Preston–Blackpool
• Trans-Pennine:
York–Leeds–Huddersfield–Manchester–Liverpool.

The evaluation of these two schemes is currently in hand, and the portents are favourable. BR, PTEs and local authorities all keenly support the proposals, and recently the Government stated that it had firmly committed itself to the support and development of rail services, as a partial alternative to the building of new roads and the widening of others, a recognition of the fact that new roads merely create more traffic, which then overloads the existing road system, leading to demands for yet more roads; a never-ending spiral. But the Government faces an extremely powerful lobby in its oft-repeated aim of transferring freight traffic and passengers from road to rail as an alternative to building new roads — a lobby composed of the road construction industry, road vehicle builders and repairers, 20 million car owners, the road haulage industry, and all those whose lives are blighted by heavy traffic and want bypasses and new roads to take traffic out of towns and villages. Complicating all this is the revised railway organisation which came into effect on 1 April 1994, as a prelude to ultimate privatisation.

The signalling on the Manchester–Bolton–Preston–Blackpool line has been immunised against interference from traction currents as far north as the fringe signalbox at Blackrod, but beyond that the signalling under the control of Preston power signalbox will require immunisation. A small, almost tiny, step in the electrification towards Preston will come when the route between Castlefield Junction and Salford Crescent is electrified in connection with a road scheme which will take over the site of the present turnback siding at Cornbrook.

Signalling

Piccadilly's power signalbox, opened in 1960, has been transferred away from its previous home. The old OCS control panel has been replaced by a standard 'NX' (push button) panel, and the route-relay interlocking installation controlling points and signals in the station area has been renewed. The remote interlockings remain unchanged.

Much of the signalling on the north side of Manchester is old-fashioned and life-expired, and it is planned to replace it with an Integrated Electronic Control Centre, located near Ardwick station. This IECC will eventually control the signalling in almost the whole of the Greater Manchester area, and the work is planned to be carried out in a number of stages:

1. The area currently controlled by the Piccadilly power signalbox, viz: the Manchester Piccadilly–Airport line, the Warrington line, the Bolton and Preston line as far as Blackrod, the Atherton line (to Moorside), and the Blackburn line.

This is planned to be achieved in 1995, but there may be some slippage.

2. The Manchester Victoria area (Salford to Thorpes Bridge), due to be commissioned in 1997 if funds and resources are available.

3. The Stockport area.

4. The East side services.

Stage 1 is estimated to cost £5.8 million, and stages 2–4 about another £55 million. Further stages are envisaged, covering the Wilmslow area, Rochdale and Todmorden, the Buxton line, the Hope Valley line and the Wigan line. Over 50 existing signalboxes would be closed.

The method of funding has not yet been decided, but discussions are taking place currently. One thing is certain — the existing signalling has a finite life and must be replaced, or there will be no trains. The investment will be linked to the two major electrification schemes previously mentioned and will be designed to allow for driver-only operation.

The future of the Cheetham Hill loop from Victoria East to Thorpes Bridge Junction has not yet been decided, because it is involved in plans for the Metrolink Oldham/Rochdale scheme, which would dive under Railtrack's lines at Thorpes Bridge, and join the Cheetham Hill loop as far as Smedley Viaduct, then take the former curve to Irk Valley Junction to join the line from Bury.

Freight

Of all the major changes which have taken place in the railway scene in the Greater Manchester area in the last 30 years, none has been more startling than the virtual demise of the freight railway. Apart from Trafford Park and one or two other locations, and except for through freight trains, Manchester's railways are passenger railways. The reasons for this sweeping change have been explored in the previous pages, but the railways were originally built to carry heavy bulk traffics, and the following figures are surely relevant:

Year	Output of Deep mined Coal (million tons)	Output of Steel Ingots & Castings (millions tons)	Output of Cotton Cloth (million linear yards)
1948	197	14.9	1,933
1958	202	19.6	1,429
1968	157	26.3	731
1978	108	20.8	380
1988	84	19.0	240
1992	66	16.2	156

(UK total output)

Since 1992, the coal output figures have declined further, but the loss of home-produced traffic has been balanced to some extent by imports of coal.

One new and relatively profitable source of traffic in recent years has been the disposal of municipal waste. Modern society produces enormous quantities, which creates problems for public bodies such as the Greater Manchester Waste Disposal Authority, which is constantly searching for new holes to fill. In 1992, a landfill site at Appley Bridge was chosen and daily trains were run from Dean Lane, Brindle Heath and Northenden. The following year a contract was signed with BR for the movement of over 1/2 million tons of domestic waste annually, necessitating a fourth daily train, from Bredbury. The Appley Bridge site is now full and trains run to a new site consisting of old gravel pits at Walton Old Junction, Warrington. The quantity of waste is so great that a second daily train may be required from Dean Lane.

There are a number of stone terminals in the area, at Dean Lane, Miles Platting, Brindle Heath, Hope Street and Ashburys, but not all are receiving railborne traffic at the present time. The only other freight terminals are Conoco at Weaste and Duncan Transrail (Otis) at Ordsall Lane.

The Freightliner Service has had a disappointingly chequered career, and the Longsight terminal was closed in 1987, one of nine closures out of a total terminal strength of 22 in an attempt to improve the profitability of Freightliners Ltd. The following year Freightliners merged with BR's Railfreight Division to try to cut costs even further. There may be some crumbs of comfort in the announcement by Roger Freeman, the Public Transport Minister, in January 1994 that an estimated £43 million would be available for rail freight during 1994–96. This will cover both the freight facilities grant (previously known as Section 8, 1974 Railways Act), and the new track access grant which is being provided to offset Railtrack's increased charges.

The Channel Tunnel is confidently expected to provide a substantial source of freight traffic for the railways, and an £11-million Euroterminal was opened at Trafford Park in August 1993. The terminal is equipped with two cranes and a reach stacker, and has the capacity to handle up to 100,000 containers and swap bodies a year. Initially the trains will run to the Wembley depot, where they will be amalgamated with traffic from other regional terminals to form block trains for

Right: No 47079 with train 6P18 10.08 from Crewe to Ordsall Lane on 12 August 1991.
Paul D. Shannon

direct transit to European destinations.

A second Euroterminal is being planned for development on a 45-acre site at Guide Bridge as a private venture by Tameside Borough Council and Tarmac.

Conclusion

The story of Manchester's railways divides neatly into two parts — (1) almost a century of continuous and profitable expansion, 1830–1914, and (2) three-quarters of a century dogged by financial problems, 1919–1995. Problems since 1919 have arisen from four main sources:

• The decline in Britain's basic industries — coal, steel, shipbuilding and textiles, which provided the railways with vast quantities of profitable traffic
• The inexorable rise of competition from cars, buses, coaches, lorries and aircraft
• The unequal financial and structural basis of much of the competition, biased against railways
• The constant struggle by railway management and, since nationalisation in 1948, by government, to put the railways on a sound financial basis; a struggle that has been a resounding failure, compounded by a string of reorganisations and constant shifts in government policy.

However, as far as Manchester is concerned, the future looks reasonably favourable. The PTE is a considerable supporter of railways. Metrolink is a success and looks likely to develop. Electrification of two key routes will surely come, and the Channel Tunnel will surely create much additional traffic, both passengers and freight. Finally, the government frequently declares that the railways must play a greater part in the nation's transport system, but it controls the purse-strings and it must make the resources available if that aim is to be achieved. Funding is the crucial issue, and without the provision of financial resources the development of Manchester's railways will not take place.

At the same time, a dark cloud of uncertainty hangs over the railway, arising from privatisation. There can have been few measures forced through Parliament against considerable opposition whose outcome was more obscure and unpredictable than the Railways Act 1993. One can only wait and see. And hope. Perhaps the ultimate question is this — Would the railway promoters and shareholders who willingly poured such enormous amounts of capital into railway development in the 19th century in the expectation of a reasonable return, have done so if they were faced with the mass of legal requirements, regulations, regulatory bodies, associated quangos and all the bureaucracy and uncertainty that faces the potential railway investor or entrepreneur today? I fear that the answer would be that they would not, at least so far as the potential train operating companies are concerned. On the other hand, there is, I believe, considerable scope for private investment in rolling stock and the infrastructure — ie, in tangible assets, and that leads me to hope that 1995 may come to be regarded as the start of a new Golden Age of Railways. Amen to that.

Above: No 47194 passes the Ordsall Lane freight depot with train 6E51 17.46 Warrington Arpley-Port Clarence on 6 March 1993. *Paul D. Shannon*

Below: A fairly new traffic, which ought to be profitable if Railtrack's charges are not too high. City authorities throughout the country are anxious to find big holes in the ground in which to dump their waste. No 45040 arrives at Dean Lane Waste Disposal Depot with a train of empties, 6J75 10.08 from Appley Bridge on 30 August 1985.
Paul D. Shannon

11 Metrolink — A Dream Come True

On Friday 17 July 1992 an important event took place in St Peter's Square, Manchester, which signified the realisation of hopes and aspirations dating back to the beginning of the century. At long last Manchester had a through north–south rail route serving the city centre, and it was entirely fitting that the opening ceremony should be performed by HM The Queen. It was also in all probability the first and last time that the Royal Train will be formed by a Metrolink tram, the Queen being conveyed in triumph to Bury in one of the Metrolink twin-sets.

The story of the north-south route is one of a lack of firm government resolve. Successive governments, both Conservative and Labour, refused to fund the Picc-Vic scheme, and it was not until 1983 that Greater Manchester Council grasped the nettle and proposed a regional light rail network as the cheapest way of improving public transport in the area. The plan was revolutionary.

The study, undertaken jointly by BR, Greater Manchester Transport and Greater Manchester Council, made the following recommendations:

• Conversion to light rail operation of the following lines radiating from Manchester:

    a) Altrincham
    b) Bury
    c) Marple/Rose Hill
    d) Glossop/Hadfield
    e) Rochdale via Oldham

• Construction of a light rail route on the former Midland Railway line to Chorlton and Didsbury
• Street-running through the city centre, with stops at High Street, Piccadilly Gardens, St Peter's Square and Deansgate and providing through communication between Victoria and Piccadilly stations
• The Bury line to be the first to be converted.

Total cost was put at £85 million, with £47 million being allocated to infrastructure and £38 million to rolling stock.

The following year, 1984, Parliamentary approval was sought for street-running through the city centre, and in 1985 a second Bill was promoted for conversion to light rail of the Bury and Altrincham lines. However, the Government, which must have seemed to impartial observers to regard Manchester as a lost cause, continued to vacillate over the question of funding, and insisted on private sector finance.

GMPTE submitted the Metrolink proposals for a Section 56 Infrastructure Grant in 1984, but it was a year before the Department of Transport accepted the justification of the scheme. The Department then insisted that Metrolink would have to be evaluated against the forthcoming bus deregulation under the 1985 Transport Act, and it was not possible to re-evalute until 1987 after there had been sufficient experience of the situation following bus deregulation.

Finally, in January 1988, the Transport Secretary announced in Parliament that he was satisfied that a case had been made for a light rail system for Manchester, and that he was inviting options for the involvement of private sector finance. Ultimately a consortium was formed to design, build and operate the system, the members being GEC, Mowlem, AMEC and Greater Manchester Buses Ltd. A new company, known as Greater Manchester Metro Ltd (GMML), was formed in January 1990 to undertake the work and operate the system, the four members of the consortium being joined by the Greater Manchester PTE. They were awarded a 15-year operating concession. The capital cost of the Metrolink scheme had now grown to £130 million.

Also in 1988 the parliamentary powers applied for in 1984/85 were granted, and on 24 October 1989 Michael Portillo, the Transport Minister, announced that a grant under Section 56 of the Transport Act 1968 would be paid at 50% of the eligible capital costs, now expected to reach £110 million. The grant would be conditional, he added, on private sector participation in both construction and operation.

The assets, including the rail vehicles, track, stations and depot, belong to Greater Manchester PTE but the whole system is leased to GMML for 15 years. Revenue from passengers will have to cover running costs, the lease rental, maintenance and profit for the operating partners. There is NO operating subsidy.

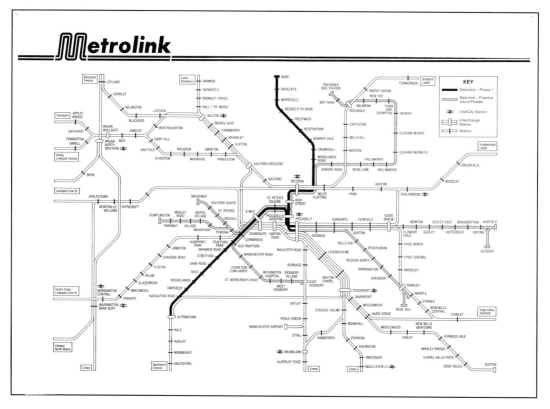

Above: Map showing present Metrolink system, and proposed extensions.

The System

The first Metrolink route to be brought into operation runs from Bury to Altrincham. From Bury the Metrolink trains run over the former L&Y third-rail electrified line, now converted to an overhead system, as far as Victoria, where street-running commences. The route to Piccadilly BR station has intermediate stations at High Street, Market Street and Piccadilly Gardens. Metrocars reverse at Piccadilly and return to Piccadilly Gardens then turn left along Mosley Street (where there is a station) to St Peter's Square station, and continue to a station alongside the G-Mex Centre (the former Central station). Alternate trains from each outer terminus now run direct Bury–Altrincham and vice versa, via the third side of the triangle at Piccadilly Gardens.

The three city-centre stations, High Street, Market Street, and Mosley Street, are uni-directional only. From G-Mex station the new line runs along the Cornbrook Viaduct, with an intermediate station at Deansgate, until it joins the former BR Altrincham line. The Cornbrook Viaduct had lain unused since the closure of Central station in 1969, but was found to be in surprisingly good condition. The necessary restoration work has been carried out with very pleasing visual results.

The Metrolink scheme required the ownership of the Bury line (from Footbridge to Bury) and the Altrincham line (from just north of Trafford Tunnel) to Deansgate Junction (exclusive) to be transferred to GMPTE (the Altrincham line is reputed to have been sold by BR for £1), and this required the diversion of the train service which had formerly been routed from Oxford Road/Piccadilly to Chester over the MSJ&A and via Northwich. The service now runs via the Crewe line to Stockport, thence via the former CLC route through Northenden to Altrincham.

Signalling and Control

On the former BR lines to Bury and Altrincham, colour light signals are used to control trains. These can show only two aspects — red (stop) and green (clear). There is no preceding distant signal as would be normal in BR practice, except at a few locations where sighting is restricted by curvature of the line etc, but station warning boards are erected in place of distant signals at braking distance from the station platform. A form of track circuit block working is in operation, which

Above: A Metrolink set leaves Victoria for the G-Mex Centre on a wet 9 May 1992. Street-running mode is adopted before the train leaves Victoria. *Paul D. Shannon*

maintains a signal at red until the preceding train has passed the next signal ahead. The signals work automatically, but can be restored to, or maintained at, red by the Control Centre in case of emergency.

An automatic train-stop device is installed at all colour light signals, consisting of a train-mounted antenna and a track-mounted beacon. When the signal is at red the system will apply the brakes if the driver fails to stop at the signal.

For street-running, completely different considerations apply, as the route of the metrocars may be obstructed by pedestrians, road vehicles or other obstacles. A normal railway signalling system would be quite inappropriate because it would not, and could not, control the movements of road vehicles sometimes competing for the same road space. For that reason the metrocars are driven 'on sight', as is done with any other vehicle on the road, and the driver must be prepared to stop at any time if the way ahead is obstructed. In other words, it is driven like a tramcar. However, some form of control signal has to be given to Metrolink drivers to indicate when they may proceed at road junctions and other locations where a normal road traffic signal might mistakenly be acted upon by a road vehicle driver. These control signals take the form of a white bar on a black background, which is horizontally displayed to indicate 'stop', and

vertically displayed for 'proceed if clear to do so.' The signals are given by fibre-optics.

There are other complications which have to be provided for. At Victoria and G-Mex stations, before leaving the segregated track section to commence street-running, the driver must switch to street-running mode. This has the following effects:

- the audible warning device changes from a railway-type horn to a chime whistle
- The headlights and rear tail-lights change to road-vehicle-style lights
- brake lights come into operation
- direction indicators become operative
- a rear-view mirror is extended.

At junctions in the city centre the points are controlled by the approaching vehicle, through the GEC Alsthon Vehicle Recognition System, known as VRS. Information relating to the intended route is entered into the VRS equipment at the start of a journey, and this transmits information to be detected by loops buried in the track. VRS not only sets the points as required but also enables priority to be given at road/rail intersections, and is an integral part of the central monitoring of the location of the Metrolink units. The driver has a 'Train Ready to Start' button in his cab, which generates a request for clearance of a signal at a station located immediately before a road junction. The operation of points in the track for an approaching Metrolink unit is delayed until it is very close, to avoid the points moving whilst a pedestrian is walking over them. By delaying the movement of the points, it is assumed that pedestrians will already have moved off the track in the face of the closely approaching Metrolink unit.

Manchester's pedestrians are still going through a learning curve, which is understandable considering that most of them are too young to remember trams. Some pedestrians deliberately rely upon the Metrolink units running at low speed, and ought to be taken across the Channel for a salutary lesson in Dutch and German cities, where light rail vehicles run through congested city centres at higher speeds than Metrolink, and where pedestrians have long been accustomed to keeping out of their way.

Metrolink units are akin to trains when operating on former BR tracks, but are more like tramcars when operating in the street. It is difficult to know what to call them. Metrolink literature calls them Supertrams, which seems reasonable. It is catchy, sounds modern and rolls off the tongue easily.

One of the major problems encountered in running through the city centre is the number of road junctions that have to be crossed, and the degree of precedence that ought to be given to Metrolink supertrams. As a principle it might be said that a supertram, possibly carrying 100 passengers, ought always to have priority at traffic lights over private cars carrying a handful of people, but where buses are involved the equation is somewhat different. There are 15 such intersections, and Metrolink has priority at 10 of them. None the less, where journey time through the city centre is important an argument could be adduced for giving supertrams absolute priority, if only to encourage more and more people to use them. Priority to supertrams is given through an inductive loop set in the road surface approaching a junction, which registers the approach of a rail vehicle and puts the road traffic signals to red as appropriate.

Rolling Stock

Each metrolink unit consists of two separate cars, articulated over a centre bogie to allow sharp curves to be negotiated in the city centre. A two-car unit is 96ft long and weighs 45 tonnes. There are seats for 82 passengers but there is plenty of standing capacity, the nominal maximum number of passengers being 206. Public address is provided, used by the driver. Each car has two doorways per side, with pneumatically-powered twin-leaf sliding doors operated by the driver. When the supertram stops at a station, the driver releases the door locks, enabling passengers to open the doors as required.

The 26 Metrolink units are stabled and maintained at the Queens Road Depot, on the site of the old BR carriage sidings. The Operations Centre is also located there.

Station Supervision and Passenger Security

Unstaffed stations, lightly loaded off-peak trains, and what is perceived to be an increasingly hostile environment have a definite effect on passengers' willingness to travel on public transport. Whether the threat to personal safety has actually increased, or whether its growth is a popular misconception, is not the issue. People are more apprehensive, and public transport operators must take this into account if they are to attract more passengers, especially during the evenings. Whilst it would be reassuring to see a policeman at every station and on every train, it would require about 200 officers to achieve this, which would just about double Metrolink's payroll.

In the absence of such a positive safeguard it has become the practice on urban rail systems of a metro type to provide closed-circuit television surveillance of unstaffed stations. Manchester's Metrolink has followed this policy, providing continuous surveillance of station platforms, subways and ticket machines on a cyclic basis, through a bank of television screens in front of the controller in the Operations Centre at Queens Road. In addition, passengers on a station platform can speak to the controller by pressing an emergency call button, which causes a video camera to record the scene and simultaneously display it in the Control Centre. Within the trains themselves there are emergency call points where passengers can speak to the driver. These systems are similar to those in operation on the Docklands Light Railway, which appear to have been quite effective.

However, whilst it has to be said that nothing can replace a railway or police uniform as a means of making passengers feel more secure, the Metrolink trains do run at very frequent intervals, and there are Mobile Controllers and roving Customer Service Inspectors. Experience so far seems to indicate that the Metrolink system is perceived by passengers to be safe.

The Future

In 1987 the PTE promoted a Bill, known as the Greater Manchester (Light Rapid Transit System) No 3 Bill, seeking powers to extend the Metrolink system to Salford Quays, and a year later it promoted another bill to convert the existing BR Rochdale via Oldham line and part of the Didsbury line to light rail operation. Further bills, Nos 4 and 5, were promoted in 1990, including an extension to Trafford Park and an extension to Rochdale town centre from the railway station.

The PTE believed that the Metrolink concept would be a success, and so it has turned out to be. Traffic levels in the first full year of operation were 20% higher than forecast, and shopkeepers in central Manchester, and in both Bury and Altrincham, are thought to have benefited greatly from Metrolink, which gives every encouragement to the PTA to extend the system. Where Metrolink takes over former BR lines and services, and does so on the type of contract applicable to the Bury–Altrincham service, it relieves the PTE of any responsibility for Section 20 support payments, an important consideration in the government's drive to reduce public expenditure.

Above: A town planner's nightmare — trams, buses and shoppers all mixed up together; but it works. The scene is the Market Street/High Street junction on 9 May 1992. *Paul D. Shannon*

Parliamentary powers are already in place for the extension to Salford Quays, and a route has already been earmarked to take the system from the city centre along the Cornbrook Viaduct to Pomona Docks and over the Ship Canal into Salford, to a terminus at Broadway. There are hopes that the route could subsequently be extended to Eccles. Urban renewal on a large scale is already planned for the area that this route would serve. Stations are proposed at Pomona, Ordsall, Salford Quays and Anchorage.

The success of the BR service to Manchester Airport has encouraged the Greater Manchester PTE to apply for permission under the Transport & Works Act 1992 to build a Metrolink light rail route to the airport from Trafford Bar to provide better transport facilities both for travellers from the Manchester area and for workers at the airport.

The neighbouring Trafford Park redevelopment area could also have its own branch, leaving the

Salford Quays line at Pomona and proceeding through stations at Wharfside, North Village, Village, Mosley Road and Parkway, and terminating at Dumplington, where a huge out-of-town shopping complex is being planned. However, the development of both these lines depends on an injection of private-sector finance, a reasonable condition bearing in mind the benefits that the developers would receive from having a Metrolink connection.

It might be mentioned that out-of-town retail developments are now regarded by the government as a mixed blessing, owing to their environmental disbenefits. In the first place they create increased car use because they are not well served by public transport. Dumplington would fall into that category, even with a Metrolink connection. In the second place, they lead to city-centre decay as shops move out to the new retail development. The city centre then attracts fewer shoppers, many of whom would previously have used public transport, plentifully supplied by buses, Metrolink and BR. It is not an attractive scenario.

High on the agenda, too, is the development of a Metrolink service to Oldham and Rochdale, using existing BR tracks. The Oldham line service is one of BR's Cinderellas and in dire need of upgrading — indeed the Manchester–Oldham line seems always to have been at the bottom of BR's priority list. Yet had it not been for the Grouping in 1923 the L&Y might well have gone ahead and electrified the line. Metrolink plans would radically improve the service, and not just by the running of a more frequent service with modern Metrolink units. The main problem as far as BR has been concerned is that the stations in Oldham and Rochdale are not well situated in relation to the town centres, and Rochdale suffers particularly in this respect. This factor has long inhibited the use of the railway for short-distance journeys, and bus competition is, and always has been, fierce.

Metrolink plans to overcome this handicap by building a short diversion in Oldham to take the line through the town centre and to extend the line in Rochdale from the existing BR station into the town centre and the bus station, which would be a fine example of public transport integration. New stations would be built in Oldham at Manchester Street and Union Street, adjacent to the two shopping complexes and the bus station, providing good bus/train interchange. In Rochdale, the Metrolink units would run along Maclure Road and down Drake Street to Smith Street, with an intermediate station at the rather infelicitously named Wet Rake. From a PTE point of view, this route must be an early candidate for upgrading, if only to escape the present heavy support payment to BR under Section 20 of the 1968 Transport Act,

now running in the region of £2 million a year, and the need to renew existing BR assets if the line is not converted to Metrolink operation in the near future. About 1½ million passengers a year use the BR service. Metrolink expects to improve this to five million. In the meantime, the GMPTE is planning to double the service frequency on this line to 15min intervals from May 1995.

However, funding for the Oldham/Rochdale Metrolink has not yet been obtained, and there may be problems in obtaining private capital under the conditions which applied to the Bury–Altrincham line.

Finally, parliamentary powers have been obtained for a line to East Didsbury via Chorlton. This would leave the Altrincham line near Trafford Bar station and use the trackbed of the former Midland main line. Intermediate stations would be provided at Manchester Road, Chorlton-cum-Hardy, St Werburgh's Road, Withington Hospital, West Didsbury and Didsbury Village.

It is very heartening to see the Greater Manchester Passenger Transport Authority forging ahead in such a positive manner after so many wasted years, but the Metrolink concept of street-running through town and city centres, and the taking over of BR tracks for out-of-town stretches (or building its own) is an idea that had to wait until the time was ripe. The big problem now is funding and the private sector must play a prominent role in this. Would this alter with a change of government? It seems unlikely, given the undoubted success of the Metrolink 'design, build and operate' concept.

Perhaps, then, the day is not far off when Manchester's streets will once again look as they did in those old photographs — full of trams and few cars. But this time they will be sleek Metrolink supertrams, running quite quickly through the city centre (pedestrians will have learned by then to keep out of the way) and with absolute priority at all intersections. Indeed, it will be essential to keep the supertrams on the move — there will be so many of them.

One final point. This is a municipal tramway renaissance, and not a conventional railway success story. The trams have won at last. But shed no tears. Metrolink has a bright expanding future because the municipal authorities believe in it. The railway branches which have been taken over were struggling to survive and required hefty subsidies. Metrolink is one of the outstanding success stories of the Greater Manchester PTA, but do not forget that the same PTA also supports many BR local services and will continue to do so as far as can be seen. The citizens of the PTA area should erect a monument to Barbara Castle. Perhaps a suitable location could be found in Piccadilly Gardens.

Appendices

Locomotive Allocation

(a) Longsight (Shed No 16) 1933 (1934 Renumbering shown)

Class	Type				Total
4P	4-4-0	Std	Compound	1130-32	3
1P	0-4-4T	Mid		1274/6/8	3
4P	2-6-4T	Std		2303-05, 2314, 2355-58, 2363/4	10
5P4F	2-6-0	Std		2856-59	4
4F	0-6-0	Std		4126, 4348/9	3
3P	4-4-0	LNW	'George the Fifth'	5187(Reb) *Helvellyn*, 5347 *Elkhound*, 5348 *Coronation*, 5349 *British Empire*, 5350 *India*, 5351 *Canada*, 5383 *John Mayall*, 5385 *William Froude*	8
4P	4-6-0	LNW	'Prince of Wales'	5696, 5705, 5768, 5824	4
5P	4-6-0	LNW	'Claughton'	5947, 5959*, 5967 *L/Corpl J A Christie VC*, 5985*, 6015* *Private E Sykes VC*, 6018* *Private W Wood VC*, (* Became 'Patriot' class Nos 5502, 5503, 5537, & 5536 respectively)	6
6P	4-6-0	Std	'Royal Scot'	6131 *The Royal Warwickshire Regiment*, 6165 *The Ranger (12th London Regiment)*, 6166 *London Rifle Brigade*, 6167 *The Hertfordshire Regiment*, 6168 *The Girl Guide*, 6169 *The Boy Scout*	6
3P	4-4-2T	LNW		6800-07	8
1P	0-6-2T	LNW		6896	1
3F	0-6-0T	Std		7341-5, 7369/70, 7400/1, 760	10
2F	0-6-0	LNW		8271/3/5/6, 8345/7/8	7
4F	4-6-0	LNW	19in Goods	8700-03, 8706, 8791, 8803, 8826	8
6F/7F	0-8-0	LNW		9283-87	5

Standard — 36, Ex-LNW — 47, Ex-Mid — 3   Total — 86

(b) Patricroft (Shed No 34) 1933 (1934 Renumbering shown)

Class	Type				Total
3P	2-6-2T	Std		12, 65-67	4
3P	4-4-0	LNW	'Precursor' & 'George the Fifth'	5207 *Eglinton*, 5211 *Aurania*, 5212 *Harrowby*, 5216 *Herald*, 5218 *Pandora*, 5223 *Snake*, 5254 *Daphne*, 5257 *Locke*, 5352 *Australia*, 5355 *South Africa*, 5397 *Planet*, 5398 *Meteor*, 5399 *Lord Stalbridge*, 5400 *Llandudno*, 5401 *Windermere*	15
4P	4-6-0	LNW	'Prince of Wales'	5727/8, 5729 *Lucknow*, 5730-35, 5736 *Disraeli*, 5737-42, 5743 *Prince Albert*, 5744/5, 5747-49	22
5P	4-6-0	LNW	'Claughton'	5953 *Buckingham*, 6017 *Breadalbane*, 6021 *Bevere*, 6024	4
2P	2-4-2T	LNW (Wirral)		6762	1
4P	4-6-2T	LNW		6966-72, 6977, 6980/2/3	11
2F	0-6-0T	LNW	Special Tank	7232	1
3F	0-6-0T	Std		7392, 7604/5	3
6F	0-8-2T	LNW		7871/3/4	3
2F	0-6-0	LNW		8117, 8120/6, 8128-31, 8133, 8293, 8577/8, 8581/4/5	14
4F	4-6-0	LNW 19in Goods		8744, 8747-50, 8752	6
6F/7F	0-8-0	LNW		8901-07, 9103, 9130, 9252-55, 933	14
2P	2-4-2T	L&Y		10641/8	2

Standard 7, Ex-LNW 91, Ex-L&Y — 2   Total — 100

(c) Newton Heath (Shed No 1) 1934

2P	4-4-0	Std		580/1, 588/9, 676/7, 691	7
5P4F	2-6-0	Std		2700, 2707-14, 2720/1/4/5/8, 2860/1	16
4F	0-6-0	Std		4209-12, 4214/5, 4460/5/7, 4475/6, 4537, 4540	13
4P	4-6-0	LNW	'Prince of Wales'	5795, 5802/4/5, 5841	5
3F	0-6-0T	Std		7386, 7507-09, 7577-79	7
7F	0-8-0	Std		9590-95, 9651-57	13
2P	4-4-0	L&Y		10108	1
5P	4-6-0	L&Y		10406, 10429, 10438, 10441/3/6, 10450/1/4/9, 10465	11
2P/3P	2-4-2T	L&Y		10655/7, 10693/9, 10729, 10733/8, 10751, 10768, 10781, 10810/4/5, 10828, 10835/9, 10865/7/8, 10870, 10883, 10909, 10911/5, 10923, 10934/5/8, 10941/4, 10950	31
5P	4-6-4T	L&Y		11110-13	4
0F	0-4-0T	L&Y		11234	1
2F	0-6-0T	L&Y	Saddle Tank	11328, 11347, 11363/5/6, 11400, 11436/8, 11496, 11502/8,11510	12
3F	0-6-0	L&Y		12100, 12143, 12156, 12164/9, 12176/7, 12204/6, 12214/9, 12238, 12258,2281, 12323/6/7, 12337/8, 12345, 12351/8, 12363/4, 12387, 12390, 12415, 12432/7, 12440, 12517/8, 12537, 12540/5/6/9, 12552-55, 12559, 12588	43
7F	0-8-0	L&Y		12715, 12741, 12790, 12822/7, 12861, 12876/7, 12886, 12911/6, 12952/3/9	14

Standard — 56, Ex-L&Y — 117, Ex-LNW — 5   Total — 178

(d) Manchester Midland (Shed No 21) 1933 (1934 renumbering shown)

2P	4-4-0	Mid	485, 514-16	4
3P	4-4-0	Mid	743/4/6/7/8	5
4P	4-4-0	Mid & Std Compound	1014-22, 1062/4, 1089/90	13
1F	0-6-0T	Mid	1838	1
3P	0-6-4T	Mid	2004, 2007-10, 2020/2	7
4P	2-6-4T	Std	2372-74	3
5P4F	2-6-0	Std	2754/8, 2828	3
2F/3F	0-6-0	Mid	2991/2/7, 3047, 3168, 3215, 3300, 3321, 3361/4, 3482/8, 3550, 3596/9, 3605-07, 3612/4, 3638, 3658, 3716/8, 3723/5	26
4F	0-6-0	Mid & Std	3927, 3940/1, 3943-47, 4016, 4022-26, 4129, 4130/1, 4283-87, 4550-53	26
3F	0-6-0T	Std	7276	1
3P	2-4-2T	L&Y	10901	1
2F	0-6-0T	L&Y	Saddle Tank	11321, 11520-24	6
3F	0-6-0	L&Y	12121, 12138	2

Standard — 23, Ex-Mid — 66, Ex-L&Y — 9   Total — 98

(e) Gorton 1934

B2	4-6-0		5424 *City of Lincoln*, 5427 *City of London*	2
B3	4-6-0		6168 *Lord Stuart of Wortley*, 6169 *Lord Faringdon*	2
B7	4-6-0		5031/4-7, 5072/3/8, 5458, 5465, 5470/6/7/9, 5482/4	16
B9	4-6-0		6105/6/7/9, 6111/2	6
B17	4-6-0	LNER Std 'Sandringham'	2816 *Fallodon*, 2824 *Lumley Castle*, 2834 *Hinchingbrooke*, 2840 *Somerleyton Hall*, 2841 *Gayton Hall*, 2842 *Kilverstone Hall*	6
D10	4-4-0	'Director'	5429 *Prince Henry*, 5433 *Walter Burgh Gair*, 5438 *Worsley-Taylor*	3
D11	4-4-0	'Director'	5503 *Somme*, 5508 *Prince of Wales*, 5511 *Marne*	3

F1/F2	2-4-2T			5574-77, 5579, 5581-84, 5586/9, 5593/6/8/9, 5729-33, 5736, 5743, 5776, 5581/4	25
J10/J11	0-6-0			5079/83, 5124, 5130, 5202/6, 5211, 5221, 5237, 5242, 5254, 5290, 5302, 5319, 5786/9, 5795, 5818, 5820/1/4, 5836, 5845, 5850, 5952, 6004	26
J39	0-6-0	LNER Std		1255, 1263/5, 1274, 1298, 1496-98, 2691-93, 2702/5/7,2962/3	16
J69	0-6-0T	Ex-GE		7086	1
K3	2-6-0	LNER Std		1121/5	2
L1	2-6-4T			5275	1
N5	0-6-2T			5520/3, 5525-28, 5530-32, 5534/5, 5540/1/3, 5903, 5918/9, 5920/4, 5932/6, 5942/6	23
O4	2-8-0			6255, 6260/8/9, 6273/6, 6283/7, 6292/3, 6300-03, 6306, 6310/5/9, 6325/7, 6330/1/7, 6341, 6350, 6365/9, 6375/6, 6567, 6576, 6625/7/8, 6633	35

LNER Std — 24, Ex-GC — 142, Ex-GE — 1   Total — 167

(f) Trafford Park CLC 1937

B9	4-6-0		6107, 6108	2
C13	4-4-2T		5018, 5020/7/8, 5047, 5188, 5453, 6055/7	9
D6	4-4-0		5855/6, 5863	3
D9	4-4-0		6023, 6033	2
F1	2-4-2T		5582	1
J10	0-6-0		5096, 5819, 5832/6, 5846/8	6
J39	0-6-0	LNER Std	1255, 1275, 1497, 2693 2962/3	6
J69	0-6-0T	Ex-GE	7198, 7273, 7351, 7371/83	5
K3	2-6-0	LNER Std	3817	1
N5	0-6-2T		5189, 5515, 5520/9, 5768, 5772	6

LNE — 7, Ex-GC — 29, Ex-GE — 5.   Total — 41

(g) Trafford Park LMS (19G) 1939

3P	2-6-2T	Std		88, 89, 168	3
4P	4-4-0	Mid Compound		1014, 1020/1/4	4
3F	0-6-0	Mid		3612, 3638	2
5P5F	4-6-0	Std		5036, 5071, 5092	3
5XP	4-6-0	Std	'Silver Jubilee'	5570 *New Zealand*, 5572 *Eire*, 5665 *Lord Rutherford of Nelson*	3

Total— 15

(h) Longsight (9A) 1938 (Up to No 6169 only)

3P	2-6-2T	Std		106	1
2P	4-4-0	Mid		356, 403, 446	3
4P	4-4-0	Std Compound		1050, 1106, 1111/8	4
1P	0-4-4T	Mid		1278, 1286	2
4P	2-6-4T	Std		2355-58, 2395-99	9
4P	2-6-4T	Std Stanier		2458, 2460/2/9, 2540, 2608/9, 2615/6	9
5P4F	2-6-0	Std		2775/6, 2810/1/3, 2854/6/8, 2938, 2940	10
3F	0-6-0	Mid		3275, 3717	2
4F	0-6-0	Std		4078, 4080, 4303/8, 4368	5
5P5F	4-6-0	Std		5024/5, 5074, 5109, 5256-58, 5295/6, 5347	10
5XP	4-6-0	Std	'Patriot'	5539 *E C Trench*, 5541 *Duke of Sutherland*, 5542/3/5	5
5XP	4-6-0	Std	'Silver Jubilee'	5625 *Sarawak*, 5653 *Barham*, 5666 *Cornwallis*, 5668 *Madden*, 5683 *Hogue*	5
6P	4-6-0	Std	'Royal Scot'	6111 *Royal Fusilier*, 6131 *The Royal Warwickshire Regiment*, 6148 *The Manchester Regiment*, 6165 *The Ranger (12th London Regiment)*, 6167 *The Hertfordshire Regiment*, 6169 *The Boy Scout*	6

Standard — 64, Ex-LNW — Nil, Ex-Mid — 7   Total — 71

3P	2-6-2T	Std		13-15, 56-63	11
2P	4-4-0	Std		584/8/9, 676/7, 685, 690	7
4P	4-4-0	Std	Compound	1101-04, 1191	5
4P	2-6-4T	Std		2310-12, 2383/4, 2406-08, 2411-14	12
4P	2-6-4T	Std	Stanier	2425/6, 2618-20	5
5P4F	2-6-0	Std		2709, 2710/3/4, 2721/4/5/8, 2730-32, 2753, 2796, 2838, 2860/5	16
5P5F	4-6-0	Std		5101-07, 5222-24, 5336/7	12
5XP	4-6-0	Std	'Patriot'	5546 *Fleetwood*, 5547, 5548 *Lytham St Annes*	3
5XP	4-6-0	Std	'Silver Jubilee'	5661 *Vernon*, 5695 *Minotaur*, 5696 *Arethusa*, 5697 *Achilles*, 5700 *Britannia*, 5701 *Conqueror*, 5702 *Colossus*	7
3F	0-6-0T	Std		7386, 7508-10	4
7F	0-8-0	Std		9560, 9595, 9627, 9636, 9640/1, 9651-57	13
2P/3P	2-4-2T	L&Y		10828, 10835, 10865, 10883, 10893, 10915, 10923, 10934, 10941/4, 10950	11
2F	0-6-0T	L&Y	Saddle Tank	11207, 11234, 11343, 11365, 11400/4, 11422, 11436/8, 11460, 11472, 11496, 11502/8, 11510	15
3F	0-6-0	L&Y		No of engines allocated	35
7F	0-8-0	L&Y		12856, 12861, 12916, 12952/9	5

Standard — 95, Ex-L&Y — 66   Total — 161

Locomotive Allocations — Post World War 2

Class	Type				Total

(a) Longsight (9A) 1954

3P	2-6-2T	LMS		40077, 40107/36	3
2P	4-4-0	Mid & LMS Std		40405/82, 40539, 40674/93	5
4P	4-4-0	LMS	Compound	41159/68	2
2P	0-4-4T	LMS		41905-07	3
4P	2-6-4T	LMS		42308/22, 42350/1, 42391, 42397-99	8
4P	2-6-4T	LMS	Stanier	42427/30, 42467/78, 42542, 42575, 42594/9, 42608	9
6P5F	2-6-0	LMS		42772/6/8, 42814/48, 42858, 42886/7/9, 42923-25, 42930/2, 42935-38, 42960	19
3F	0-6-0	Mid		43275, 43457, 43717	3
4F	0-6-0	LMS		44069, 44349/57	3
5	4-6-0	LMS		44686/7, 44741/2, 44748-52, 44760, 44935/7, 44941, 45109, 45385	15
6P5F/7P	4-6-0	LMS	'Patriot'	45500 *Patriot*, 45501 *St Dunstan's*, 45520 *Llandudno*, 45530 *Sir Frank Ree*, 45536 *Private W Wood VC*, 45539 *E C Trench*, 45540 *Sir Robert Turnbull*	7
6P5F	4-6-0	LMS	'Silver Jubilee'	45553 *Canada*, 45555 *Quebec*, 45556 *Nova Scotia*, 45578 *United Provinces*, 45587 *Baroda*, 45595 *Southern Rhodesia*, 45624 *St Helena*, 45631 *Tanganyika*, 45632 *Tonga*, 45638 *Zanzibar*, 45644 *Howe*, 45680 *Camperdown*, 45689 *Ajax*, 45709 *Implacable*, 45723 *Fearless*	15
7P	4-6-0	LMS	'Royal Scot'	46111 *Royal Fusilier*, 46114 *Coldstream Guardsman*, 46115 *Scots Guardsman*, 46120 *Royal Inniskilling Fusilier*, 46122 *Royal Ulster Rifleman* 46125 *3rd Carabinier*, 46130 *The West Yorkshire Regiment*,	

			46131 *The Royal Warwickshire Regiment*,		
			46143 *The South Staffordshire Regiment*,		
			46160 *Queen Victoria's Rifleman*, 46161 *King's Own*,		
			46169 *The Boy Scouts*		12
3F	0-6-0T	LMS		47267, 47341/3/5/7, 47369/95, 47400, 47528, 47673	10
8F	2-8-0	LMS		48389, 48425/8, 48500/1, 48516, 48633, 48731/44	9
7F	0-8-0	LNW		49428, 49439	2
7P6F	4-6-2	BR	'Britannia'	70031 *Byron*, 70032 *Tennyson*, 70033 *Charles Dickens*,	
				70043 *Lord Kitchener*, 70044 *Earl Haig*	5
4	2-6-4T	BR		80039	1

BR — 6, LMS — 117, Ex-LNW — 2, Ex-Mid — 6   Total — 131

(b) Trafford Park (9E) 1954

3P	2-6-2T	LMS		40009, 40017	2
4P	4-4-0	LMS	Compound	40910, 41066/98, 41112/54, 41161/70/3	8
4	2-6-4T	LMS		42064/5, 42452/69, 42676/83	6
4F	0-6-0	LMS		44236/75, 44350/92	4
5	4-6-0	LMS		44717, 44938, 45239, 45347	4
6P5F	4-6-0	LMS	'Silver Jubilee'	45618 *New Hebrides*, 45622 *Nyasaland*,	
				45628 *Somaliland*, 45629 *Straits Settlements*,	
				45652 *Hawke*, 45655 *Keith*	6
8F	2-8-0	LMS		48411, 48680, 48698, 48741	4
D10/	4-4-0	GC		62653 *Sir Edward Fraser*, 62658 *Prince George*,	
D11/1				62661 *Gerard Powys Dewhurst*, 62662 *Prince of Wales*,	
				62664 *Princess Mary*, 62668 *Jutland*	6
J10	0-6-0	GC		65138/44/6, 65153/6/7, 65167, 65170/1, 65181/4,	
				65186/7, 65191/7/8, 65205/9	18
J69/1	0-6-0T	GE		68583, 68595/8	3
N5/2	0-6-2T	GC		69255, 69304/26, 69335/6, 69343/7, 69358, 69361/4, 69370	11

Ex-LMS — 34, Ex-GC — 35, Ex-GE — 3   Total — 72

(c) Patricroft (10C) 1954

2P	4-4-0	Mid & LMS		40434/48, 40450, 40635	4
4	2-6-4T	LMS		42442, 42560/1/3, 42574/91, 42662	7
5	4-6-0	LMS		44708, 44808, 45005/37, 45042/57, 45095, 45137/42,	
				45147/82, 45188/99, 45231/59, 45290/4, 45302/4, 45312/29,	
				45352, 45377/8, 45401/10, 45411/20, 45424/6/8, 45442/4	33
6P5F	4-6-0	LMS	'Silver Jubilee'	45558 *Manitoba*, 45559 *British Columbia*, 45563 *Australia*,	
				45600 *Bermuda*, 45645 *Collingwood*, 45668 *Madden*	6
3F	0-6-0T	LMS		47364/5, 47399, 47430, 47621	5
7F	0-8-0	LMS		48926, 49027/87, 49094, 49199, 49209, 49234/54,	
				49335/40, 49386, 49400/21/6	14
2F	0-6-0	LMS		52016/24, 52031/45	4
5	4-6-0	BR		73043/4	2

BR — 2, Ex-LMS — 52, Ex-LNW — 14, Ex-L&Y — 4, Ex-Mid — 3   Total — 75

(d) Newton Heath (26A) 1954

3P	2-6-2T	LMS		40013/5, 40063/5	4
4	2-6-4T	LMS		42278-90, 42486, 42550, 42618, 42621-25	21
6P5F	2-6-0	LMS		42701-05, 42707-11, 42713-15, 42750, 42766/89,	
				42820, 42871/8	19
4F	0-6-0	LMS		44311, 44543	2
5	4-6-0	LMS		44696/7, 44734-36, 44890/1, 44893-95, 44933/4, 45102-05,	
				45202/3, 45220, 45223-25, 45232-34, 45336	26
6P5F	4-6-0	LMS	'Silver Jubilee'	45635 *Tobago*, 45642 *Boscawen*, 45661 *Vernon*,	
				45671 *Prince Rupert*, 45700 *Amethyst*,	

				45701 *Conqueror*, 45702 *Colossus*, 45706 *Express*, 45710 *Irresistible*, 45712 *Victory*	10
2	2-6-0	LMS		46410/1, 46418/9, 46484	5
3F	0-6-0	LMS		47577, 47586	2
7F	0-8-0	LMS		49508/57, 49560/70, 49666/7	6
2F	0-6-0T	L&Y	Saddle Tank	51436/47, 51457/8, 51470/2, 51496	7
3F	0-6-0	L&Y		52089, 52108/37, 52159/65, 52271, 52300/28, 52334/58, 52360/89, 52390, 52455/61	15
4	2-6-4T	BR		80049-53	5
8F	2-8-0	WD		90105/13, 90222/45, 90248/83, 90289/91, 90327/38, 90360/6, 90376/88, 90389/90, 90523/5, 90530/3, 90535/48, 90558/61, 90576/89, 90669/75, 90706/8, 90715	31

BR — 5, Ex-LMS — 95, Ex-L&Y — 22, Ex-WD — 31   Total — 153

(e) Agecroft (26B) 1954

4	2-6-4T	LMS		42645-48	4
6P5F	2-6-0	LMS		42721-25, 42730/4, 42753/5, 42819/38, 42860/4, 42868	14
5	4-6-0	LMS		44781/2, 44823, 44987, 45337/8	6
2	2-6-0	LMS		46412, 46485	2
3F	0-6-0T	LMS		47574/8/9, 47583-85	6
7F	0-8-0	LMS		49555 49578, 49603, 49627	4
0F	0-4-0T	L&Y	Saddle Tank	51207, 51230, 51240	3
2F	0-6-0T	L&Y	Saddle Tank	51500, 51512	2
3F	0-6-0	L&Y		52293	1
8F	2-8-0	WD		90102, 90254, 90306/7, 90324/54, 90546/64, 90632, 90713	10

Ex-LMS — 36, Ex-L&Y — 6, Ex-WD — 10   Total — 52

(f) Belle Vue (26G) 1954

1F	0-6-0T	Mid		41702, 41814	2
3F	0-6-0	Mid		43612, 43630/8, 43756	4
4F	0-6-0	Mid & LMS		43927, 44022/5, 44040/2, 44114/9, 44291, 44486	9
5	4-6-0	LMS		44803/45, 45031, 45284, 45450	5
3F	0-6-0T	LMS		47336, 47440	2
2F	0-6-0T	L&Y		51484, 51510	2
2F	0-6-0	Mid		58128	1
8F	2-8-0	WD		90122/6, 90140, 90163/97, 90204, 90552	7

Ex-LMS — 13, Ex-Mid — 10, Ex-L&Y — 2, Ex-WD — 7   Total — 32

(g) Gorton (39A) 1954

B1	4-6-0	LNE		61161, 61265	2
K3	2-6-0	LNE		61808/32, 61865, 61910/3, 61966	6
04	2-8-0	GC		63573/5, 63582/98, 63600/3, 63631/41, 63681/6, 63700/9, 63713/6, 63719/21, 63739/43, 63767/94, 63805/48, 63862/95	24
J11	0-6-0	GC		64294/8, 64304/6/11/6, 64322/6/32/3, 64342/6/57/63, 64368/78/82/3, 64401/9, 64413/5/26/34/35/7/40/50	28
J39	0-6-0	LNE		64717/8, 64740/2/3/5/8	7
C13/14	4-4-2T	GC		67401/3/5/7, 67415/7, 67421/3, 67425-27, 67431/7/8, 67440/ 1/4/5/7/8, 67450/1	22
J94	0-6-0T	WD	Saddle Tank	68012/64/79	3
Y3	0-4-0T	LNE	Sentinel	68169	1
N5	0-6-2T	GC		69250/60, 69270/96, 69307/8, 69328/33, 69338/53	10
A5	4-6-2T	GC		69805/6, 69817, 69823/9	5

Ex-LNE — 16, Ex-GC — 89, Ex-WD — 3   Total — 108

List of Signalboxes on Main Routes — 1960

(Signalboxes which controlled only goods lines, etc are not listed)

	Distance between Signalboxes (yd)	Additional Passenger Lines Up	Additional Passenger Lines Down
Manchester Victoria to Swinton			
Victoria East Junction			
Victoria West Junction	402	3	3
Deal Street	498	3	4
Salford Station	687	1	1
Windsor Bridge No 1	588	1	1
Windsor Bridge No 2	866	1	1
Windsor Bridge No 3	358	1	1
Pendleton Broad Street Station	676	1	1
Irlam	900	1	1
Brindle Heath Junction	551	1	1
Pendlebury Station	1m 510	1	1
Swinton Station	1,088	1	1
Windsor Bridge No 3 To Bolton			
Windsor Bridge No 3			
Brindle Heath Sidings	1m 228		
Agecroft Junction	821		
Clifton Junction	1m 409		
Pepper Hill	670		
Kearsley Junction	2m 725		
Moses Gate	1m 1,711		
Burnden Junction	1,296		
Bolton Trinity Street East Junction	488	1	
Manchester Victoria to Bury Bolton Street			
Victoria East Junction Millgate	300	1	1
Newtown No 1	367	1	1
Irk Valley Junction	1,078		
Queens Road	634		
Woodlands Road	1166		
Crumpsall Station	1021		
Heaton Park Station	1m 830		
Prestwich Station	834		
Whitefield Station	1m 623		
Radcliffe Central South	1m 894		
-do- North Junction	884		
Hagside Level Crossing	1100		
Bury Bolton Street Loco Junction	889		
Buckley Wells	654		
Bury Bolton Street South	324	1	
Manchester Victoria to Rochdale			
Victoria East Junction			
Footbridge	581	1	1
Cheetham Hill Junction	819	1	1
Smedley Viaduct	504	1	1
Monsall Lane	1,273	1	1

	Distance between Signalboxes (yd)	Additional Passenger Lines Up	Additional Passenger Lines Down
Thorpes Bridge Junction	923	1	1
Newton Heath Junction	618	1	1
Moston Colliery	577		
Moston Junction	1,257		
Vitriol Works	1m 243		
Middleton Junction West	702		1
-do- East	145		
Mills Hill	905		
Castleton South Junction	2m 827		
-do- East Junction	667		
-do- Station	496		
-do- Sidings	1633		
Rochdale West	711		1

Thorpes Bridge Junction to Oldham Mumps

Thorpes Bridge Junction			
Hollinwood Station	2m 686		
Oldham Werneth Station	1m 1154		
Oldham Mumps No 1	1,671		

Manchester Victoria to Stalybridge

Victoria East Junction			
Millgate	264	1	1
Newtown No 1	367	1	1
Newtown No 2	384	1	1
Collyhurst Street	725	1	1
Miles Platting Station Junction	449	1	1
Ashton Branch Sidings	368		
Philips Park No 1	497		
Park Station Junction	503		
Baguley Fold Junction	605		
Clayton Bridge Station	1,407		
Droylsden Station Junction	1m 548		
Ashton Moss North Junction	1m 91		
OA & GB Junction	698		
Ashton (Charlestown) West	481		
-do- East	394		
Stalybridge No 2	1m 187		

Ardwick Junction to Godley Junction

Ardwick Junction			
Ardwick No 1	115		
Ashburys West Junction	1,056		1
Ashburys East Junction	585		
Priory Junction	698		
Gorton Junction	1,018	1	1
Fairfield Junction	1m 102	1	1
Stockport Junction	1m 278	1	1
Ashton Junction	355	1	1
Guide Bridge East Junction	586		1
Hyde Junction	1,438		

	Distance between Signalboxes (yd)	Additional Passenger Lines Up	Additional Passenger Lines Down
Newton Station	1,754		
Godley Junction	1m 201		

Ashbury's East Junction to Romiley Junction

Ashburys East Junction			
Belle Vue Engine Shed	353		
Belle Vue Station	1,439		
Reddish North Station	1m 385		
Reddish North Junction	1m 216		
Lingard Lane Colliery Sidings	1,232		
Bredbury Station	1,675		
Romiley Junction	1,709		

Manchester London Road to Stockport (before power signalling)

London Road No 3			
-do- No 2	179		
-do- No 1	415	1	1
Ardwick Junction	541	1	1
Longsight No 4	954	1	1
Longsight No 1	672	1	1
Slade Lane Junction	1,237	1	1
Levenshulme Station	800	1	1
Heaton Norris Junction	2m 455	1	1
Stockport Edgeley No 2	1,190	1	1

Oxford Road to Altrincham & Bowden

Oxford Road Station			
Castlefield Junction	799		
Cornbrook Junction East	1,343		
Old Trafford Junction	590		
Old Trafford Station	727		
Warwick Road Station	754	1	1
Stretford Station	1,531	1	1
Mersey Bridge	1,516	1	1
Sale Station	1,526	1	1
Brooklands Station	1,290		
Timperley Junction	1m 173		
Deansgate Junction	392		
Navigation Road	534		
Altrincham North	689		

Manchester Central to Heaton Mersey Station Junction

Manchester Central			
Cornbrook West Junction	1m 70	1	1
Throstle Nest East Junction	493	1	1
-do- South Junction	470		
Chorlton-cum-Hardy Station	1m 495		
-do- Junction	902		
Withington & West Didsbury Station	1m 691		
Didsbury Goods Yard	1,678		
Heaton Mersey Station Junction	1m 40		

	Distance between Signalboxes (yd)	Additional Passenger Lines Up	Additional Passenger Lines Down
Manchester Central to Glazebrook East Junction			
Manchester Central			
Cornbrook West Junction	1m 70	1	1
Throstle Nest East Junction	493	1	1
Trafford Park Junction	1,300		
-do- Station	775		
Urmston Station	1m 1,705		
Flixton Station	1m 117		
Irlam Station	2m 687		
Glazebrook East Junction	1,397		
Deal Street to Patricroft Station			
Deal Street			
Ordsall Lane No 2	1,3001	1	
-do- No 4	789	1	1
Cross Lane Junction	892	1	1
Eccles Station	1m 1,392	1	1
Eccles Junction	1,172	1	1
Patricroft Station	715	1	1

List of Signalboxes on Main Routes — 1995

Manchester Piccadilly Signalling Centre

Fringe signalboxes:-

Deal Street
Walkden
Crow Nest Junction (Hindley)
Blackrod (Horwich)
Bromley Cross (Blackburn Line)
Ashburys
Heaton Norris Junction
Wilmslow PSB (Styal Line near Gatley)
Eccles
Glazebrook East Junction

Manchester Victoria to Rochdale

Victoria East Junction
Cheetham Hill Junction
Thorpes Bridge Junction
Vitriol Works
Castleton East Junction
Rochdale

Thorpes Bridge Junction to Rochdale via Oldham

Thorpes Bridge Junction
Oldham Mumps
Shaw Station

Manchester Victoria to Stalybridge

Victoria East Junction
Collyhurst Street
Miles Platting Station Junction
Philips Park No 1
Baguley Fold Junction
Ashton Moss North Junction
OA & GB Junction
Stalybridge

Ardwick Junction to Godley

Ashburys
Guide Bridge
Dinting

Other Signalboxes

Brewery Sidings (Miles Platting)
Denton Junction
Philips Park No 2
Romiley Junction

Newspaper Trains from Manchester — 1950s

From Piccadilly

23.25 Crewe
01.10 Chester
01.25 Cleethorpes

From Victoria/Exchange

21.50 Heysham
23.20 Glasgow
00.12 Newcastle
00.20 Leeds
02.05 Wigan
02.25 Leeds
03.05 Blackpool
03.15 Southport
03.23 St Helens
04.00 Colne

Express Freight Trains — 1939

From Liverpool Road

7.5pm	Fitted Freight No 2	Carlisle
8.8pm	Express Freight (G W)	Bristol
9.20pm	Express Freight*	Mold Junction
9.35pm	Express Freight*	Carnforth
10.55pm	Express Freight*	Edge Hill
11.25pm	Through Freight (G W)	Saltney

From London Road

7.55pm	Express Freight*	Birmingham
8.28pm	Fitted Freight No 2	London
8.50pm	Express Freight (G W)	Oxley Sidings
9.10pm	Express Freight*	Sudbury Junction
9.40pm	Express Freight	Shrewsbury
10.15pm	Express Freight*	Birmingham
10.40pm	Express Freight	Hillhouse
10.55pm	Express Freight	Burton

*Continuous brake in use on not less than four vehicles

Timetable Freight Services — 1995

Passing Through Piccadilly, Platforms 13 & 14

Down	*Passing Time*
4M99 17.14 SX FLR Southampton MCT to Trafford Park Sdgs	00.40
6M77 19.05 TThFO UKC Park Royal Guinness	
to Ordsall Lane Euro Transrail	01.52
4M78 19.00 SX FLR Parkeston CT to Trafford Park ET	02.43
4H32 03.00 MX FLR Crewe Basford Hall	
to Trafford Park Euro Terminal	03.57
4M53 20.42 SX FLR Felixstowe N FLT to Trafford Park ET	04.05
4M37 22.05 SX FLR Tilbury RCT to Trafford Park ET	04.38
6M08 00.26 TSO PET Haverton Hill to Glazebrook BTP	04.50
6M10 00.15 MFO PET Port Clarence to Glazebrook BTP	04.50
6M18 01.00 ThO PET Lindsay Oil Ref to Glazebrook BTP	04.50
4H06 01.52 MO CTI Wembley EFOC to Trafford Park Sdgs Q	05.51
4H05 02.52 MX CTI Wembley EFOC to Trafford Park ET Q	06.40
4H34 06.30 MSX) CTI Wembley Euro Frt Ops Centre	
06.20 SO) to Trafford Park Euro Terminal Q	10.32
4M45 03.08 MSX) FLR Felixstowe North FLT	
03.01 SOQ) to Trafford Park Euro Terminal	(11.32
4H30 09.16 SX FLR Allerton DMUD to Trafford Park ET	(12.32
4H35 08.40 MSX) CTI Wembley Frt Ops Centre	12.32
08.10 SO) to Trafford Park Sidings Q	13.32
4M46 10.27 SX FLR Felixstowe N to Trafford Park ET	20.02
4H38 17.30 SO) CTI Wembley Euro Frt Ops Centre	(21.18
19.43 MSX) to Trafford Park Euro Terminal Q	(23.34
4H58 20.53 SX FLR Crewe Basford Hall SSN	
to Trafford Park Euro Terminal	21.53

4A18 01.36 MX CTI Trafford Park ET to Wembley EFOC Q	01.57
4K55 02.16 MX FLR Trafford Park Euro Terminal	
to Crewe Basford Hall SSM	02.38
4K66 03.25 MX FLR Trafford Park Euro Terminal	
to Crewe Basford Hall SSM	03.47
4A10 05.14 MO CTI Trafford Park ET to Wembley EFOC Q	05.26
4S91 05.28 MX CTI Trafford Park Euro Tml to Moseurt Q	05.42
4L72 10.10 MSX) FLR Trafford Park Euro Terminal to	
4A72 10.10 SO) Felixstowe N FLT (MSX),Wembley EFOC(SO)	10.27
6E20 09.48 TSO PET Glazebrook BTP to Haverton Hill Ex S	10.52
4A11 11.10 SX CTI Trafford Park ET to Wembley EFOC Q	11.27
6E67 11.48 ThO PET Glazebrook BTP to Lindsay ORF	12.
4A13 13.10 CTI Trafford Park ET to Wembley EFOC Q	13.27
6E61 12.48 MFO PET Glazebrook BTP to Port Clarence	13.52
4F31 14.10 SX FLR Trafford Park ET to Allerton DMUD	14.27
4O30 15.10 SO FLR Trafford Park ES to Southampton MCT	15.27
4L98 20.32 FSX FLR Trafford Park ET to Tilbury RCT	20.45
4O08 20.15 SX FLR Trafford Park ET to Southampton MCT	21.27
4L83 21.30 SX FLR Trafford Park ET to Parkeston SS	21.43
4A14 21.52 SX CTI Trafford Park ET to Wembley EFOC	22.03
4L82 22.31 SX FLR Trafford Park ET to Felixstowe S FLT	22.43

Passing Through Manchester Victoria

Down

6M62 20.05 TThO UKC Hull Saltend BP to Arpley Sdgs	00.15
7M61 22.35 SX TLC Milford West Sdgs to Fidlers Ferry	00.25
6M56 22.05 SX UKC Humber ORF to Stanlow LPG Sidings	01.26
6M43 21.55 FO UKC Humber ORF to Holyhead RTZ Sdgs	01.29
6M32 00.50 TThO PET Lindsey ORF to Ashton in Mak KS	04.23
7M62 03.04 MX TLC Milford West Sdgs to Fidlers Ferry	05.00
6M80 01.59 MSX PET Lindsey ORF to Oakleigh Sdgs	
or Lostock Works Q	05.09
6F75 06.15 SX CON Dean Lane RT Sdgs to Warrington RTS Q	06.26
6M31 02.20 TO PET Lindsey ORF to Weaste Junc	06.29
7M52 06.35 TLC Milford West Sdgs to Fidlers Ferry	09.37
7D06 10.03 SX DEP Guide Bridge to Penmaenmawr Quarry	10.25
6M81 09.00 SX Dept'mtl Healey Mills to Arpley Sidings	11.28
6F77 11.28 SX REF Dean Lane RT Sdgs to Warrington RTS Q	11.38
6C09 08.59 SX DEP Arpley Sidings to Workington SS	12.22
6M21 11.19 SX TLC Healey Mills SS to Seaforth CT Q	13.22
7M25 11.09 SX TLC Milford West Sdgs to Fidlers Ferry	13.26
6M54 09.56 SX PET Leeds Shell Sdgs to Stanlow Shell AS	14.23
6M54 08.59 SO PET Leeds Shell Sdgs to Stanlow Shell Sdg	15.22
7M57 14.33 SX TLC Milford West Sdgs to Fidlers Ferry	17.40
7M18 18.35 SX TLC Milford West Sdgs to Fidlers Ferry	20.28
6M60 06.28 MO UKC Dalry Roche to Arpley Sdgs	21.22
6M47 17.02 WO UKC Haverton Hill Ex Sdgs to Bescot Yard	22.21
6M52 17.00 MO UKC Boulby Potash to Stanlow Shell AS	23.04

Up

6E04 22.00 MThO UKC Bescot Yard to Haverton Hill ES	01.55
6E95 02.04 MX TLC Walton Old Jnc to Milford West Sdgs Q	02.48
6E37 02.04 MX PET Stanlow Shell DS to Leeds Shell Sdgs	03.38

6E29 05.58 SX TLC Walton Old Jnc to Milford West Sdgs Q   06.51
6J75 08.35 SX CON Warrington RTS to Dean Lane RT Sdgs Q   09.36
6C09 08.59 SX DEP Arpley Sdgs to Workington SS   09.42
6E64 09.52 SX TLC Walton Old Jnc to Milford West Sdgs   10.37
6E39 06.45 MWFO UKC Arpley Sdgs to Hull Saltend BP   10.57
6E35 07.05 TThO UKC Holyhead RTZ Sdgs to Humber ORF Q   11.39
6E24 12.31 TO PET Weaste Junc. to Lindsey ORF   13.12
6E30 13.27 SX DEP Arpley Sdgs to Healey Mills SS   14.09
6J77 13.47 SX CON Warrington RTS to Dean Lane RTS14.36
6E66 13.35 SX TLC Fidlers Ferry to Milford West Sdgs   15.39
6S61 15.02 TO UKC Arpley Sdgs to Dalry Roche   15.43
6E22 17.00 SX TLC Fidlers Ferry to Milford West Sdgs Q   18.43
7H19 16.10 SX DEP Penmaenmawr Quarry to Guide Bridge   18.49
6E88 17.23 MSX PET Lostock Works or Oakleigh Sdgs
          to Lindsay Oil Refinery
6E23 18.30 SX TLC Seaforth CT to Healey Mills SS Q   20.33
6E05 20.07 SX UKC Stanlow LPG Sdgs to Humber ORF   21.49
6E97 21.05 SX TCL Fidlers Ferry to Milford West Sdgs   23.11

Other freight trains are operated at short notice and are not in the permanent timetable.

Abbreviations

AS	— Arrival Sidings	EUR	— Railfreight Distribution — European
CON	— Trainload Freight Construction	FLR	— Freightliner
CT	— Container Terminal	LPG	— Liquid Petroleum Gas
CTI	— Railfreight Distribution — Channel Tunnel Intermodal	ORF	— Oil Refinery
		PET	— Trainload Freight — Petroleum Products
DEP	— Departmental Train	Q	— Runs when required
ES	— Exchange Sidings	RTS	— Refuse Transfer Station
ET	— Euro Terminal	SS	— Sorting Sidings
EFOC	— Euro Freight Ops Centre	TLC	— Trainload Freight — Coal
		UKC	— Railfreight Distribution — UK Contracts

List of Freight Terminals in the Manchester Area1995 (Not all currently receiving traffic)

Pendleton Brindle Heath	Greater Manchester Waste Disposal
Salford Hope Street	Peakstone Stone
Miles Platting	Tilcon Stone
Dean Lane	Greater Manchester Waste Disposal
" "	Quickmix Concrete Co
Ashburys	ARC Stone
Bredbury	Greater Manchester Waste Disposal
"	Tilcon Stone
Trafford Park	Freightliner
" "	Channel Tunnel Freight terminal
" "	Manchester International Freight Tml
" "	Containerbase Ltd.
" "	Harris Distribution
" "	Cerestar
" "	Norton Metals, Scrap
" "	Castle Services, Steel
Ordsall Lane	Otis Euro Transrail Ltd
Weaste	Lancs Tar Distillers

List of Abbreviations

BICC — British Insulated Callenders Co
BR — British Rail(ways)
BREL — British Rail Engineering Ltd
BTC — British Transport Commission
CLC — Cheshire Lines Committee
CME — Chief Mechanical Engineer
DMU — Diesel Multiple Unit
EEC — European Economic Community
EMU — Electric Multiple Unit
GC — Great Central (Railway)
GJR — Grand Junction Railway
GMC — Greater Manchester Council
GMML — Greater Manchester Metro Ltd
GMPTE — Greater Manchester Passenger Transport Executive
GN — Great Northern (Railway)
GPO — General Post Office
GW — Great Western (Railway)
IECC — Integrated Electronic Control Centre
LMS — London, Midland & Scottish (Railway)
LNER — London & North Eastern Railway
LNW — London & North Western (Railway)
L&Y — Lancashire & Yorkshire (Railway)
M&BR — Manchester & Birmingham Railway
Mid — Midland (Railway)
MSJ&A — Manchester, South Junction & Altrincham (Railway)
MS&L — Manchester, Sheffield & Lincolnshire (Railway)
NCL — National Carriers Ltd
NFC — National Freight Corporation
NS — North Staffordshire (Railway)
NX — Entrance-Exit
OA&GB — Oldham, Ashton-under-Lyne & Guide Bridge (Railway)
OCS — One Control Switch
PTA — Passenger Transport Authority
PTE — Passenger Transport Executive
RAF — Royal Air Force
REC — Railway Executive Committee
SELNEC — Southeast Lancashire/Northeast Cheshire
VRS — Vehicle Recognition System

Bibliography

Magazines and Periodicals

Modern Railways
Railnews (BR house journal)
Railway Gazette
Railway Gazette International
Railway Magazine
Railway Observer (magazine of the Railway Correspondence & Travel Society)

Reports, Pamphlets, etc

British Rail Track Diagrams — LMR, Quail Map Company
The Reshaping of British Railways, BRB/HMSO1963
The Development of the Major Railway Trunk Routes, BRB 1965
BR and Constituent Companies Sectional Appendices
Locomotive & Multiple Unit abcs, Ian Allan
Locomotive Allocations (various dates), RCTS
Locomotive Stock books (various dates), RCTS
Loco Shed books, Ian Allan
Modernisation & Re-equipment of British Railways, BTC
Passenger and Freight Timetables
Railway Accident Reports: The Railway Inspectorate, HMSO

Books

British Railways Engineering, Johnson, John & Long, Robert A.
The Cheshire Lines Railway, Griffiths, R. P.
Gradients of the British Main Line Railways, Railway Magazine, The (1936)
Great Central (2 vols), Dow, George
The Great Northern Railway (3 vols), Wrottesley, John
The Lancashire & Yorkshire Railway in the Twentieth Century, Mason, Eric
The LMS & LNER in Manchester, Rose, R. E.
The LMS at War, Nash, George C.
LNER Locomotives, Casserley, H. C.
Locomotive and Train Working in the Latter Part of the 19th Century, Ahrons, E. L.
The Locomotives of the LNWR, Livesey, H. F. F.
The Locomotives of Sir Nigel Gresley, Nock, O. S.
The Midland Railway, Its Rise & Progress, Williams, F.S.
A Regional History of the Railways of Great Britain, Volume 10: The North West, Holt, Geoffrey O.
Roads & Rails of Manchester 1900–1950, Joyce, J.
Scenes from the Past (3) Manchester Railway Termini, Johnson, E. M.
Scenes from the Past (8) Railways in and Around the Manchester Suburbs, Johnson, E. M.
Scenes from the Past (16) The Midland Route from Manchester, Johnson, E. M.
Town & City Histories — Manchester, Kidd, Alan